A PLUME BOOK
THE GREAT NEW YORK SPORTS DEBATE

ROGER RUBIN has been a sportswriter in New York since 1988. He has worked at *Sports Illustrated*, *Newsday*, and, since 1995, the New York *Daily News*. His stories have received awards from the AP Sports Editors and he can frequently be heard espousing opinions about college basketball and baseball on New York talk radio. Rubin is a graduate of Columbia University and lives on Manhattan's Upper West Side.

DAVID LENNON has been a staff writer for *Newsday* since 1991. He is a member of the Baseball Writers' Association of America and a Baseball Hall of Fame voter. He is a frequent guest on talk radio and on NY1's sports shows. A graduate of the College of the Holy Cross, Lennon currently lives on Manhattan's Upper East Side.

The GREAT
NEW YORK
SPORTS DEBATE

Two New York Sportswriters
Go Head-to-Head on the
50 Most Heated Questions

ROGER RUBIN and DAVID LENNON

A PLUME BOOK

PLUME
Published by Penguin Group
Penguin Group (USA) Inc., 375 Hudson Street, New York, New York 10014, U.S.A.
• Penguin Group (Canada), 90 Eglinton Avenue East, Suite 700, Toronto, Ontario,
Canada M4P 2Y3 (a division of Pearson Penguin Canada Inc.) • Penguin Books
Ltd., 80 Strand, London WC2R 0RL, England • Penguin Ireland, 25 St. Stephen's
Green, Dublin 2, Ireland (a division of Penguin Books Ltd.) • Penguin Group (Aus-
tralia), 250 Camberwell Road, Camberwell, Victoria 3124, Australia (a division of
Pearson Australia Group Pty. Ltd.) • Penguin Books India Pvt. Ltd., 11 Community
Centre, Panchsheel Park, New Delhi – 110 017, India • Penguin Books (NZ), cnr
Airborne and Rosedale Roads, Albany, Auckland 1310, New Zealand (a division of
Pearson New Zealand Ltd.) • Penguin Books (South Africa) (Pty.) Ltd., 24 Sturdee
Avenue, Rosebank, Johannesburg 2196, South Africa

Penguin Books Ltd., Registered Offices: 80 Strand, London WC2R 0RL, England

First published by Plume, a member of Penguin Group (USA) Inc.

First Printing, November 2006
10 9 8 7 6 5 4 3 2 1

℗ REGISTERED TRADEMARK—MARCA REGISTRADA

LIBRARY OF CONGRESS CATALOGING-IN-PUBLICATION DATA

Rubin, Roger.
    The great New York sports debate : two New York sportswriters go head to
head on the 50 most heated questions / Roger Rubin and David Lennon.
        p. cm.
    ISBN 0-452-28754-5 (trade pbk.)
    1. Sports—New York (State)—New York—Miscellanea.
I. Lennon, David. II. Title.
GV584.5.N4R83 2006
796.09747'1—dc22
                                                                    2006019276

Printed in the United States of America
Set in Janson

For Mom, who always has been there for me;
and for Dad, who I miss very much.
—R.R.

For Mom, Dad, and Chris, the top three on my list.
—D.L.

Acknowledgments

David Lennon and Roger Rubin would together like to thank the following people:

- ○ Glen Macnow and Angelo Cataldi for originally suggesting that we do a book like this, for their trailblazing innovation, and for preparing us for such a major undertaking.

- ○ Mike Vaccaro of the *New York Post* for showing us the path.

- ○ Greg Dinkin and Frank Scatoni of Venture Literary for teaching us some of the publishing ropes and helping make a good idea even better.

- ○ Plume editors Jake Klisivitch and Cliff Corcoran for their hard work improving the manuscript.

- ○ Our friends David Gordon and Pete Conway for giving us insight into the psyche of New York sports fans, like it or not, and for being great sounding boards.

- ○ Our brothers—Peter Rubin, Chris Lennon, and Marc Rubin—for their assistance and encouragement in every aspect of this undertaking.

○ And those who took the time to kindly share their thoughts and "settle the score" for us on some issues: John Calipari, John Davidson, Will Leitch, Tom Glavine, Jim Larranaga, Kevin Millar, Bob Oliva, Gary Sheffield, Darryl Strawberry, and Mary Wittenberg.

Roger Rubin would also like to thank the following people who, whether they realize it or not, provided inspiration and support along the way: Adam Berkowitz, Peter Botte, Leon Carter, Jack Curry, Chris Fallon, Ed Fay, Mark Fratto, Eric Gelfand, Joe Gergen, Evan Grossman, Marc Hanes, John Harper, Frank Isola, Suzanne B. Kling, Bill Madden, Janet Paskin, Bill Price, Jim Rich, Lenn Robbins, A.E. Roseman, Heidi Rubin, Mark and Shana Siegel, Arthur Staple, Teri Thompson, Larry Torres, Dick Weiss, and Claire Broyles Williams.

Also thanks go out to Mort Zuckerman, Martin Dunn, Bill Boyle, and the rest of the incredibly hard-working staff at the *Daily News*.

David Lennon also offers thanks to: Bob George, whose excitement for the book was appreciated more than he knows, even from a Bostonian; Janny Hu, a talented writer but an even better friend; Susan Slusser, my West Coast role model; Mike Caponigro, who knows New York, even though he grew up in Walpole; Thu Van Dinh, for listening; Todd Dextradeur, for always asking when I would write a book; Dr. Miriam Chung, for good advice, medical and otherwise; Jon Heyman, the best teammate there is; Bill Eichenberger, my *Newsday* ally for the project; and Roger Rubin, thanks for making all this possible. I owe you one, buddy.

Contents

Introduction

Why There Is No Chapter About Babe Ruth in This Book

Rubin says: Dave, I think people are going to wonder why they're not going to read about whether Babe Ruth was the greatest player in the history of organized sport.

Lennon says: It's a fair point.

Rubin says: Of course, I also don't think people are sitting around America's bars, living rooms, and kitchen tables talking about The Immortal Babe at all these days . . . unless it's in the context of Barry Bonds.

Lennon says: Tough break for the Babe, being dragged from the grave into that steroids mess. At least he wasn't on anything stronger than hot dogs and Ballantine Ale.

Rubin says: See, there's something else no one's going to be seeing much of in the coming pages: Ballantine Ale. You know why? I drive a Toyota, not a time machine. And Ballantine is not something you can find on tap at every corner saloon anymore, just as the Babe's feats aren't something people are discussing over a pint of it. It's a little passé.

But I can tell you this: If they were, you can bet we'd be putting our two cents in on him.

Lennon says: I don't even think Babe Ruth really existed. How could a guy hit that many home runs and not be on the juice? You see the size of those ballparks back then? I think the whole thing was rigged by the commissioner's office to save the game after the Black Sox scandal. Kind of like how baseball turned a blind eye to McGwire's and Sosa's "workout regimens" during the great Maris chase of 1998.

Rubin says: In your own inimitable way, Dave, you've managed to be on-target without being on-target. Let me put it more succinctly. The 1998 home run race is what people are still talking about these days, just like A-Rod, Jason Giambi, or the "New Mets." It's because it's something they saw, read, or caught a glimpse of at the ballpark or on television. People aren't debating Ruth, because very few of us were alive to see him. We're talking about things we saw, like Bucky Dent's home run or Willis Reed limping onto the court.

Lennon says: Sorry for the rant, Rog. And thanks for steering us back on course. It's easy to take off on a tangent when discussing sports, but at least we've managed to stick to the last thirty-five years so everyone can feel like they're a part of the dialogue.

Rubin says: Keeping us on point is what I'm all about, Len-o. But don't apologize for the rant. This book is all about rants. It's just that you won't find any rants about whether Joe Gordon was the Yankees' best second baseman, because that's just not what people discuss.

Lennon says: True. I never hear anyone talking about that either. But there's not a Yankee fan alive who doesn't think Don Mattingly was a better first baseman than Keith Hernandez (something we'll get to a little later).

Obviously, he wasn't. But, like I said, that's a debate for a different page.

Rubin says: And, while completely wrong, you are at least proving the point. People debate about what they know and what they see. Most of the time when people like Ruth or Carl Hubbell or Duke Snider come up, it's when they're being compared to modern-day athletes.

Lennon says: Not that there's anything wrong with that. We're just trying to set some new standards, an update on the classics, if you will. And by including Generation X, along with Y and Z, we can apply some fresh perspective.

Rubin says: "Set new standards"? "Update the classics"? Sounds pretty highbrow there, *Newsday*.

Let me say it more plainly: If they're reading this book, there's a good chance they have an opinion on most of the subjects we're discussing. I think everyone can understand that.

Lennon says: So we're just bringing this debate into the twenty-first century. Sorry, Babe, no offense intended.

Okay, Rog. It's on.

The GREAT
NEW YORK
SPORTS DEBATE

1

Who Is the Most Despised Villain?

Rubin says: There are natural laws when it comes to sports in this city, just like those that dictate predator and prey. Yankees fans will always dislike the Red Sox. Jets fans will always despise the Patriots. And if you like the Knicks, then you probably share no love for anyone on the Pacers or Celtics or Heat.

There is one man that can unite New Yorkers in hate, regardless of which team or sport he or she calls a favorite. The mention of his name boils people's blood all over the region and ignites a strong visceral reaction. His arrival in town could mobilize entire units of the NYPD onto protective detail and crowd control.

No villain has been more hated in this town than John Rocker.

This is not about performance; Rocker became a great closer while with the Braves, but Mets fans never held him responsible for dashing a season's hopes. And it's not about being part of a rival team; even after he was dealt from Atlanta to Cleveland, he got invective at Yankee Stadium.

John Rocker is Sports Enemy No. 1 because he's a bigot who dared to turn his sights on our fair city and everything it stands for.

Multiculturalism and diversity are American cornerstones, and no place embodies them better than New York. It is truly a great melting pot, with people from many nations, lifestyles, and ethnicities living side by side because they can. Rocker's screed—given in several interviews, most notably in *Sports Illustrated*—insulted many of those people and perpetuated a number of negative stereotypes about the city.

We were already getting an idea of what an ass Rocker might be like from his on-field behavior during the 1999 National League Championship Series when the Braves played the Mets for three games at Shea Stadium. Before the games he would jaw with the fans, give them the finger, or spit in their direction. While shagging balls in the outfield he would show pleading spectators a ball as though he were going to flip it to them and then either feign the throw or intentionally toss it short of the stands. It's no wonder that his first appearance was greeted with chants of "Ass-hole! Ass-hole!"

"Met fans, the majority of them, are not even human," Rocker said after Game 3. "The majority are subhuman."

"They're the worst fans in the league."

In the *Sports Illustrated* article, Rocker was asked his thoughts on playing in New York and responded "I would retire first."

"Imagine having to take the number 7 train to the ballpark, looking like you're [riding through] Beirut next to some kid with purple hair next to some queer with AIDS right next to some dude who just got out of jail for the fourth time, right next to some twenty-year-old mom with four kids. It's depressing."

He also offered this: "The biggest thing I don't like about New York are the foreigners. I'm not a very big fan of foreigners. You can walk an entire block in Times Square and not hear anybody speaking English. Asians and Koreans and Vietnamese and Indians and Russians and Spanish people and everything up there. How the hell did they get in this country?"

John, way to make sure you don't leave anyone out.

Rocker made some efforts to apologize, but none of them, not even the one that was splayed across the Shea Stadium scoreboard before the first Braves-Mets game of 2000, rang sincere. With the water of the fallout rising above his ears, he still held reporters to blame for quoting him accurately and outing his intolerance.

After that Rocker was never alone at Shea, always guarded by police security details. He was even escorted from the park by police on the day he was traded to the Indians.

There's little funny in the Rocker saga, except for its epilogue. Rocker, two years out of baseball and hoping to make a comeback, signed with the independent minor league Long Island Ducks. Rocker had to come to New York for a last chance.

New Yorkers are famous for giving athletes a second chance. Jason Giambi was embraced at the start of last season, even in the wake of reports that he testified to a grand jury that he'd used steroids. It was enough to make you wonder if Rocker would be given the same kid-glove treatment, even though you knew there was almost no chance.

Lennon says: Got to give you some credit, Rubin. You picked a real winner in John Rocker. When it comes to villains, nothing beats a bigoted, homophobic racist, and speaking as a New Yorker, from the South, no less, it would be difficult to invent someone as perfect for that role as Rocker.

But I'll tell you where I get you on this one. For all of Rocker's despicable words, they were just that: words. We can get all jacked up about his New York–bashing monologue, and the bomb threats, but I'll stick with the guy that really stuck it to New Yorkers, and that's the Indiana Pacers' Reggie Miller.

It wasn't just that Miller was born and bred on the West Coast, attended UCLA, and then was drafted into the Hoosier heartland. He had the nerve to come into Madison Square Garden, smack dab in the center of Midtown, and start rearranging the furniture in the world's most famous arena.

Miller flopped. He whined. He soaked up the boos and antagonized the crowd right back, not to mention jawing with Knick über fan and Brooklyn-born director Spike Lee. Miller mocked Lee, clad in his oversized Ewing jersey and Knicks cap, and made everyone feel like he was about to do whatever he wanted during his forty-eight-minute stay on Seventh Avenue. And you know what, Miller often did.

In the 1994 Eastern Conference Finals, with the series tied at two, Miller made a bet with Lee on the outcome. If the Pacers won, Lee would have to put Miller's wife, Marita Stayrou, in his next movie. If the Knicks won, Miller had to visit Mike Tyson, who was serving a prison sentence in Indiana.

Indiana was getting blown out, 70–58, when Miller shredded the Knicks for twenty-five points in the fourth quarter, including five three-pointers, and many of his shots came right in front of Lee. Each time down the floor, Miller would taunt Lee, and at one point clutched his throat in the now infamous choking sign.

That gesture alone was enough to anoint Miller as an all-time villain, and though the Pacers lost that series, a bitter rivalry was born.

"He just fed off the crowd. They hated him. He loved to be the villain," former Knicks guard John Starks told *Newsday*. "Reggie had a way of getting under everyone's skin."

Starks knew what he was talking about. He once got so frustrated with Miller's trash-talking antics that he head-butted him during a game. But it was nearly impossible to slow Miller down, and especially at the Garden.

During the Eastern Conference Finals in 1995, Miller did the unimaginable, scoring eight points in 8.9 seconds to give the Pacers a stunning Game 1 victory. With Indiana trailing by six points, Miller nailed a three with 16.4 seconds left, then stole Anthony Mason's inbounds pass, dribbling backward to drain another three with 13.3 seconds left. Finally, Miller was fouled rebounding a Patrick Ewing miss and hit two free throws for the game-winning points.

Want more? There was Miller's thirty-eight-point performance in the Pacers' overtime victory in Game 4 of the 1998 Eastern semifinals, which included the tying three he drained to force the extra period. Two years later, Miller helped deny the Knicks a trip the NBA Finals by scoring thirty-four points—seventeen in the fourth quarter—in the clinching Game 6. By that point, Knicks fans were so beaten down by Miller they were too humiliated to boo.

That's the difference here, Rubin. Your boy Rocker was nothing more than a dopey left-hander with an acid tongue. Miller had the talent and the guts to treat Madison Square Garden like his personal playground, and New Yorkers hated him for it.

2

Which Was the Best Trade?

Lennon says: Ever listen to talk radio, when the guy calls up, says he's got a trade proposal, and it goes something like this: two Double-A retreads and a .188-hitting reserve infielder for Vladimir Guerrero? Or Roger Clemens? Or Jim Edmonds?

That's the American dream. Something for nothing. All gain, no pain. And for every GM who insists he wants to make a fair and balanced trade that will "help both teams," you can bet every Benjamin of that $200-million payroll he's lying. Which is why it's not enough for the best swap in New York history to simply benefit the locals—it has to be a plain-daylight Brinks robbery, with the other team left pleading insanity to its fleeced fan base.

And no one did it better than Yankees' GM Gene Michael, who flat-out stole Paul O'Neill from the Reds for Roberto Kelly in a November 3, 1992, trade that helped lay the groundwork for the pin-striped dynasty that began with the 1996 World Series title. Oh, and the Yankees got minor-league first baseman Joe DeBerry, too.

Here's why Stick is a genius. While saying publicly that the club's No. 1 off-season priority is pitching—not much changes, eh?—and the media howling for either David Cone, Greg Swindell, or John Smiley, Michael goes back door to Cincy for O'Neill, the left-handed bat he's wanted all along.

The pouting, petulant O'Neill evidently wore out his welcome at Riverfront, but the same could be said for Kelly in the Bronx. Kelly was the Yankees' lone all-star during the 1992 season, but the rap on him was unrealized potential, and he put up his best numbers—.302 batting average, twenty homers, and forty-two stolen bases—in separate seasons.

"I have a chance to play for a winning team, a team that can go to the playoffs and the World Series," Kelly said on his way out the door. "There's no way I can be disappointed."

Imagine that. Well, as you might expect, Kelly never did that with the Reds, playing 125 games in Cincinnati over two seasons before he was traded to the Braves. But O'Neill, his career resurrected, was instrumental in getting the Yankees back to the playoffs for the first time in fourteen years (with a wild-card berth in 1995) followed by four World Series titles over the next five years.

Not only was the feisty O'Neill a spiritual leader—his tantrums now written off as competitive fire—he was a pivotal cog in the Yankees' championship machine. O'Neill never hit .300 for the Reds, but he won the American League batting title in 1994 with a .359 average.

On the Yankees' 1998 club, which some hailed as the "best ever" after winning 125 games, including a sweep of the Padres in the Fall Classic, O'Neill had his most balanced season at the age of thirty-six. He batted .317 with twenty-four homers, 116 RBI, and even fifteen stolen bases. As for Kelly, he played in seventy-five games for the Rangers that year—the Yankees knocked Texas out in the Division Series—and a total of ninety-seven games over the next two seasons before retiring, ironically, from the Yankees. Kelly never made it to the World Series, or even a League Championship for that matter, and batted .294 in ten playoff games, with no home runs and one RBI.

As for O'Neill, he never got a ring for the thumb, but it wasn't for a lack of trying. O'Neill played in seventy-six postseason games for the Yankees, hitting .281 with ten home runs and 35 RBI.

Furthermore, O'Neill was immortalized as the original "warrior" by George Steinbrenner, who loved nothing more than to see one of his players tomahawk a water cooler or shatter a bat out of frustration.

As for Michael, the brains behind that trade, he was soon bumped up to the newly created position of "superscout," a well-deserved promotion. O'Neill made a winner out of everyone involved with that deal. What a steal.

Rubin says: Go big or go home, Dave, that's what I always say. While lots of people might go for the Paul O'Neill–for–Bobby Kelly deal, I think we can ratchet things up at least one more notch. O'Neill was a key component in four World Series champions, but what if he were the sole reason for winning those titles?

Then, my friend, Paul O'Neill would be named Mark Messier, and the Yankees would be called the Rangers. Not only was the Rangers' 1991 deal for Messier the kind of broad-daylight heist that this answer requires, it is the one event that directly translated to the Blueshirts shaking off fifty-four years of frustration to win the 1994 Stanley Cup.

At a time when the trend in the NHL was not to acquire a player in his thirties, Rangers then–general manager Neil Smith was willing to take a gamble on Messier, who was thirty. In the 1991 trade with the Edmonton Oilers, the Rangers gave up aging Bernie Nicholls—who'd never score more than twenty-two goals in a season after that—along with Steven Rice and Louie DeBrusk (that's right: You've never heard of them).

In return, the Rangers got something beyond measure. They got an outspoken winner with a championship pedigree and a cultured personality that fit perfectly in New York. Messier redirected the can't-win-it mind-set that had befallen the Blueshirts and singlehandedly changed the losing culture of the organization.

The Rangers always had enough talent to be considered among the better NHL teams, yet they always seemed to underachieve. Messier was exactly what was needed: a bold talker and motivator who could back up his words with his actions.

Who could imagine that he would guarantee a victory in the 1994 Eastern Conference Finals and then score a hat trick in Game 6 to get the job done? New York hadn't seen that kind of dedication to triumph since Willis Reed with the Knicks.

Messier may have been overshadowed in his early years with the Oilers by Wayne Gretzky. It's understandable. Lou Gehrig was overshadowed by Babe Ruth and the comparison of Gretzky with Ruth applies. But so does the comparison of Messier with Gehrig. We're talking about the kind of guys who exemplify championship play.

"I had one general manager, I'd rather not say who, who told me trading for Mark Messier would be the worst thing I could ever do," Smith told the *Hartford Courant*. "If Mark had turned out to be another [player past his prime], I would have been dead here. But it was the best trade I ever made."

In the first couple seasons with the Rangers, Messier was able to identify that head coach Roger Neilson wasn't using a style of play that would allow the Rangers to win it all. Many say Messier was the one who orchestrated Neilson's ouster, but there were no objections to the hiring of Mike Keenan, who took them to the Promised Land.

More credit to Messier: He won in Edmonton after Gretzky left, was playing productively ten seasons after he was deemed "too old," and turned Rangers games into must-see events like Yankees games are today. The Rangers were fun to watch throughout his first stint with them.

The aging stars of the current era seem to always find a way to play for the team that is favored to win a crown or offer a big final payday (note that Randy Johnson would accept a trade only to the Yankees). Messier believed enough in his abilities that he would go to a team that hadn't won in half a century.

The O'Neill trade is one of the great ones a New York baseball team has made. The Mets' 1987 trade of backup catcher Ed Hearn and two prospects to the Royals for David Cone is another. In fact, so is the Yankees' 1995 dealing of minor-leaguer Marty Janzen to Toronto that brought Cone back to the Big Apple to be a part of those same four World Series champion teams that O'Neill played for. But none of them can compete with the Messier deal.

Those baseball players were important, but no one can say they were *the* reason for winning like they can with Messier.

THE TOP 10 TRADES

1. Paul O'Neill: The Yankees obtained a cornerstone to their modern dynasty by acquiring O'Neill from the Reds in 1992 for outfielder Roberto Kelly and minor-league first baseman Joe De-Berry. General manager Gene Michael deserves credit for seeing the silver lining in the tempestuous O'Neill, who shook off his underachieving label in Cincinnati to win the American League batting title in 1994 and then anchored the Yankees' lineup through its four successful World Series runs through 2000.

2. Mark Messier: It takes more than one player to end a fifty-four-year Stanley Cup drought at Madison Square Garden, but the Rangers probably would still be waiting if not for Messier. GM Neil Smith acquired Messier from the Oilers in 1991 for Bernie Nicholls, Steven Rice, and Louie DeBrusk—the last two not exactly household names—and the move made history when the Rangers, powered by Messier, won the Cup in 1994. No one personified the C on his sweater more than Messier, and he remains the face of the franchise's glory days.

3. Jason Kidd: The Nets were the punch line to every NBA joke until GM Rod Thorn traded the troublesome Stephon Marbury, along with Somalia Samake and Johnny Newman, to the Suns for Kidd and Chris Dudley. This swap did nothing less than transform the Nets from laughingstock to the elite of the Eastern Conference. Before Kidd, the Nets had won only one playoff series in their history. With Kidd, they advanced to the NBA finals twice. Even though they fell short in both tries, the Kidd-fortified Nets earned respect never before seen in the swamps of Jersey.

4. Mike Piazza: True, Piazza was in the walk year of his contract when the Mets acquired him in 1998 from the Marlins for Preston Wilson, Ed Yarnall, and Geoff Goetz. But if GM Steve Phillips had been unable to pull the trigger on this deal in May, and Piazza didn't finish out the season in Flushing, maybe the Mets never would have locked up the future Hall of Famer with the subsequent seven-year, $91-million contract. By trading for Piazza less than two weeks after the Dodgers shipped him to Florida, Phillips got the inside track to a player who restored respectability to the franchise.

5. David Cone (Yankees): Cone's reputation as a "hired-gun" was well deserved, and he played that role to perfection in 1995 when the Yankees practically stole him from the Blue Jays three days before the July 31 trade deadline for three minor-league pitching prospects: Marty Janzen, Jason Jarvis, and Mike Gordon. Cone went 9-2 with a 3.82 in thirteen starts after the trade, helping the Yankees end a fourteen-year playoff drought by claiming baseball's first-ever wild-card berth.

6. Bill Parcells: Insiders say the Jets began wooing Parcells in the week leading up to his Patriots' appearance in Super Bowl XXX, but it wasn't until Commissioner Paul Tagliabue brokered a trade that the Big Tuna was allowed to jump ship to New York. The Pats wanted the Jets' first overall draft pick for Parcells; Tagliabue made them settle for four picks over the next three years, and it was worth it for the Jets, who made it to the AFC title game in Parcells's second season.

7. Mike Hampton: Lacking a bona fide No. 1 starter, the Mets pried Hampton away from the Astros in December 1999 for two of their most promising young players: speedy outfielder Roger Cedeño and hard-throwing right-hander Octavio Dotel (along with minor-leaguer Kyle Kessel). Houston was worried about what it would eventually cost to keep Hampton, who was headed into his walk year, but GM Steve Phillips was more concerned about the immediate payoff, and the left-hander turned out to be the missing piece for a team on the fringe. Hampton went 15-10 as the Mets claimed the NL wild card, but showed his mettle in the NLCS, winning MVP honors with sixteen scoreless innings as the Mets dumped the Cardinals en route to the World Series.

8. Dave DeBusschere: The Knicks sacrificed center Walt Bellamy, along with reserve guard Howard Komives, in order to extract DeBusschere from the Pistons in 1968, but the move was definitely worth it. Though DeBusschere and Bellamy had similar numbers afterward, the trade allowed the Knicks to shift Willis Reed to center, and the team flourished, losing in the conference finals to the Celtics in 1969 but winning the NBA title in 1970 and 1973. The presence of the 6-foot-6, 235-pound DeBusschere made the Knicks better on both sides of the ball, and he was a five-time all-star after the trade.

9. Butch Goring: For the Islanders, a team with a recent stretch of terrible trades, acquiring Goring from the Kings in

March 1980 for Billy Harris and Dave Lewis was a masterstroke for GM Bill Torrey, who could not have imagined the unprecedented success that followed. The Islanders became a dynasty that won four consecutive Stanley Cups with Goring, and he received the Conn Smythe trophy as the outstanding player of their first championship only months after his arrival from Los Angeles.

10. David Cone (Mets): The Royals still regret the day they sent the homegrown Cone to the Mets for backup catcher Ed Hearn in March 1987. Blame it on temporary insanity. Cone split time between the rotation and the bullpen during his rookie season, but jump-started his illustrious career with a 20-3 record the following year, when he finished second in ERA (2.22) and strikeouts (213). He went 90-48 in six seasons for the Mets, and thrived in the New York spotlight, a surprising fit for someone born and raised in Kansas City.

3

Which Catcher Set the Standard?

Rubin says: This one started as a real conundrum for me, but it didn't last all that long. New Yorkers have been very lucky when it comes to catchers. The Yankees and Mets almost always fielded a good team, and few teams are very good without a good catcher. The equipment they wear may bear the nickname "tools of ignorance," but the catcher usually has the most baseball smarts on the team.

We've had Hall of Famers and future Hall of Famers. We've had wise men with great personalities who became managers and television analysts. But believe it or not, my pick is none of these and it didn't take that long to realize why.

Only one guy has a video montage attesting to his significance and greatness that plays on the scoreboard at nearly every game. Only one has a locker in the clubhouse that remains empty and untouched more than two decades since he stopped playing. Only the name Thurman Munson is spoken with reverence any time it comes up.

The video montage? The empty locker in the back left-hand corner of the Yankees' clubhouse? These are an homage to one of the most important people in the long and storied history of baseball's most decorated franchise.

Munson is not in the Hall of Fame. He didn't play enough seasons before his fatal plane crash in the summer of 1979 to be elected by voters. No matter. In any way that you measure a catcher, Munson stands tall. He may not have hit the most home runs or batted for the highest average or had the most charisma. Still, he had great credentials. Munson had a .292 lifetime average, three Gold Gloves, and won the 1970 American League Rookie of the Year Award and 1976 American League MVP.

For this and so many other reasons, Munson was The Guy.

After Lou Gehrig hung 'em up in 1939, the Yankees went more than three decades without a team captain. There just wasn't anyone who measured up in terms of performance and character. And then came Munson.

Just think about some of the players who have been named captain: This short list includes Gehrig, Munson, and Derek Jeter. That's saying something. There's a reason people stand and cheer every time that video montage plays across the big screen in center field.

Good catchers take it upon themselves to prepare a pitching staff for an opponent, call a solid game, and stifle an opposing offense with their arm. The great ones do that and also deliver victories with their offense. Munson did all those things and was a true leader.

As the Yankees grew back into a power in his early seasons, he set the tone for their burgeoning take-no-prisoners attitude in 1973 with the home plate collision and ensuing fight he had with Boston's Carlton Fisk.

He was a peacekeeper during Game 5 of the 1976 ALCS, protecting George Brett from the onrushing Yankees after a hard slide into Graig Nettles at third base.

And he was an arbiter of good will, helping ease tempestuous Reggie Jackson into the clubhouse after the Yankees acquired him in 1977.

Oh, and performance? Today we look at Derek Jeter and marvel at what he brings to the team. He is in the middle of every great moment, whether with his bat or his glove or his instinct. And when the games are most meaningful, the Yankees get his best.

Munson was Jeter before Jeter. The Yankees won three pennants and two World Series with him behind the dish. And those big games: Wow.

You want clutch? In fourteen games during three Championship Series he hit .339 with 10 RBI. In sixteen games during three World Series, he hit .373 with 12 RBI.

Dave, some people may go for a long-ball hitter. Other may like a guy with a higher average or a rocket arm. I just think that's the flash. Munson had all those *and* honor. He was style and substance.

Lennon says: Nice position you left me here, Rog. Why don't you just say, "Okay, Dave, let's hear you rip the dead guy." Of course, I'm not going to do that. There's no denying that Munson was a beloved Yankee who attained legendary status because of his tragic end. And his résumé is beyond reproach, enhanced by a life in pinstripes.

But there is a modern alternative to Munson, at the other end of the spectrum, and that is Mike Piazza. The two played in different eras, obviously. The gritty Munson made his name by knocking heads during the no-frills '70s and Piazza cashed in at the height of the free-agent spending arc during the game's late '90s renaissance.

When you're talking about a catcher transcending that typical backstop label, however, the choice is Piazza. It's not too often in baseball that someone is actually worth their inflated paycheck, but the Mets can feel comfortable they didn't get cheated on their $91-million investment in Piazza.

Piazza was everything the Mets needed him to be: cleanup hitter, media darling, and, above all, savior of the franchise. Before GM Steve Phillips pried Piazza away from the Marlins in May of 1998, his rudderless club had not been to the playoffs since 1988, and was in the midst of a shameful decade highlighted by bleacher-squirting, firecracker-flinging knuckleheads.

When Piazza first arrived, he didn't seem to fit, a laid-back West Coast playboy suiting up in a dreary stadium adjacent to swampy Flushing Bay and beneath the noisy flight plans of LaGuardia's jets. But Piazza quickly proved he had a big enough bat to make even Shea appear small, as well as a mental toughness and competitive fire to succeed in New York.

Unlike Munson, Piazza never won an MVP, though he was robbed in 1997 when he finished second to Colorado's Larry Walker, who benefited from the thin air of Coors Field. But he's a lock for the Hall of Fame as the greatest hitting catcher of his generation, if not all time. Piazza hit more than thirty home runs in eight seasons, reaching forty twice, and had five years of 100-plus RBI—with 98 in 2002 and 94 in 2001.

There's no debating those numbers, which are tremendous for any player and virtually unheard of before Piazza burst onto the scene as a sixty-second-round pick (No. 1,390 overall) from the 1988 draft. And Piazza knew how to perform on the game's biggest stage, delivering some of the most memorable moments in this city's sports history.

You didn't have to be a Mets fan, or even like baseball, to get goose bumps watching Piazza's dramatic home run against the rival Braves in the first game played in New York after the 9/11 tragedy. That takes a special player.

And Piazza rarely bristled in the unforgiving spotlight of New York's intense media glare. Some would ask what that has to do with his performance between the lines, but that's part of the job description in the twenty-first century, when nothing, however personal, is out of bounds.

How many times did Munson have to deny he was gay? Silly question, I know. But if the former Yankee captain was asked, as Piazza was on the field at Veterans Stadium, it's more likely the reporter would get a fist in the teeth than a humorous answer. It's a different world now. Munson's hard-charging style would be appreciated in this day and age. He just might not have been as good, or at least not as good as Piazza.

Munson's career was cut short by a cruel twist of fate, so it's impossible to compare him with Piazza from a longevity standpoint. That doesn't mean, however, that Piazza doesn't get points for surviving fourteen seasons behind the plate, a grueling task that took its toll in his later years with the Mets. Criticize Piazza for a suspect throwing arm, but little else. He always sacrificed himself to block balls as well as base-runners, and pitchers often praised him for his ability to call games.

By the end at Shea, Piazza bore little resemblance to the confident slugger that showed up back in 1998. But he brought the crowd to its feet just the same, hitting tape-measure home runs to places that only the elite can reach. As a catcher, Piazza truly was in a class by himself.

Did the Giants Blow It with Eli Manning?

Lennon says: The Giants believed they were getting the next Peyton Manning when they grabbed his younger brother, Eli, in a draft-day trade with the San Diego Chargers in 2004. Flawless college résumé, rifle arm, and hey, the golden offspring of tortured NFL great Archie Manning.

Well, they got a mini-Peyton all right, as anyone who watched Eli's first playoff game can attest. In that dreadful loss to the Carolina Panthers at the Meadowlands, Eli exhibited all the classic Manning traits: bowed head, shrugged shoulders, face twisted in abject look of helplessness.

It was the same body language Peyton had perfected in all of those playoff losses to the New England Patriots, and then showed once again during that stunning defeat to the Pittsburgh Steelers in the second round of the 2006 playoffs. Regular season stud, playoff dud—not what you want from your franchise quarterback, and not what the Giants expected to get in forfeiting those draft picks for Eli.

Here's what makes Eli's development even more painful to endure: Ben Roethlisberger, selected at No. 11 in that 2004 draft, already has a Super Bowl ring, and it's not like he was holding a clipboard, either. Sure, Roethlisberger was lousy that night in Detroit, and his 22.6 rating was the worst ever for a winning quarterback. But if not for Big Ben, the Steelers would have been at home watching Eli's brother in SB XL, not beating the Seahawks at Ford Field.

Roethlisberger, with a 5-1 postseason record, was money in January while Eli performed like pocket change. With the Giants expecting a big day from little Manning, Eli instead completed more passes to the Panthers (three interceptions) than to star receiver Plaxico Burress.

I don't want to hear about complicated defensive schemes or the swirling Jersey crosswinds, either. Manning was named the NCAA's top student athlete while at Ole Miss, so he should have the intelligence to break down film and read scouting reports. As for the weather, Manning's arm, which set or tied forty-seven records during his collegiate career, is supposed to be impervious to the elements.

If you want to mention growing pains, Rube, I'll listen. But in New York, high draft picks don't get very long to climb the learning curve, especially when you arrive with the hype of an Eli Manning. Remember, this was a college kid who told the Chargers he would not suit up for them if they selected him with the No. 1 overall pick.

That's not the way you want to begin your NFL career; but if not for Manning's bold power play, the Giants never would have gotten him. As a result, the Giants selected another quarterback, North Carolina State's Philip Rivers, at No. 4 and traded him to San Diego along with their first and third round picks in the 2005 draft.

Rivers, stuck behind the resurgent Drew Brees, has yet to come off the bench for the Chargers, so I can't use him as ammunition in this debate just yet. But the Chargers did turn one of those picks into linebacker Shawne Merriman, who happened to be named the NFL's Rookie of the Year in the same season that the Giants wound up woefully thin at that position.

Oh, and one other thing. Did I mention Roethlisberger was still on the board? The Giants could have traded down, added draft picks and still secured a franchise QB in Big Ben. Maybe hindsight is 20/20, but the future of organizations are made on decisions like this, and the Giants can't help but feel some regret on how that draft unfolded.

The biggest knock against Roethlisberger apparently was that Archie Manning wasn't his dad. Okay, Miami of Ohio isn't known as a football factory, and if you want to grade him on intelligence, Roethlisberger was a Phys. Ed. major and not the supposed egghead Eli was at Ole Miss.

But Roethlisberger was no secret, either. Giants GM Ernie Accorsi later admitted that if the Chargers hadn't been interested in a Manning-for-Rivers swap, he would have selected Roethlisberger at No. 4. I'll give Accorsi credit for being honest, but that's the kind of statement that comes back to haunt you. Better to just say, "Hey, this Roethlisberger guy—he sure had us fooled." No sense in reminding your fan base what might have been.

And here's a bit of trivia for you, Rog. Accorsi was on the Colts staff when John Elway, the No. 1 pick in the 1983 draft, declared he wouldn't play for Indianapolis. The Colts promptly traded him to Denver, and Elway went on to win two Super Bowls during his Hall of Fame career.

So there's your precedent, Rog. If Manning is anything short of Elway, the Giants blew it.

Rubin says: The next time I make dinner over at my place, I'll be sure to take out your argument against Eli Manning, Dave. It's got so many holes, it should be perfect for straining pasta.

Quarterbacks like Tom Brady, who arrive in the NFL and are immediately capable of winning the big one, come along once in every generation of football players. So Kid Manning isn't on as fast a learning curve as the Patriots' signal caller? That makes him even with almost every other QB who's been in the league, Hall of Famers included.

It's not entirely fair that you should make John Elway the standard by whom young Eli is measured. It's a little like saying that Sidney Crosby would be a failure if he's not as good as Wayne Gretzky or that David Wright would be a disappointment if he's not the hitter that Mike Schmidt was. However, your choice of Elway is significant because two years into his career, Manning is ahead of where John the Great was.

Hard to believe? Well, believe it.

Elway was the top pick in the 1983 NFL draft, but he sure didn't look like he was going to end up one of the best of all time based on his first couple seasons. Just as Manning did this past season, Elway laid an egg in his first playoff game, a twenty-four-point loss to the Seahawks that saw him throw for only 123 yards, with no touchdowns and an interception. He got picked off twice in a seventeen-point loss to the Steelers the next year, too.

Mr. Rush-to-Judgment, it sounds to me like you'd have dealt him away after his third season, when the Broncos didn't even make the playoffs. And you'd have missed him blossoming into the Super Bowl–winning quarterback he became the following season.

Having a poor outing in your first playoff game happens to the best of QBs. Hell, Troy Aikman won three Super Bowls but imploded in a thirty-two-point loss to the Lions in his first postseason appearance. And Phil Simms—one of your favorites—lost his first playoff game to the Niners in a zero-touchdown, two-interception outing.

Dave, if you think this is easy, you really embody the phrase armchair quarterback.

Eli Manning is already very good, and he could be great one day soon. There's no reason to think otherwise. He not only helped the Giants win eleven games and get to the playoffs in his second season behind center, he ranked fifth in passing yards and threw for twenty-four touchdowns with just seventeen interceptions.

You know how many seasons it was before Terry Bradshaw completed a season with more TDs than INTs? Try five. And all he ended up doing was leading the Steelers to four Super Bowl titles.

It's also highly questionable to hold big brother Peyton or Ben Roethlisberger against Eli.

Peyton Manning has done miserably with winning the big one in a way that can only remind us of Jim Kelly, who was the losing quarterback in the Super Bowl four straight seasons. I don't particularly feel like racing to his defense, but I think you and I both know that with the exception of New England's Bill Belichick, every head coach in the NFL would love to have Peyton suiting up for them.

I'm trying to piece together your logic on how Peyton Manning's shortcomings are going to be visited on his younger brother. Does that mean we should have expected Pedro Martinez to break down physically at age twenty-nine, just because that's what his older brother Ramon did?

It may be unpopular to rip a guy who just won the Super Bowl, but I also can't fall in step with this notion that the Giants would be better in the long run if they'd taken Roethlisberger. The Steelers were not only a much better team, they relied on the pass less than any NFL team last year; the Giants, on the other hand, went to the air more than most. And talk about that Super Bowl performance? Big Ben was 9-for-21 for 123 yards with no touchdowns and two interceptions. I'm sorry but those numbers look eerily like young Manning's did in the loss to the Raiders.

Players say that it's tougher to play in New York because of people with attitudes like yours. Eli was drafted at No. 2 so he has to be the best quarterback in the league as soon as he shows up? Almost no one is going to be able to deliver on that. Try having more patience than a two-year-old.

5

Is It Really More Difficult to Play in New York?

Rubin says: There is a theory in science known as the Heisenberg Uncertainty Principle. It explains that the act of observing and measuring an object actually causes that object to change.

It turns out sport is more like science than anyone realized.

There is no place where athletes are observed and measured more than in New York, and there is no place where the impact is more apparent.

Kenny Rogers arrived in the Big Apple to become the Yankees newest franchise pitcher and left a couple years later with a faint-of-heart reputation that remains even today. Neil O'Donnell was going to be the next Namath and lead the Jets to the Promised Land, but instead ended up the reason Gang Green went 1-15 in 1996 and lasted just two years.

The list of people who arrived with great expectation and wilted under the glare of the New York spotlight is a long one. It's not just the athletes either. Lou Holtz, Glen Sather, and Larry Brown are some of their sport's biggest winners; none of them, as coach or GM, could work their championship magic in this cauldron.

There is a litany of reasons that New York is the toughest place to play. High expectation from fans is only part of the equation. There is pressure from within, as most New York arrivals try to live up to their huge contracts or billings as a championship-maker.

And don't forget the predictably unpredictable nature in which most of the city's pro teams are run.

If we're going to get to the crux of this phenomenon, Davey boy, we have to start with the man in the mirror. Media scrutiny is a major reason so many jocks can't hack it in New York.

When a player shows up at Shea or Yankee Stadium we're already in his space. The Yankees are covered by eight newspapers, two sports talk radio stations and a handful of television outlets. There are a dozen people already around him when he starts to dress. And he knows that every one of those news outlets is going to be scrutinizing his every move. One screw-up can turn Alex Rodriguez from A-Rod to "E-Rod" on the back page of a newspaper or make Kaz Matsui into "Mutt-sui" during the afternoon drive.

All these reporters are looking for something special—a scoop—that will make his or her paper the one to read. And unlike the press corps in many other cities, we're not going to cheerlead. New York has a lot of good reporters who pick up every little schism or developing issue.

How about the folks who own the teams? These guys are either meddlesome (George Steinbrenner of the Yankees) or political (Woody Johnson of the Jets) or a little of both (Fred Wilpon of the Mets). And sometimes you get the wild card like Bruce Ratner, who buys the Nets and then lets most of the key players go with a mind to rebuild in a new location.

The New York fans? They're plenty dedicated, but have shown themselves to be tough enough to unmercifully boo even icons like Patrick Ewing or Mariano Rivera.

Could be time for a little empirical evidence of the New York impact, just a few of its greatest hits.

The Mets made Bobby Bonilla, a Bronx-born slugger, baseball's highest-paid player. But after four straight seasons as an all-star, Bonilla made it only once in his three seasons in town. After the Mets dealt him to Baltimore, Bonilla returned to all-star form. This guy just couldn't handle the spotlight, once even threatening a reporter with his infamous "I'll show you the Bronx" line.

Rogers and Danny Tartabull were both all-stars when the Yankees signed them for big bucks, and neither had an all-star caliber season in pinstripes. In the last couple years we've seen the New York spotlight turn Jeff Weaver and Javier Vazquez from aces to head cases and Jose Contreras from legend to loser.

Kiki Vandeweghe, Xavier McDaniel, and Rolando Blackmon were all supposed to be the guy to make the Knicks an NBA champion, and the New York pressure turned each from all-star to all-stink. Alexi Yashin somehow lost his game in the move from the Senators to the Islanders. Marcel Dionne averaged forty goals for the Kings yet somehow needed three seasons to score forty for the Rangers.

There's just too much here for it to be a coincidence.

Lennon says: Here's another question for you, Rog: How did you manage to type while providing a shoulder for your million-dollar babies to cry on? Spare me the lame excuses and man-in-the-mirror nonsense. As for Heisenberg, sounds like another guy who spent too much time reading articles about himself.

The last time I checked, the pitching rubber at Yankee Stadium is sixty feet, six inches from home plate, just like it is in Kansas City and Minnesota. It's still one hundred yards from end zone to end zone at the Meadowlands, same as Houston and Carolina.

So why exactly am I supposed to believe it's more difficult in the Big Apple? Because there's a few more reporters in the locker room? Give me a break. The losers on the list that you provided were either due for a fall or not that good anyway. Often, it's a big-name athlete, on the wrong side of thirty-five, seeing the end is near and going for the kind of payday that only a New York franchise, with its millions in disposable income, can provide.

The biggest concern for these players, after taking tens of millions from George Steinbrenner or Fred Wilpon, is figuring out whether to go for the penthouse on Central Park West or the estate in Westchester. Oh, and the traffic to the ballpark can be rough, too.

That said, am I surprised that Alex Rodriguez discloses that he needs not one but two therapists after his first season playing for the Yankees? No, but that has more to do with his own cravings for public affirmation than some kind of New York ego-eating virus. Bobby Bonilla? Neil O'Donnell? A fifth-grader wouldn't pick either one of them for his rotisserie team, so what the heck was a GM thinking by signing them?

Blame it on the scouting department. Shea Stadium didn't destroy Roberto Alomar; he apparently had lost interest in playing the game and the Indians simply realized that before shipping him to the Mets, who in retrospect were duped by that deal.

New York's hypercaffeinated environment just makes for a handy excuse. Think it's easy playing quarterback for the Cowboys or Eagles? How about closing games for the Red Sox? Ask Kobe Bryant how life was in Los Angeles after Shaq bolted for South Beach.

Just about every city has demanded the head of its star athlete on a stick before running him out of town. It's the nature of professional sports and hardly unique to New York. In fact, I would argue just the opposite. Big Apple fans idolize their sports heroes, elevating even middle relievers and backup QBs to star status. Think the Giants' Jesse Palmer gets to be The Bachelor if he didn't play for a New York team? No shot.

The positives far outweigh the negatives, so in the words of the late Bob Murphy, here's the happy recap: more money, more fame, and, um, did I mention more money? So you have to listen to a few boos from time to time and maybe Mike and the Mad Dog have made you their chew toy for the week.

Big deal. No big-name free agent has turned his back on New York because he can't deal with the hype, and no one ever will. The money is the biggest reason, of course, but anyone worth those millions should be able to disregard whatever distractions that may surface along the way.

Otherwise, failure is inevitable, whether it's in New York or New Orleans. I haven't seen anyone with a TV camera or a notebook make an interception yet.

SETTLE THE SCORE/GARY SHEFFIELD

(Gary Sheffield of the Yankees has played in six markets and been successful in all of them. Here are some of his thoughts on whether New York's been the toughest.)

New York has plenty of distractions that could potentially throw a player off his axis, but Gary Sheffield insists these things interfere only as much as you let them. Tune them out and you should have no problem.

Sheffield has been an all-star with five different teams. Each place he played—Milwaukee, San Diego, Miami, Los Angeles, Atlanta, and New York—there were outside influences that affected him or his teammates. The key, he says, is to ignore them and keep the game the same no matter where you play.

"There are circumstances that have a huge impact on a player, including the fans," he says. "People who talk about other issues—why they struggle—they think it doesn't have to do with themselves and that's looking for excuses.

"I look at New York and Miami and L.A. as the same. They [are] the same if you make it the same and tell yourself, 'I want to be here, I enjoy playing where I am playing, I'll try to do the best for the team.' All the other stuff I've learned not to turn my head and notice.

"[There's] a lot of things in baseball people don't realize . . . there's a lot of things that can agitate a player. You have to come to work every single day and deal with different issues and sometimes it's the same issues every day. It gets annoying and that can annoy the player to where he can't go out and perform. I turn a blind eye to [them] until I have to deal with it—I know when to fight my battles."

Sheffield says he learned this the hard way in his first seasons with the Brewers when he suffered a foot injury. When medical tests showed no structural damage, management questioned his honesty, played him hurt, and then sent him to the minors when his production flagged. Later tests bore out his claim, but the damage was done. Sheffield's relationship with the Brewers was deeply fractured, and facing that every day interfered with his play.

He says he's seen interferences of all kinds, from the friction with management in Milwaukee to fan apathy in Miami to media scrutiny in L.A. and New York.

Sheffield agrees that many players spend time adjusting to New York because it is so different from everywhere else, from its high position in lifestyle to the often fickle fans to the clubhouses and locker rooms teeming with reporters. He says that he did not—in his first season with the Yankees he hit .290 with thirty-six homers and 121 RBI—because he locked those things out of his head.

"A lot of people think that because it's New York, you're going to have to adjust to it and they come in here thinking that," he says. "It's the fact that you're adjusting to a new situation in general. I have adjusted to every situation I've gone into, like everyone else, but it has nothing to do with what the city is or how difficult it is made out to be."

Sheffield goes on to say that some of the most difficult distractions he's seen can come in places where there is little support for the team. As a Yankee, he goes to many cities where he finds more fans are rooting for his team than for the home team. He didn't like that when he played for the Marlins in Miami.

"When you don't have fans coming out to support you and you're asked to beat the best teams in the world. When the best teams come to play you at home and there's more fans for their team than for your own. Those are hard to swallow . . . I know how that can wear on the players," he says.

Though Sheffield insists that the distractions can be disregarded, it was apparent in August of 2005, as the Yankees were struggling to remain in the playoff hunt, that he isn't always able to follow his own advice: The way the Yankees were covered, he said, was affecting the team and agitating him.

"I know who the leader is on the team," he said in an interview with *New York* magazine that was interpreted as a veiled shot at Derek Jeter and Alex Rodriguez. "I know who the opposing team comes in knowing they have to defend to stop the Yankees . . . I know this. The people don't know. Why? The media don't want them to know."

Sheffield goes on to say in that interview that the intense media presence in the clubhouse has had an impact on team chemistry.

"This is the first team I've been on where no one sits at their locker," Sheffield says. "It's where you build your chemistry, just talking about life. I'm used to having six chairs around me, but here if there are six chairs, then there's going to be twenty reporters."

Gary Sheffield's performance in the field says that he excels at focusing on what matters, but he surely knows that everyone else has not.

Did the Rangers Become Irrelevant Since Winning the Stanley Cup?

Lennon says: No disrespect to the Rangers, but how could they not? This is the sporting world's version of Jumping the Shark. Once the pinnacle is reached, there's nowhere to go but down—and out of sight, as far as the general public is concerned.

Futility, when it reaches a certain depth, becomes interesting. Sympathy sells. Everyone loves an underdog. The Cubs will never be as cuddly once they win a World Series. As for the Red Sox, that's a special case because New England fans are warped to begin with. All they did was end an eighty-six-year-old curse and the Olde Towne Team has never been more popular.

When you're dealing with the NHL, however, we're talking about a niche audience, like people who enjoy anchovies on pizza or buy *Playboy* for the articles. I'm not saying that Rangers fans fit either of those profiles, but you get the idea.

Look at it this way. How many times have you been at some kind of social gathering—church picnic, bachelor party, bar mitzvah, etc.—and people are talking about the Rangers? Maybe I'm being a snob here, but the answer for me, since 1994, is a big fat zero.

Obviously, it wasn't always that way. During the winter and spring of 1994, the Rangers owned the city, actually treating the Yankees and Mets like second-class citizens. Reflecting back on those months, it's difficult to fathom. It was like some kind of alternate universe.

When the Rangers were in the playoffs, every bar was packed—to watch a hockey game, no less.

That type of behavior is practically unheard of south of Saskatchewan. But people who couldn't tell a blue line from a red line got caught up in the hysteria as soon as someone from the next cubicle told them the Rangers hadn't won the Stanley Cup since 1940. Just like that, you needed a second mortgage to sit in the rafters at Madison Square Garden, and Messier jerseys were everywhere.

For once, the Rangers finally delivered. They exorcised the demons, won the Cup, and got their ticker-tape parade down the Canyon of Heroes. Then—poof!—the lovable underdogs, now the defending champions, suddenly didn't seem so important anymore.

The next season, the Rangers had just twenty-two wins, and suddenly they just weren't that much fun. The same lovable bunch that skated around the Garden ice with the Cup only a few months earlier was now a bloated roster of overpriced underachievers, fat and happy with success. And the same fans that worshipped them were now saying "What have you done for me lately?"

But the only thing worse than ridicule for a sports franchise is indifference, and in New York, it's a difficult trend to reverse. Slowly but surely, the Rangers inevitably were dismantled, and only once did they finish higher than fourth in the Atlantic Division in the decade after winning the Cup.

Players like Messier, Mike Richter, Adam Graves, and Brian Leetch took on a mythical importance for the Rangers, and became household names for New Yorkers. Fortunately for the MSG suits, they still do, but only to a certain degree. On the day Messier announced his retirement, he didn't even get the back page to himself, which showed just how far the Rangers had fallen since 1994.

In attempting to resurrect that past glory, the Rangers have tried to buy their way back into the playoffs with deals for the legendary Wayne Gretzky, the dizzy Eric Lindros, and their current marquis name, Jaromir Jagr. In the meantime, a city of eight million yawns.

To be fair, success is relative for the Rangers. Persuade 17,000 fans to visit the Garden, keep those $7 beers flowing, and maybe get a few thousand TV sets tuned to the game on any given night. The Rangers couldn't get the back page of the *Daily News* these days if they bought it as ad space. That's not their fault, entirely. It's just where the Blueshirts reside in the city's food chain.

That's not to say the Rangers aren't heading in the right direction. They are. But to think they can ever recapture those magical Cup-chasing days of 1994 is not realistic.

But I reserve the right to change my mind. Just check back with me in 2048.

Rubin says: While I may not be out at a newsstand looking to see what I can "read" in the new issue of *Playboy*, I proudly admit that I am a fan of anchovies on pizza. That, by the way, is not some tiny niche group either. Anchovies stay on the menu because they must in our supply-and-demand world.

The Rangers are the same way. They're in the newspapers and newscasts every day because they matter to people. And I say this in spite of the fact I know there's a joke going around that they sell out every game to the same 18,200 people each night. The Rangers may have ceased to be the lead story in town for a decade, but they never faded away. And right now they may be on the cusp of a renaissance.

I think we all know what irrelevant looks like. You don't have to go too far back to remember when the Mets were having their playoff hopes turned out in August. Fans stopped going to Shea Stadium. Game accounts in the papers stopped being about games and instead focused on everything from a bright prospect who'd been called up to clubhouse dramas to the end of a season for a player in his walk year. The sports reports on the evening news would end with a highlight-less "and the Mets lost to the Braves, 7–4."

The Rangers avoided that kind of a limbo in large part because the NHL's playoff structure took so many teams. The only prolonged stretch when no one cared came during the lockout when there wasn't a season to follow.

A few concessions. Have the post–Stanley Cup Blueshirts been a bad team? Yes. Have they been a bunch of overpaid fading stars? Yes.

But have they lost their following? Absolutely not.

In every year of this decade, the Rangers have filled an average of at least 95 percent of the seats for their home games at the Garden. And when they've gone on the road, they've been one of the NHL's biggest draws.

None of the newspapers have stopped traveling with them and there's a good reason for it. If you want to put a big dent into your own circulation, dropping your coverage of an incredibly popular team is the fastest way to do it.

Sad to say, but hockey is never going to be king in this town until the Rangers again are a consistent contender. Until that happens, the only place where you'll ever find the Islanders on a back page is *Newsday*. Heck, the only day the Devils made the back pages in the city during their most recent championship season was the day they won the Stanley Cup (and if I am not mistaken they had to share it with one of the baseball teams).

The good news is that day doesn't seem so very far off. Look at what the Broadway Blueshirts have going for them now. Their defense is among the league's stingiest with emerging star goaltender Henrik Lundqvist playing behind a grinding group of defensemen that includes Michal Rozsival, Marek Malik, Tom Poti, and Fedor Tyutin. The offense may not run it up, but Jaromir Jagr is back in superstar form and rookie Petr Prucha looks like a future franchise player.

The Rangers are decades of futility away from being the national cause they became before winning it all in 1994. Their fans' starvation for success, as you pointed out, was only matched by that of Red Sox, White Sox, and Cubs fans. They gorged themselves well that year.

After a long while though, the hunger is returning; now that the team has shown real potential to make noise in the NHL again, it's like the scent of a good meal is wafting in from all directions.

With a feeding frenzy seemingly so close at hand, no one is going to turn the channel on this one.

7

Who Is the Best Coach or Manager?

Rubin says: While arguments can be made for a number of candidates, one simply stands out ahead of all the rest. That's Joe Torre of the New York Yankees. There are lots of ways that fans measure who is the best and Torre is the standard in every category.

What are the criteria for determining the best? We're supposed to be New Yorkers and so ultimately the bottom line is going to be the bottom line. To even be considered here, you have to get your team to the playoffs with regularity and then you have to win championships once you get there.

Since Torre was placed at the helm of the Yankees before the 1996 season, he has taken the Bombers to the playoffs ten times in ten seasons. That's batting 1.000 on that category and you're not going to find anyone who comes close during the past three and a half decades. Take your pick—Bill Parcells, Al Arbour, Red Holzman, Jeff Van Gundy, Jacques Lemaire, Larry Robinson, Bobby Valentine, Davey Johnson—none comes close.

Torre also has taken his Yankees to six World Series and won four world championships. The World Series is almost always the two best teams or the two teams that are playing the best, and in those circumstances, his clubs won ten straight games in one stretch.

Admittedly, Arbour has equaled him with the four titles, but can we really compare winning the World Series with taking the Stanley Cup? One is the most-covered event of the sports year; the other runs with the tire ads in the sports pages.

Now, maybe you consider yourself an aficionado, someone who appreciates the subtleties of sport. Winning the whole enchilada ain't enough for you. And you think that with all the talent afforded by the biggest, most-ridiculous payroll in sports, the Yankees actually should have done all that winning.

Before you call someone the best in the Big Apple you want to see him or her overcome the odds, handle adversity, and thrive where others will fail.

For you I have a two-word answer: George Steinbrenner. Try overcoming that.

Steinbrenner is an unpredictable force and a horrendous micromanager. He'll sign or trade a player without consulting anyone. He'll fill the newspapers with criticism and even pressure his manager to use certain players. To boot, he has packed the atmosphere around the team with an air of recklessness with his track record of firing managers (seventeen at last count) and coaches.

This guy has rained distractions on his team, from criticizing Derek Jeter for his partying ways, to overriding Torre's decision to send Jose Contreras to Triple-A Columbus with an assignment to Tampa, to publicly feuding with former bench coach Don Zimmer.

Torre has found a way to insulate his team from The Boss's insanity. He takes the hits for them. And as the most successful manager in baseball, he tames Steinbrenner with the trump card of walking away.

Handling the Yankees is no cakewalk either. Any time you put seventeen all-stars in one room, you're not going to have enough space for all the egos and conflicting personalities. Torre has created a clubhouse that feels almost like a corporate office. No one expects to be treated any differently from the rest because they know that self-interest blocks the path to winning. There have been times Torre's had four pitchers capable of being the closer on most teams and only he could get three to accept lesser roles as set-up men for Mariano Rivera.

Torre's management of the clubhouse doesn't end there. Throughout the season and especially in the playoffs, he allows his players to focus on the games by deflecting the scrutiny of New York's overzealous media with his charm and candor.

The Yankees may have the most impressive payroll, but they also have some of the toughest circumstances to thrive in. Just ask Jeff Weaver. Or Kenny Rogers.

Torre is the best when it comes to winning and losing, but he also is the best in so many other departments. He is a media darling, a peacemaker, a strategist, and a therapist all at once. There's no beating a combination like that.

Lennon says: You're too predictable, Rubin. I would have expected nothing less than you joining the ranks of the Torre-worshippers, the disciples of Saint Joe, if only because of your unabashed love for America's pastime. With all due respect to Mr. Torre—as Derek Jeter unfailingly refers to his skipper—the key to the Yankees' success under his tenure has more to do with money than management.

That's why I give the nod to the big Tuna, Bill Parcells, for guiding the New York Giants to two Super Bowl titles in four years. Maybe it's unfair to compare two completely different sports like football and baseball, but let's look at the unique challenges Parcells faced, even if Giants owner Wellington Mara is no George Steinbrenner.

For one, Parcells had to do more than simply keep his players from popping off to the newspaper, though he did have his share of characters. How do you think Torre would have handled LT? Sort of makes Gary Sheffield seem like an altar boy. And Parcells has to lord over a roster that is twice the size of a baseball team, with far more moving parts and a greater risk of injury.

How about preparation? Does it even matter to Torre who is pitching for the Royals? Or the Devil Rays? With the highest-priced lineup in the game, Torre basically uses a rubber stamp for most of the summer, maybe pausing to think when the Red Sox are in town. No wonder Torre always looks well rested. His biggest concern usually involves finding a corner table at the best Italian restaurant in (insert city here).

Think it's a coincidence that Parcells knows as much about angioplasty as he does about a two-deep zone? That heart bypass surgery goes with the job description of an NFL coach? Stress is devising a game plan to stop Walter Payton or slow down the Bills' prolific K-gun offense, which Parcells's Giants somehow did in pulling the huge upset in Super Bowl XXV.

Schemes like that aren't hatched over a plate of lobster *fra diavolo*. It takes weeks of no sleep, cold coffee, and stale doughnuts to draw up a strategy that wins a regular-season game, never mind a conference championship or a Super Bowl. Parcells did surround himself with a great staff—his chief lieutenant, Bill Belichick, is now the mastermind of the New England Patriots.

But Parcells not only knows his Xs and Os, he's also one of the game's premier motivators, and all you had to do was watch those Giants teams play to see that fire burn through. His Giants had talent, no question about that, but there's no Lombardi Trophy without Parcells. In eight seasons patrolling the Meadowlands, Parcells compiled a 77-49 record. That might be just an ordinary season for the Yankees, but in the NFL, that's a dynasty, and it won't be happening again anytime soon in New York.

Maybe the best indication of Parcells's greatness is what happened to the Giants after he left. In comes Ray Handley, and the defending Super Bowl champions limp to an 8-8 record, and the

Super Bowl has been a distant memory ever since, aside from the blowout loss to the Ravens.

Parcells achieved greatness with the Giants, but after leading the Patriots to the Super Bowl in 1996, he returned to New York and almost got the Jets there, too. That's the mark of a truly great coach or manager. Not only rebuild one team, but also show the ability to do it over and over again, something that Torre will struggle to do if he ever leaves the Bronx—not to mention his failures before he arrived and inherited Steinbrenner's payroll.

Even though Parcells heads the hated Cowboys now, his Jersey roots and unmatched success in the Meadowlands make him without peer among the all-time coaching ranks in New York.

THE FIVE BEST AND FIVE WORST MANAGERS OR COACHES

Best

1. Joe Torre/Yankees (1996–present): His résumé speaks for itself. When Torre was hired by the Yankees for the start of the '96 season, baseball's most storied franchise had not won a World Series since 1978—the longest title drought in the Bombers' history since the arrival of Babe Ruth. Not only did Torre's club win a ring in his first October, they claimed four World Series crowns over the next five seasons.

2. Bill Parcells/Giants (1983–90): The Tuna didn't get off to a legendary start in New York, finishing 3-12-1 in his first season. But over the next three years, riding a suffocating defense and a cool quarterback named Phil Simms, Parcells groomed the Giants into champions—not once but twice, in Super Bowls XXI and XXV.

3. Al Arbour/Islanders (1973–86; 1988–94): The Islanders won only twelve games in their inaugural season, but when Arbour arrived the following year, he transformed the expansion franchise into one of the most successful in NHL history. With Arbour on the bench, the Islanders won four straight Stanley Cups, and he is second only to Scotty Bowman in wins and games coached.

4. Pat Riley/Knicks (1991–95): In his short but sweet tenure that failed to produce an NBA title, Riley brought star power—and success—to the big stage on Thirty-third Street. In 1993, Riley led the Knicks to their best regular-season record in franchise history and pushed them to the NBA Finals in 1994, when they lost to the Rockets in seven games.

5. Davey Johnson/Mets (1984–90): Johnson was hired after leading Tidewater to the Triple-A World Series title, and three years later, he did the same with the Mets, who rallied from an 0-2 deficit to beat the Red Sox in the 1986 Fall Classic. The Mets under Johnson were an extremely talented bunch—featuring Darryl Strawberry and Dwight Gooden—but it took a special skill to balance a clubhouse full of big egos and even bigger partiers.

Worst

1. Rich Kotite/Jets (1995–96): Kotite has to rank at the very top of the Jets' long list of coaching mistakes. Despite some success with the Eagles, he was a complete disaster after being hired to replace Pete Carroll, finishing 4-28 in his two seasons for the Jets, who had the NFL's worst record each time, including 1-15 in 1996. Kotite lost thirty-one of his final thirty-five games, and has not returned to NFL since being chased out of New York.

2. Art Howe/Mets (2003–04): Owner Fred Wilpon hired Howe within minutes of meeting him, saying he "lit up the room" during the interview. While Howe was a decent enough guy, it would be difficult to find a manager more ill-suited for New York, and the performance of his team reflected his uneasiness in the corner office. The Mets finished thirty-four and a half games behind the Braves in 2002, and twenty-five games out in Howe's final season, when he managed the last two weeks as a lame duck.

3. Ray Handley/Giants (1991–92): As the offensive coordinator under Bill Parcells, Handley seemed like an okay choice to continue the Tuna's legacy in the Meadowlands. But with the Giants coming off their second Super Bowl victory in four seasons, the timing was not great for a rookie head coach, and Handley flunked badly. The Giants slipped to 8-8 in his first season, and after a turbulent 6-10 campaign the next year, Handley was fired, much to the delight of the New York media.

4. Stump Merrill/Yankees (1990–91): Here's all you need to know about Merrill: He once benched Don Mattingly for refusing to get a haircut. Regardless of the numbers—and the Yankees weren't good under Merrill—feuding with one of the most respected players to ever put on the pinstripes is not a smart career move. Ultimately, Merrill lost the clubhouse, and eventually his job after a 71-91 finish to the 1991 season.

5. Brian Mahoney/St. John's (1992–96): Lou Carnesecca's right-hand man for many years, Mahoney seemed like a natural choice to succeed the Hall of Fame coach when he retired. He got off to a great start, too, with a nineteen-win debut season and a trip to the NCAA Tournament's round of thirty-two. Things didn't go well after that. Even though Mahoney recruited two players who would go on to the NBA, including heralded Felipe Lopez, his Johnnies didn't finish over .500 for the next three years. His final record was 56-58.

8

Is It a Sin Against Mankind to Be a Fan of "Both Teams"?

Lennon says: I'll use an example that most of us, even those outside of New York, can understand. How many people do you know went around saying during in the 2004 election, "I just can't decide who to vote for. I like both George W. Bush and John Kerry." Sounds insane, doesn't it? But why not? We're all Americans, right? They're both Americans? Aren't we all on the same team?

Not exactly. Just because millions of fans share a piece of real estate, side by side, stretched out over a large chunk of the Northeast, it doesn't necessarily make them friends. Only neighbors. And cheering for every team just because it has New York (or New Jersey) on its uniforms doesn't work, particularly when the two teams are not only trying to beat each other, but humiliate them.

Break it down any way you want: Yankees, Giants, Rangers, or Mets, Jets, Islanders. (The Knicks cross the boundary because no one really knows what to make of the Nets, but that's the only exception). When you grow up in New York, you pick a side—usually passed on from generation to generation—and you stick to it.

The resurrection of the Subway Series, a byproduct of Commissioner Bud Selig's beloved interleague play, was like squirting lighter fluid onto the eternal flame that burns inside fans of the Yankees and Mets. Instead of just arguing about who is the better team, now the bragging rights are settled every season. Even if the Mets suck, win the six-game series and the fans can tell their pinstripe-loving pals to shut their pieholes.

Not that it happens very often. And just like life, these New York rivalries have their winners and losers. The Mets and Jets have been the clear underdogs in the last two decades, accumulating only one world championship between them since 1986. Of course, the Yankees have four World Series rings during that span and the Giants have two Lombardi trophies.

There has been some evidence of crossing over. The weak-willed, bandwagon types can be found sneaking into the other's arena during the good times, as the overflowing crowds at Yankee Stadium these days can attest. The House that Ruth Built was empty during the Mets' rise in the mid- to late-'80s, and that would be difficult to explain if the true believers stuck behind their respective teams. These fair-weather fans are pariahs in New York, traitors that belong in one-team towns.

Thankfully, the Big Apple's civil war rages every time the Rangers battle the Islanders ("Potvin beats his wife! Potvin beats his wife!"). Who can forget the 2003 meeting at the Nassau Coliseum when a flood of Santas skated onto the ice between periods and one stupid St. Nick pulled up his costume to reveal a Rangers sweater underneath. He was immediately dragged to the ice and pummeled senseless by the rest of the Islander-loving Santas, who clearly enjoyed the early Christmas present.

It's probably a good thing that the Jets and Giants play each other infrequently during the regular season because corralling two unruly mobs in the Meadowlands is never a good idea, especially after four hours of tailgating tune-up with Miller Lite and Wild Turkey. These blood feuds make the Great Santa Massacre seem like a night at the Rockettes.

I can see children growing up in New York, asking their dad or mom why they can't wear both a Mets and a Yankees cap. All their parents have to do is pull out a videotape of Roger Clemens denting Mike Piazza's helmet with a ninety-six-mph beanball. It's that simple.

And it's never enough for your team to be doing well. The other one has to be miserable. If the Jets are cruising toward the playoffs, the Giants must be pathetic losers, and vice versa. Nothing brings their respective fans greater pleasure. And that's how it should be.

Rubin says: Dave, my friend, you have a closed-minded view of the world. You don't see the best in New Yorkers. You don't see the potential for them to experience a cornucopia of good feelings. In fact, you promote a mind-set that discourages it.

I find it almost ironic that you would use the example of the 2004 presidential election as an example because I know you're not a red-stater, even though you sound like one right now. You profess to quell all dialogue by shouting down others who don't agree with you.

There are plenty of people in the Big Apple who like both the Jets and the Giants, who like both the Yankees and the Mets, who like both the Knicks and the Nets.

The Rangers and the Islanders? Maybe not so much.

You know what they get to enjoy that the people in your world do not? On every NFL Sunday, they have a team to root for at 1 P.M. and another at 4 P.M. In late September, they have two baseball pennant races to follow. During the NBA season, they can marvel at both Jason Kidd and Stephon Marbury and not feel guilty about it. And when the hot-stove fires roar in New York each winter as the Mets and Yankees maneuver to build their teams for next season, they get something to talk about at the water cooler almost every day.

For people who can feel more than one allegiance, there are stories in the newspapers they don't have to blow past. For six months there always is a home baseball game to attend. And every weekend during the football season, there is a reason to load up the SUV, head out to the Giants Stadium parking lot, and fire up the barbecue. And wouldn't it be nice to do that more than eight times each autumn?

Can you see a beautiful world coming into view, Dave? I think you can.

For the people who live the kind of life I describe, there are going to be confounding moments. The Mets and Yankees play each other six times each season because of the abominable introduction of interleague play. The Knicks and Nets meet four times each season. The Giants and Jets only face each other once in a blue moon. So there we have an average of ten days each year where one feels conflict.

I believe that things were different before the Giants and Dodgers packed up for the West Coast. They played in an eight-team division where only one team would make it to the postseason and they met twenty-two times per season. That's too many contests at too close a range and with too much at stake to be able to cheer for both clubs. Though it would have been something if they'd played into the 1960s in New York and we'd all gotten Mays and Marichal against Koufax and Drysdale every couple weeks.

Those might not be six to ten days that my people look forward to, but at least there is the debate. Everyone loves to talk sports, take a position, and debate. When the Mets and Yankees are facing each other on the same field, the level of discourse in the city escalates. My people have a position to take no matter what circumstances they find themselves in.

And they never get pelted with beer by other fans in The House that Ruth Built.

New Yorkers are bigger than the types who wish ill upon their neighbors who root for a different team. Yankees fans can pray for a Boston collapse. Mets fans can relish a Braves injury. But when Yankees fans describe their good feelings about winning the World

Series in 1996 or 1998, I assure you that none of them say "and what made it even better was that the Mets blew."

I don't believe that Giants fans didn't like Namath, or that Mets fans don't appreciate Jeter or that Knicks fans hate Jason Kidd.

New Yorkers have room in their hearts for all the area teams.

It's a beautiful world out here, Dave. Come see what it's like.

9

A-Rod: Money Player or Just Plays for the Money?

Rubin says: New York has passionate and attentive sports fans, but this is the question they ask that baffles me the most. I am astonished to find there are people in this town who think Alex Rodriguez is anything other than one of the best baseball players in the game. Hell, he might even be *the* best.

Did Rodriguez stink up the joint during the 2005 postseason? No question about it. But did he also win the 2005 American League MVP? You bet he did and, as always, he was a dominant performer in many aspects of the game.

I have to believe the genesis of a question like this somehow lies in the ludicrous amount of money the guy makes. The $252 million deal he managed to score off the Rangers before the 2001 season has somehow turned people against him. And this is something that's completely stupid. He got a great deal! Someone was willing to pay him that! Can you honestly say that any of us would turn such an offer down? I think not!

And while I'd like to go on a tangent about how great our free market economy is, I instead will continue to wonder what his mad cash has to do with anything.

Rodriguez could end up the best player of a generation. Before age thirty he had four hundred home runs. And he could certainly end up passing Hank Aaron's 755 home runs in his career. And here's what makes it even better. Unlike some big home run hitters of the past decade, no one is going to suggest that A-Rod rode the juice to reach his heights.

The other thing that strikes me as ridiculous about the questioning of A-Rod is this notion that he's a selfish player and this works to the detriment of his team. Rodriguez may have some character flaws and he may be self-absorbed—though that may be the rule with elite athletes—but he wants to win a championship and he cares about doing it with a team that has made him feel at home.

Rodriguez so wants to be part of a winner that when the Red Sox were on the cusp of making a deal to bring him to Boston, he offered to lessen the value of his contract by about $12 million. And to facilitate the trade that brought him to the Yankees he wasn't so selfish as to demand to play shortstop, even though most considered him the best defensive shortstop in baseball as well.

A-Rod's personality quirks have come out and brought him his share of bad moments on the diamond and in the clubhouse. The prelude to his lunching on Jason Varitek's mitt during the 2004 regular season wasn't pretty. And it was nothing short of embarrassing when he slapped the ball out of Bronson Arroyo's glove during the 2004 ALCS (though it did inspire a hilarious photo on the Internet of the play with a woman's purse superimposed on his arm).

And it's also pretty clear that Rodriguez somehow rubs some of his teammates the wrong way. They've never reacted well when he's tried to step in front of Jeter as the voice of the team.

I won't apologize for any of that either. But I will say this: I'll take it every time as long as it comes with a .315 average, forty-five home runs, 125 RBI, and twenty stolen bases every season. And did I mention that he's also become one of the best-fielding third basemen in just two seasons since the position switch?

Maybe the Rodriguez thing couldn't work in Texas. Maybe on the Rangers budget they could not afford to surround him with enough good players while paying that monstrous salary. That's just not the case with the Yankees. And I don't think it's fair that A-Rod is always in the crosshairs. In 2005, Mike Mussina got $19 million to go 13-8 and Kevin Brown got almost $16 million to pitch less than seventy-five innings. Even at $25 million, you can see Rodriguez is a much better value.

He seems pretty money to me.

Lennon says: When it comes to numbers, Roger, you're absolutely right. No one's better than Alex Rodriguez. Just ask his agent, Scott Boras, who produced a binder the size of a Dallas phone book when it came time to negotiate that ludicrous $252-million deal with the Texas Rangers.

Not that there's anything wrong with that. Baseball, after all, is a business, and I'll never fault a player for squeezing every last dime he can get from a billion-dollar industry. But maybe Steve Phillips was on to something when he said the Mets didn't want A-Rod because of the 24-and-1 mentality it would create in the clubhouse.

Of course, Phillips, GM at the time, was merely covering for owner Fred Wilpon, who wanted no part of paying Rodriguez. There is, however, some truth in that statement. A-Rod, like that tiki idol Bobby Brady finds in Hawaii, brings nothing but bad luck to whatever franchise strings him around its neck.

The Mariners were good with A-Rod. But the year he bolts for the megabucks in Texas, Seattle breaks the Yankees' record for regular-season victories and the Rangers plummet in the American League West standings. Not that it bothers Rodriguez any. Two years later, with Texas in disarray, A-Rod hits forty-seven home runs and wins the MVP for a team that finishes in last place and twenty games under .500.

When the Rangers finally realized they couldn't win as long as A-Rod was bleeding them dry, they unloaded him on the Yankees. But in a delicious twist of irony, the team that was thwarted in their efforts to get Rodriguez—the Red Sox—reversed an eighty-six-year-old curse and beat A-Rod's Yankees en route to their first World Series title since 1918. Coincidence? Methinks not.

So what is it about Rodriguez? Is he just too high-maintenance to have on a championship team? Could be. Whatever is going on with the Yankees, it always seems to come back to A-Rod. Last year, when the media was buzzing about his futility against the Red Sox, Rodriguez reportedly saved a young boy from oncoming traffic in front of the team's hotel in Copley Square. Not long after, A-Rod and his wife appeared on the front page of the *Daily News*, extolling the virtues of psychotherapy.

I know what you're saying. What's that got to do with anything? And I ask you this: How many times have you seen Derek Jeter on the front page of the tabloids blabbing about his personal stuff? Zero, that's how many. The only time you'll catch Jeter in the front section of the newspaper is when he's photographed swimming with supermodels, and that's during the offseason. That's not entirely why Jeter has four World Series rings, but that's four more than A-Rod, so draw your own conclusions.

Which brings us to last October, the only month that really matters to the Yankees. During the regular season, Rodriguez earned his second MVP trophy by batting .321 with forty-eight home runs and 130 RBI. It was a spectacular year for him, and crucial to the Yankees, who rallied to overtake the Red Sox for the division title during the final month of the season.

But when it came time for the playoffs, A-Rod vanished against the Angels, and he should consider himself lucky that The Boss chose not to dust off the Mr. May nickname he stuck on Dave Winfield more than two decades earlier. Rodriguez batted .133 (2-for-15) in that Division Series and didn't drive in a run.

If any moment defined Rodriguez during that series it was the ninth inning of Game 5, when the Yankees trailed by the score of 5–3. Jeter, who batted .333 with two homers and 5 RBI in the

ALDS, led off with a single, and A-Rod, the tying run, immediately grounded into a double play. The only thing more perfect than his timely failure was his comments afterward.

"I had a great year, something I'm very proud of," Rodriguez said. "I left my guts on the field, I left my heart out there, so I'm not going to hang my head. I'm just going to go out and learn from it and become a better Yankee."

For $252 million, a team should get more than a pretty face and flowery comments. Rodriguez always has great years. That's why he's the richest player in baseball and a bona fide lock for the Hall of Fame. Just get used to watching other teams in the World Series as long as he's on your roster.

10

What Was the Greatest Sporting Event Held at Madison Square Garden?

Lennon says: I could get all sarcastic here and make some joking reference to Bruno Sammartino and Ivan "The Polish Hammer" Putski, but only because there's no real debate involved when it comes to this question.

"The Fight of the Century"—otherwise known as Ali-Frazier I—goes right at the top of the list, and everything else that happened at the corner of Thirty-third Street and Seventh Avenue finishes a distant second.

I know that boxing means little to the Nintendo generation, but I'll try to paint a picture for those who think *Rocky III* was a documentary. As for the fight fans who remember the night of March 8, 1971, and the weeks leading up to that historic date, there's not much I can say to embellish that evening.

Not only was the first Ali-Frazier clash the greatest event ever staged at the Garden, many consider it one of the most significant sporting experiences in history. Right up there with David upsetting Goliath, only with a bigger television audience.

This was one of those rare occasions where the fight actually lived up to the hype. And you couldn't invent two better combatants. When Muhammad Ali signed on to face Joe Frazier, the Supreme Court was still deciding whether or not to jail him for refusing the draft. Can you imagine the type of media circus that would create now? With twenty-four-hour news channels and the Internet? Ali's news conferences alone would be pay-per-view episodes.

But this was about more than Ali's politics and a nation divided. There was a heavyweight belt on the line, too. Ali was 31-0 with twenty-five knockouts heading into the title bout, but had been stripped of his title because of his legal battle. Frazier was 26-0 with twenty-three KO's and was the reigning champion only because of Ali's feud with the U.S. government.

Don King wasn't promoting fights at the time, but maybe somebody related to him was—Ali and Frazier each received only $2.5 million instead of getting a cut of the gross profits, which would exceed $30 million.

Even the weigh-in was a spectacle. Ali's presence that day caused a riot outside the Garden, and he was cautioned to stay inside the arena to avoid the stampeding crowds. When it was finally time for Ali and Frazier to step into the ring later that night, the scene was surreal, according to people lucky enough to witness it.

"That night the Garden was like a combination of New Year's Eve and the Easter Parade," MSG publicist John F. X. Condon told Ali biographer Thomas Hauser. "I don't think there's ever been a night like it. It was one of those evenings where everybody who was anybody was there. I look in the press section and I see Frank Sinatra [shooting photographs for *Life* magazine]. I'd just finished kicking out Dustin Hoffman and Diana Ross."

And this generation thinks it's a big deal when Mike Tyson chomps on Evander Holyfield's ear like it was a Slim Jim. For all of Ali's bluster and badgering of Frazier, it was Frazier who delivered the most startling—and prophetic—words before the fight. He didn't care about sharing his strategy either.

"He can keep that pretty head," Frazier said of Ali. "I don't want it. What I'm going to do is try and pull them kidneys out."

For pure shock appeal, it's not Tyson saying he's going to eat

Holyfield's children, but Frazier made good on his promise. He slowed Ali with a vicious body attack, and by the later rounds, managed to hurt Ali in a way he had never been hurt before.

In the eleventh round, Frazier shook Ali with a thunderous left hook, and then knocked him down with the same punch in the fifteenth. The sellout crowd of 20,455 was stunned to see Ali on his back, even though he bounced to his feet almost as quickly.

"He was going to get up if he was dead," Ali's corner man, Ferdie Pacheco, said. "If Frazier had killed him, he'd have gotten up."

But in the end, it didn't matter. Frazier won by a unanimous decision, setting the stage for a string of rematches that never lived up to the original. The Garden was only three years old when it hosted "The Fight of the Century" and nothing has come close ever since.

"Just lost a fight, that's all," Ali told reporters the next morning. "Presidents get assassinated, civil rights leaders get assassinated. The world goes on. You'll all be writing about something else soon."

That was a different era, but the impact of that night at the Garden still resonates to this day.

Rubin says: Dave, you have picked one of the shaping moments in sports as your choice and I commend you on it. I'm never going to throw stones at this selection, one of the great nights in American sports history. But I consider the first Ali-Frazier fight as the runner-up in this category. I think there is one seminal moment from the Garden's history that supersedes even that.

On the afternoon of May 8, 1970, the entire city of New York was having a massive panic attack. The Knicks were to face the Los Angeles Lakers in Game 7 of the NBA Finals and were looking at the prospect of doing it without their team captain and leading scorer. Then, moments before tip-off that evening, badly injured center Willis Reed limped out of the tunnel that led from the

'Bockers' locker room to the Garden floor. In one moment, one man would swing all the momentum of an entire NBA season and send the hometown team to its first NBA crown.

Reed's courageous effort that night became the standard, for all of sport, for playing in pain. Kirk Gibson's 1988 home run against the Oakland A's—when he could hardly swing a bat and barely make it around the bases—was simply amazing theater and only a fraction of what Reed did. To this day—and surely for eternity—when someone overcomes an injury to perform in a critical game, Reed's name will be invoked.

"Madison Square Garden used to seat 19,500, maybe 19,600," Reed said in a recent interview with Frank Isola of the *Daily News*. "But the count is now up to 200,000 because that's how many people told me they were there that night."

Reed pulled his right thigh muscle in Game 5 and had to miss Game 6 in Los Angeles. There, without Reed to play defense, Lakers center Wilt Chamberlain scored forty-five points as they knotted the series with the Knicks. All of New York could only pray that Reed would make an improbable—make that impossible—return to be the difference maker in the series.

That he did, though he was nowhere close to game condition. He didn't know if he'd be able to play when he arrived at the Garden that night, and felt able to suit up and play only after getting treatment and a shot of Carbocaine.

Reed knew full well that he wasn't going to be able to make a difference with his play on the court. He was too hobbled to either stop the Big Dipper or make an offensive impact. But he also knew that by making a courageous effort and getting into the game, he would be able to shift the psychological advantage back into the Knicks' favor.

When Reed made his way out of the tunnel and into the pregame layup line, accounts of the game say the Lakers stopped in their tracks and just watched him. And he'd only begun to provide his team with the inspirational lift that would carry them to victory.

Reed was clearly incapacitated by the injury, but he scored New York's first points on a jump shot and then made another to push the lead to 5–2. That was almost all of the statistical contribution he would be able to make that night.

The stat line shows Reed finished with four points and three rebounds in twenty-seven minutes, but just the same he is considered the reason New York prevailed in that game. Almost no one remembers the phenomenal effort of Walt Frazier, who totaled thirty-six points and nineteen assists in the contest. Willis Reed won the Knicks that title.

"People always talk about [how] last shots win games," Reed said, "but I think the first shot won a game.

"If ever there was any doubt my teammates could get this done, I think all doubt was erased when I went out on the court."

THE TEN GREATEST GARDEN EVENTS OF THE LAST THIRTY-FIVE YEARS

1. Muhammad Ali vs. Joe Frazier: The first meeting of these heavyweight titans on March 8, 1971, lived up to its hype as the "fight of the century." The undefeated Ali had been stripped of his title for refusing the draft. The undefeated Frazier had been anointed the champion and still was the underdog. Frazier prevailed in a unanimous decision after putting Ali on the canvas in the fifteenth round.

2. Willis Reed hobbles to the court: In a single heroic moment on May 8, 1970, the badly injured Knicks captain provided his team with the inspiration to win Game 7 of the NBA Finals and claim the franchise's first championship. After suffering a severely pulled thigh muscle that forced him to miss Game 6, Reed's appearance and four first-quarter points inspired the Knicks to beat the Lakers 113–99.

3. The Rangers win the Stanley Cup: The Blueshirts shook off fifty-four years of frustration and captured Game 7 of the Finals against Vancouver by a 3–2 score on June 9, 1994. The image of captain Mark Messier, who'd been bold enough to guarantee a Game 6 win in the Conference Finals and then delivered it with a hat trick, strikes an enduring image as he hoists the Cup. In the stands one fan holds a sign that reads "Now I Can Die In Peace."

4. Ali gets payback: It was never going to match the hype of their first contest some three years earlier, but the twelve-round heavyweight championship bout on January 28, 1974, was still one of the great nights in boxing. Frazier, closing in on the end of a great career, was saved from a second-round knockout by a referee's error and then stunned Ali in the seventh with the same left hook he'd used to floor him in the final round of their first meeting. Ali prevailed with a twelve-round unanimous decision.

5. "Matteau! Matteau! Matteau!": The Rangers' drive to the 1994 Stanley Cup was filled with ridiculously exciting moments and on May 27, 1994, they won Game 7 of the Eastern Conference Finals over the rival New Jersey Devils in overtime. The Rangers managed to reach a seventh game only after Mark Messier delivered, with a hat trick, on a guarantee of a Game 6 win at the Meadowlands. The Devils tied the game with less than ten seconds left in regulation on Valeri Zelepukin's goal, but Stephane Matteau lifted the Rangers with his wraparound score past Martin Brodeur.

6. The "Sweater Game": In 1985 the hottest ticket at the Garden was not for a boxing match or a Knicks game or a Rangers game. It was for St. John's February 27 meeting against Big East archrival Georgetown. The Chris Mullin–led Redmen were No. 1 in the country. The Patrick Ewing–led Hoyas were No. 2. And before tip-off Georgetown coach John Thompson came out wearing a sweater identical to Lou Carnesecca's trademark lucky sweater. Georgetown prevailed behind Ewing's twenty points, 85–69.

7. The "Double-nickel": Michael Jordan always enjoyed playing against the Knicks at the Garden, but after missing all of the 1994 season and most of the 1995 season in a failed attempt to become a big-league baseball player, no one was sure what he'd be like in his return. Jordan answered all doubters with fifty-five points in just his fifth game of that season. He also made the pass to Bill Wennington in the final seconds that provided a dunk and a 113–111 win.

8. Perfect 10: Before March 28, 1976, no gymnast had ever scored a perfect 10.0 score in an international competition. That was the day that Soviet fourteen-year-old Nadia Comaneci competed in the American Cup. The eighty-six-pounder got 10s in the floor exercise and the vault and won all four events she was entered in. Three months later she would capture gold in Montreal.

9. Class of the Masters: For four hours and forty-two minutes on December 5, 1988, Boris Becker and Ivan Lendl hammered each other in the final of the Nabisco Masters, one of the best tennis matches ever played on U.S. soil. Becker, who'd become an overnight sensation by winning Wimbledon three years earlier, ended Lendl's run of three straight titles with a five-set victory, 5–7, 7–6, 3–6, 6–2, 7–6. It was as close as a match could get, with Becker winning 164 points and twenty-eight games to Lendl's 162 points and twenty-seven games.

10. A fine "Mess": It was January 12, 2006, when the Rangers honored their greatest hero, Mark Messier, by retiring his number and raising a banner to the rafters. The Rangers captain transformed a snake-bit franchise into a Stanley Cup champion in just three seasons and the night he was honored will stand as one of the great nights in franchise history.

11

Dwight Gooden and Darryl Strawberry: Tragic Heroes or Wasted Careers?

Rubin says: This is really a question of "what is" and "what should have been."

Here's the "what is": Dwight Gooden and Darryl Strawberry were key players for the Mets in the mid-1980s, helped the club to a very significant World Series title in 1986, and then surprisingly hung on to play small roles when the Yankees won four titles between 1996 and 2000.

Here's "what should have been":

○ Strawberry should have become Reggie Jackson, a player who must always be mentioned in a discussion of baseball's all-time best power hitters;

○ Gooden should have become a modern-day Tom Seaver, a part of any realistic conversation about the best right-handed pitchers of a generation;

○ And the Mets should have grown into New York's dynasty baseball team, led to handfuls of World Series titles by a pair of certain Hall of Famers.

It should be seen as nothing short of a tragedy that things ended up one way and not the other. As New Yorkers, we must appreciate their contributions to some of our finest moments. Each was a part of a couple of great October celebrations. Still, if you feel anything but shortchanged by what we got from these two, you may be the one who needs to reevaluate.

Strawberry and Gooden cheated themselves and us with by running afoul with drugs and the law. Instead of being part of the fabric of baseball, they are footnotes. Worse still, they robbed millions of fans—from kids who looked up to them as role models to season ticket holders who essentially paid their salaries—of something that could have been very special.

Maybe, Dave, you're going to be one of their many apologists. There are lots of them, a myopic group that says "they helped the Mets win in '86 and gave us a summer to remember." Maybe instead you'll say "they owed more to themselves and so we should not lament." But like it or not, a great baseball player can be a beacon who touches many people. These two flamed out much too soon.

In the early 1980s, Strawberry and Gooden had the world laid out before them.

The five-tool Strawberry needed less than three seasons in the minors and burst onto the scene with a freshman season that earned him the NL Rookie of the Year award. And for nine seasons he would average more than thirty home runs a year and make the all-star team eight times.

But that really ended up being it. He averaged less than forty-five games per season during the last eight years of his career, a period laden with incidents of spousal abuse, three drug suspensions, and numerous stints in rehab for cocaine and alcohol abuse. The 1994 tax evasion indictment and 1999 solicitation arrest also weren't high-water marks.

That Strawberry was able to work himself back to play bit roles on the 1996, 1998, and 1999 Yankees teams could be viewed as impressive. Of course one might consider that at ages thirty-four and thirty-six, Jackson was one of the best players in baseball and won the home run title both years.

Gooden was the NL Rookie of the Year in 1984 at age nineteen and the NL Cy Young Award winner in 1985. He had a hundred wins before the age of twenty-five and had helped the Mets capture the '86 Series. He had the best curveball in the majors, prompting those who call the pitch "Uncle Charlie" to dub his "Lord Charles."

Gooden's drug problems first tripped him up during the off-season after the World Series and plagued him the rest of his career. By the time he tested positive for cocaine in 1994, he'd crossed the line enough times to be banned from the game for the entire 1995 season.

Many would say there was a small measure of redemption in 1996 when he went 11-7 for the Yankees and pitched his no-hitter against the Mariners. Instead, I felt something else watching him hit the mid-90s on the radar gun that day. Gooden's demons claimed more than a half dozen seasons that could have been special.

In the cases of both Strawberry and Gooden, their struggles against addiction are lamentable. But no one looks on unmet potential and sees greatness.

Lennon says: Perhaps in a perfect world—that is, one without career-busting temptations—Dwight Gooden and Darryl Strawberry would be standing at the podium in Cooperstown one day. But there are no guarantees in this life, regardless of how fast you can throw a baseball or how far you can hit it, and Doc and Straw are two examples of the wide gulf between potential and reality.

I can't argue with you, Rog, when you talk about the talent each of these troubled players possessed. But I do have a problem with the perception of "what should have been." You talk about Doc and

Straw like you deserve a refund, as if these two offended the sensibility of a city and its fans.

But they did nothing more criminal than hold up a mirror to a metropolis that spun wildly out of control during the coked-up '80s, and are as important as tragic role models today as they were winning World Series rings in both Flushing and the Bronx. It's a familiar story, building celebrities up so they can be torn down at a later date, and Doc and Straw had the misfortune of hitting their stride during a time that was not kind to addictive personalities with millions in disposable income.

The Manhattan club scene was awash in cocaine during the Reagan '80s—or Bolivian Marching Powder, as penned by Jay McInerney—and there was no bigger player on that stage than the brash, bullying Mets. They owned New York by 1986, and none shined brighter than Doc and Straw. Even their nicknames were made for the back page, and their antics, both on the field and off, generated plenty of headlines for the front of the newspaper, too.

But that, in a strange way, was part of the bad-boy charm. And as you mentioned, Rog, both of them were more than just sideshow attractions. It's not like Gooden flamed out before ever getting to the majors. Winning the Rookie of the Year award at nineteen and the Cy Young the following season is a rare accomplishment in its own right. As for Strawberry, he also was a Rookie of the Year and an eight-time all-star. Not too shabby.

But the most compelling storylines for these two involved their second chances across town with the Yankees. Gooden was suspended for the entire 1995 season after testing positive for cocaine, but on George Steinbrenner's invite, mounted his comeback in the Bronx and threw his first career no-hitter on a magical night at Yankee Stadium. And not against some patsies like the Twins or Expos, either. Gooden silenced the mighty Mariners.

Strawberry lasted longer in pinstripes, and proved that he could still be as formidable as a role player, just as long as he had a bat in his hands. I remember what it was like in the Bronx when Strawberry was called on to pinch hit. Just the sight of him heading toward the on-deck circle brought the crowd to its feet, and after one of his high-arcing shots landed in the upper deck, there wasn't a soul who thought about his troubled past.

Doc and Straw were supposed to spend their careers performing those same heroics for the Mets, but it just didn't work out that way. Instead, now that their playing days are over, they caution others not to make the same mistakes. Delivering those cautionary tales probably has more value to society at large than anything Doc and Straw did on a baseball field. Sure they were fun to watch, but that was never the whole story. And being human is nothing anyone needs to apologize for.

So Doc and Straw won't have plaques in Cooperstown. They still have more than a few mementos in the building, and it's not like they'll ever be forgotten in this city. Both ascended to a larger-than life status that only a precious few reach in New York, and they even picked up a couple of World Series rings along the way. They might not have turned out to be the best ever, but they left their mark on baseball history, and are still helping to change lives beyond the game.

Who Is the Most "Significant Other"?

Lennon says: I know what some of you are saying out there. "What in the name of Brigitte Nielsen does this have to do with anything?" And I'll tell you that this is a burning issue that needs to be addressed.

Why? Look what happened to Kris Benson. Five minutes after his wife, Anna, was talking with *Playboy* about a photo shoot, the Mets were trying to trade him to Kansas City. Coincidence? I don't think so.

But don't confuse significant with self-destructive. Shoot, hooking up with Marilyn Monroe probably was not one of Joe DiMaggio's best moves, either, though you can't blame a guy for trying. What I'm looking for here is the most media-friendly of the bunch, the ones that attract as much attention, if not more, than what's happening in the game.

Right at the top of that list is Carol Alt, a fixture on Rangers' broadcasts during her marriage to defenseman Ron Greschner. This was as big a power couple as you could get in the NHL, which, for some reason, has always attracted more than its share of attention from supermodels.

Greschner was no slouch, either. Before Brian Leetch came along, Greschner was the Rangers' all-time leader in points, goals, and assists. His marriage to Alt, however, helped him bridge the gap from the back of the newspaper to Page Six.

Back then, there were no Web sites to post inflammatory comments, and the most outrageous thing Greschner and Alt did together was make a workout video. Oh, and a couple of bad Italian movies. Apparently, Alt was the darling of Italian filmmakers, and Greschner was an extra in one of their movies.

And Alt was in a different league than Anna Benson, who needs to make outrageous comments to sell her pictorials in fringe men's magazines. Alt, nicknamed "The Face," helped launch the *Sports Illustrated* swimsuit edition by gracing the very first cover. If that wasn't enough, *Playboy* dubbed Alt, "The Most Beautiful Woman in the World." No wonder she was a favorite of the TV cameras at the Garden. Alt was worth a few ratings points on her own.

But there was more to Alt's city appeal than swimsuits and magazine covers. She was one of New York's own—raised in East Williston, L.I. and was discovered as a student at Hofstra. As for her affection for the NHL, Alt said it had more to do with the players than the game.

"I grew up on Long Island," Alt told ESPN.com. "I didn't even know the Islanders existed. I mean, the only guy I ever went to see at Nassau Coliseum was Bob Dylan."

All that changed when she married Greschner in 1983. But it was after her divorce, thirteen years later, that she changed her home ice from Thirty-third Street to Hempstead Turnpike. Much to the disappointment of Rangers' fans, Alt changed allegiances to the Blueshirts' hated adversary when she married Islanders defenseman Alexei Yashin.

That stands as one of the biggest trades between the two bitter rivals, but Alt never caused much of a stir beyond roiling up the fans at the arenas. And she never became a divisive force in either organization, which is more that can be said of many others.

Whether it's Mark Gastineau's turbulent relationship with Nielsen, which led to his premature retirement, or the more recent episode involving Antonio Davis's wife, Kendra, and her scuffle in the stands, a player's wife or girlfriend can easily become a factor in the success of a franchise. When Alex Rodriguez's wife, Cindy, opened up about their therapy visits, it was on the front page of the *Daily News*, for better or for worse.

Of course, none have been blamed as directly as Anna Benson was for the trade of her husband, and Alt's marriages to a pair of NHL stars probably had the opposite effect for those franchises. Having her around made it worth holding on to the husbands.

Rubin says: Dave, while credit goes your way for not picking D-list celebrity Anna Benson (or is that Double-D list?), I'm afraid to say that years of keeping Carol Alt's *SI* swimsuit cover under your mattress doesn't qualify her as the most "significant other" to anyone but you.

A staggering beauty? You bet. She's got a huge fan right here. But the only significant thing she did on the sports scene was make the Rangers' and then Islanders' telecasts just a little more fun to watch. Divorcing a Ranger and later marrying an Islander was certainly newsworthy, but she never commanded the headlines or overshadowed her husband's team.

Marilyn Peterson and Susan Kekich, on the other hand, did both of those things when they pulled a little switch of their own before spring training in 1973.

Yankees pitchers Fritz Peterson and Mike Kekich actually swapped wives before spring training in 1973, embroiling the club in a huge morality scandal just as George Steinbrenner was taking the reins of the franchise. You think getting on Page Six is a big deal, Davey Boy, try owning the front pages for a long run.

Yes, we're talking about something that happened in the wake of the Swinging Sixties and not something from the current Republican Victorian age, but this still was shocking stuff. The two left-handers (like there was any chance they'd be anything else) not only swapped wives, they swapped kids, houses, and pets.

"We didn't swap wives, we swapped lives," Peterson said at the time.

"We didn't do anything sneaky or lecherous," Susan said. "There isn't anything smutty about this."

Right. Got it. Nothing smutty.

The pitchers became teammates when Kekich was traded from the Dodgers before the 1969 season, and grew to be fast friends. They socialized at home and on the road and the two couples would sometimes double date. It was on one such occasion that someone in the group initially floated the idea.

Now, it seems pretty obvious that this isn't something that people would just go ahead and do without, um, seeing what it might be like. So it's pretty safe to assume that the double dates from that point on were more like something out of a porn movie than a Rockwell painting.

The Yankees didn't have a clue how to handle the situation, and so the intrigue roiled along all through the spring, with players alternately making jokes about the situations and insisting that neither player's performance would be affected.

But all of baseball felt the shockwaves. Commissioner Bowie Kuhn said he was appalled by the behavior of the two pitchers. Suddenly all of baseball had to deal with the public speculation about the kinds of things that were happening behind closed doors in the sport, not unlike the conjecture the NBA grappled with over rumors of rampant narcotics use later in the decade.

As it turned out, Marilyn and Susan's "moves" ended up having an enormous impact on the Yankees' season and both their husbands (ex-husbands? Oh, well, whatever).

Peterson had averaged seventeen wins a season for the Bombers during the previous four seasons, but slumped to 8-15 with an ERA close to 4.00. Kekich lost his spot in the starting rotation and, after going 2-5 with a 7.52 ERA in twenty-one appearances, got traded to Cleveland for the estimable Lowell Palmer.

Peterson was dealt in the middle of the following season—also to the Indians—in a move that brought Chris Chambliss to the Bronx. By then Kekich had been released.

The mixing of couples ended up in mixed results as well. Susan and Fritz were married in 1974. Marilyn and Mike split up after only a few months.

Carol Alt might have been the best New York spouse to look at, but Marilyn Peterson and Susan Kekich were ones they actually wanted to talk about.

SETTLE THE SCORE/WILL LEITCH

(Will Leitch, the editor of the wildly popular Web site Deadspin.com, knows a thing or two about the off-the-field allure of sports culture. We figured that made him a reliable source to settle this score.)

It's got to be Anna Benson. The thing about some of the things she says is that she would not get away with them if she were not an attractive woman. And for the record, she's not even *that* attractive. She *is* attractive, but she's not *that* attractive, which somehow makes her even more of a character and more enjoyable.

I guarantee you there are players who have more attractive wives than Anna Benson. People pay attention to her because she's loud, and because she's willing to wear a baseball bikini. Obviously, she's very good at self-promotion and knows how to play the media.

The funny thing about her, for somebody that's so obviously over-covered, is that she's actually crazier than people realize. The loony part of her personality never quite gets out there. She's almost too crazy for people to report on. So much of her seems self-promotional. But the stuff she writes on her Web site—those little rants—that's not self-promotional at all. It's just kind of scary.

If you go to her Web site, she looks legitimately unhinged. It's not just that she writes, "I think PETA takes the defense of animals to an extreme." She writes, "Hey, sometimes I like to eat the cute little bunnies!" You know? It's not enough that she says, "Hey, I think the gun control people have gone a little overboard." She says, "Sometimes I get a gun and the most exciting thing is to shoot at something and kill it!"

Another funny thing about Anna Benson is that, for somebody that's supposedly a model, there are, like, seven pictures of her. I mean, one of the things she says on her Web site is that she's one of the most downloaded women on the Internet. Well, it's because there's only seven pictures. And there were, like, two before she came to New York. Now there's seven, and most of them are when she plays Santa at a press conference or something.

It's so interesting that she's become this . . . I don't know what. She's like a mad genius. If you remember their press conference [when Kris Benson was traded to Baltimore], she said they found out about the trade from a reporter while they were doing [the *FHM*] photo shoot. And then they go to Kris, and Kris always has this blank "What are you going to do?" look on his face every time she goes off like that. The first thing Kris says is that he found out about the trade when he got off the plane to New York. And for the smallest second, you see Anna's face twitch, and you just know he's getting his ass kicked. That's the thing. She's so good that she realizes it's not enough that they were traded—it was right in the middle of her *FHM* photo shoot!

Part of her is very calculating, and wants to control everything in the media, but then there's this other side of her that is just nuts. She's both calculating and yet kind of unhinged, and to me, no matter what else she is, she's just endlessly entertaining to watch, almost in spite of herself. She's always one of our most popular features.

Which Is the Greatest Single Performance?

Rubin says: Because this is New York and because it has hosted every kind of sporting event imaginable, we've seen a myriad of spectacular efforts by some of the greatest athletes in every sport. We've seen phenomenal performances in the boxing rings and on the baseball diamonds, from the hardwood and ice of our arenas to the asphalt courts at the National Tennis Center.

And here's what I think: You could take the best effort from every one of those—the perfect games and the hat tricks and straight-set victories—and pile them on top of one another and it still wouldn't nearly stack up to what we saw on June 9, 1973, at Belmont Park. That was the day Secretariat completed the first Triple Crown in twenty-five years with the greatest horse race ever run.

We don't have many moments from sports history that are like that one. In that moment the finest athlete a sport has ever known realized every ounce of his potential, and left a nation of sports fans talking about it for decades.

Wilt Chamberlain can have his one hundred-point game—something most people consider the best single-day performance by any competitor in any sport. Secretariat's record-setting win at the Belmont Stakes is not just the most superlative effort in New York history. It's the preeminent single performance since Cain and Abel raced to the far side of the backyard.

The final moment of that race has produced one my favorite sports photos ever. We've all seen that shot of Secretariat at the finish. You can barely make out that there were any other horses in the race. It's like the race was over and they hadn't even gotten to the stretch. Big Red was the winner by a breathtaking thirty-one lengths in a time of 2:24 for 1½ miles, the all-time record on a dirt track.

There have been many records we think can never be broken. Some have fallen, like Lou Gehrig's 2,130 consecutive games or Bob Beamon's long jump of 29'2½" or Sandy Koufax's four no-hitters. And there are those that will probably live up to the promise, like Joe DiMaggio's fifty-six-game hitting streak. Secretariat's Belmont goes firmly in that second category.

Three decades have produced some of the finest thoroughbreds in racing and none have come within two seconds of that time. It's untouchable. And so was Secretariat that day.

Big Red had already set a world record for 1¼ miles at the Kentucky Derby and was clocked to a Pimlico track record for 1³⁄16 miles at the Preakness (albeit there is some dispute because of a malfunctioning clock). That's why he went off as a 1–10 favorite that day. But if you look at his splits for the Belmont you will see he was moving a far sight faster than he did in either of those.

The archrival that season was named Sham, and this was supposed to be the competitor who could run with the favorite. In a matter of three-quarters of a mile, Secretariat turned Sham to Shame by forcing him to expend all he had just to keep up. Sham was only two lengths back halfway through the race and finished dead last, more than forty-five lengths in the dust.

Stunned onlookers at the track that day saw Secretariat, with Ron Turcotte up, break away from the pack, and feared that his tank would empty before he could finish. Just two weeks before racing at Churchill Downs, Big Red seemed incapable of winning a race as long as 1¼ miles and this was two furlongs more.

But Turcotte knew better. This was a paramount athlete on his finest day. He would say that Secretariat could have set the track record pulling up at the end, but wanted no part of it. He was increasing his speed in the final stretch and Turcotte let him go another two furlongs after crossing the finish before slowing him down.

"He's just the complete horse," Turcotte told the *New York Times* following the race. "I let him run a bit early to get position in the first turn. Once he got in front of Sham, he wasn't about to give anything away. I kept looking back. The last seventy yards or so I [saw] on the toteboard teletimer I was breaking the record pretty good, so I let him go on a little. Just a hand ride. I never hit him once."

Lennon says: A horse? Roger, you're making this a little too easy for me, don't you think? I'm not even sure a horse qualifies as an athlete. But I'll give you the loophole that we didn't disqualify any species for the sake of argument. What next? A panda that shoots free throws? Maybe a Dalmatian that shags fly balls?

Well, before I let this degenerate into an episode of "Stupid Pet Tricks," how about we return this discussion to human beings? My vote for the two-legged species is Reggie Jackson, who earned mythical status on the night of October 18, 1977.

Unlike Secretariat's feat, impressive as it may be, Jackson's performance really doesn't require much background. Everyone already knows what he did in Game 6 of the World Series that year, and for those who don't, you're reading the wrong book right now. Put this one down and head for the aisle that has Dr. Phil.

For the record, Jackson not only slugged three home runs that evening at Yankee Stadium, he did it on three pitches. Incredibly, Jackson only tied the record because Babe Ruth hit the trifecta twice, in 1926 and in 1928, but there is no indication that even the Sultan of Swat did it on consecutive swings.

Hitting three home runs in one game, while a neat trick, is no guarantee of immortality. Fifteen players have belted four, most recently Carlos Delgado in 2003, but that and a quarter, maybe, gets you the lead story on *SportsCenter* that night. Do it in April or June, and people already have forgotten you by October.

That's what makes Jackson's three-spot so great. Okay, so he came up big in the World Series. But it was the deciding game, in the Bronx, and the first homer turned a 3–2 deficit into a 4–3 Yankees' lead they never relinquished. The official attendance for that Game 6 was 56,407, though it's probably ballooned to a half-million by now, and I'll just take a few moments to recount some of the more spectacular details.

As the *Washington Post*'s Thomas Boswell wrote, Jackson put on a show during batting practice, crushing a few balls deep into the right-field upper deck and sending another roughly five hundred feet to the back rows of the bleachers. For that reason, Boswell surmised that Dodgers starter Burt Hooten walked Jackson on four pitches in his first at-bat. Looking back, that was the only way to keep him in the ballpark on this particular night.

Jackson probably figured he wasn't going to get another pitch to hit, so he went first-pitch swinging the next time up against Hooten and hooked a line drive that shot over the right-field wall like Jackson had used a three-iron. Hooten was gone when Jackson came to the plate again, and reliever Elias Sosa must not have been paying attention because he served up an identical pitch that wound up in nearly the same spot.

According to accounts from that night, Jackson refused to answer the fans' beckoning for a curtain call after the second home run. But knowing his flair for the dramatic, Jackson was most likely saving himself for the hat trick. This time, it was against Charlie Hough, and Jackson hammered his signature knuckler for a five hundred-foot blast that landed in the blacked-out section of the center-field bleachers.

Even the Dodgers, their title dreams kaput, had to feel lucky they were on the field to witness what was nothing less than a Ruthian performance for the modern era. It was as if Jackson had channeled The Babe for one mighty encore, and that's the way it must have felt for everyone in the building.

"I must admit," L.A. first baseman Steve Garvey said afterward, "when Reggie hit his third home run, and I was sure nobody was looking, I applauded in my glove."

Finally, Jackson was ready for his close-up, and he granted the sellout crowd the curtain call they had been screaming for. There have been hundreds of special performances in this city, in every arena, but none can touch Reggie for what he did and when he did it.

Sorry, Rog. I can't go with Mr. Ed here. The winner is Mr. October.

George Steinbrenner: Good or Evil?

Lennon says: Obviously, this depends on whom you ask. Think Dave Winfield has the same opinion of The Boss as Alex Rodriguez? How about Buck Showalter and Joe Torre? Or maybe Steinbrenner's limo driver and the thirtysomething Yankee fan tending bar in Hoboken?

There are two kinds of people in Steinbrenner's world. Those on his payroll, who take his millions as well as his abuse, and the ticket-buying, YES-watching public, which gets to watch the Yankees make their perennial playoff run from a safe distance.

Both groups have nothing to complain about, and here's why: If you like to win, and you like money, then Steinbrenner's your guy. He's practically a pin-striped Santa Claus, only instead of handing out presents once every 365 days, Steinbrenner never stops giving.

He delivers suitcases of cash to the most coveted free agents, and buys the brightest superstars for his adoring fan base. What's not to love? Steinbrenner made Torre the richest manager in baseball, wealthier beyond his dreams. Doesn't that entitle him to get a little cranky at times? Remember how your dad grumbled to himself when he sat down to pay the bills?

Of course, Steinbrenner wasn't always viewed as the generous patriarch of the Yankees. It's tough to put a positive spin on his hiring of Howie Spira to dig up dirt on Winfield, or his characterizing of his suspension from baseball as a little misunderstanding.

Then there are the stories of him firing secretaries for bringing him the wrong sandwich, bullying young office workers, screaming at Yankee underlings. Hey, nobody's perfect. Plus, how else could he have held his own on *Seinfeld* if he wasn't yelling for a calzone?

It's gotten easier to like Steinbrenner. When he demanded that Jay Buhner be traded for Ken Phelps, Yankee fans were outraged. Nearly two decades later, the Mariners are still waiting for a World Series title—or to even attend one without buying a ticket. The Yankees have four rings since then, and lost two others. Doesn't seem like such a big deal now, does it?

But most people will never embrace Steinbrenner, and that's because not everyone in this world is a Yankees fan. It only seems that way. Steinbrenner remains the embodiment of whatever is wrong with the national pastime. He spends three times as much on payroll as other teams, basically because he can, and then gripes about sharing his revenue with Kansas City and Tampa Bay.

It's plain jealousy. That's all. If everyone else is so smart, then why didn't they get a group together and buy the Yankees from CBS for $10 million back in 1973? These days, that's not enough to rent A-Rod for half a season.

The Yankees wouldn't be the Yankees without Steinbrenner, and there will come a day when he's no longer seen ranting and raving from his luxury box. Even now, he's slipped more into the background, reduced to issuing press releases through his PR firm rather than holding court with dozens of reporters.

No one has ever owned the back pages of the city's tabloids like Steinbrenner, and it is likely that no one ever will. He was always larger than life, perfect for the New York stage, and should be remembered as more of a hero than a villain for what he did for the Yankees. Plenty have bemoaned their lot in life toiling for Steinbrenner, but they always had the door as a fallback option, and few took that route unless they were fired, sometimes over and over again, like Billy Martin.

Steinbrenner may not have treated those employees particularly well, but there's no question he's been good for the Yankees, in his own inimitable way.

Rubin says: Oh good lord, Dave! What's next? A blind item on Page Six of the *New York Post* that describes you and The Boss canoodling at Elaine's? You sound like practically everyone on his payroll, making excuses for his boorish and destructive behavior.

Steinbrenner is all about Steinbrenner and always has been. From his meddling edicts to the team to his proclamations that all money he throws around is just to "give the New York fans the championship they deserve," this guy has never been about what's good and pure in baseball and the world.

Oh yeah, and those proclamations? They're being issued as statements from the public relations firm he hired with the two bucks a month he extorts from every fan who just want to see the games on his YES network.

If Steinbrenner is so good, how come he is the only MLB owner to have been suspended from baseball? How come he's been caught trying to "get dirt" on his players? How come he's done egregious things like sign a big-time free agent and then revoke the office staff's dental insurance the next day?

To me this sounds more like a guy who's on the express bus to hell.

If the guy has done anything truly good here, it is this: He's given New Yorkers a team that is worth watching all season long, every season. And this is probably why so many people like you are getting snowed.

As I sat down to write this, I found myself going through an exercise that sounded a little like this: "How evil is Steinbrenner? Let me count the ways." And I came up with a lot of them.

He makes things more difficult for the fans by giving them a team worth watching and then taking 130 of 162 games off of the free airwaves. Plus he's made Yankees tickets among the most expensive in baseball; it costs a real working-class person a week's pay to take the spouse and kids to the park for a single game.

He makes things more difficult for the people in uniform. Do you think any of the seventeen managers he fired feels good about him? I'd say that even the current one, Joe Torre, has issues. Anyone remember two summers ago? Torre wouldn't even respond to The Boss's criticisms because he felt like it was distracting the team.

How about messing with members of Torre's staff, like undercutting pitching coach Mel Stottlemyre his last few years or no longer paying for Don Zimmer's transportation to the park? Or messing with players, like questioning whether Derek Jeter was living too fast a lifestyle or calling Dave Winfield Mr. May or labeling Hideki Irabu a "fat toad?"

Steinbrenner has been embroiled in the Watergate scandal, associated with notorious people, and is about to rob the Bronx of Macombs Dam Park, mangling it to build a new stadium.

But I see one evil he's done above all other things. Steinbrenner has helped drive a wedge between baseball fans and baseball players across this great nation. How did he do it? His free spending has escalated player salaries to a critical place.

In the major markets, where the clubs can afford to pay a handful of stars enough money to keep them out of his grasp, spectators actually resent the players for their bloated salaries. In the smaller markets, he's made it so teams cannot even contend. This robs the people in Kansas City and Pittsburgh and Denver of the chance to fall for their teams; after all, who wants to go see a perennial loser?

That, I think, is evidence of George Steinbrenner's true evil genius. He doesn't go out and overtly try to destroy anything, he just slowly coaxes the relationship between baseball and its supporters along a steady downward spiral.

Best Quarterback: Phil Simms or Joe Namath?

Rubin says: Joe Namath is an easy target today. He made himself into one over the years with his indulgent lifestyle and his tendencies toward excess. The nationally televised "I want to kiss you" interview with Suzy Kolber was only the moment when it became clear to the world that the Hall of Famer has the same weaknesses as we all do.

It's a shame that it happened, because it obscures for youngsters a view of what Namath was when he was the superstar signal caller for the Jets. The guy was much more than a football hero; he was a sports god in this town and there hasn't been a quarterback with either NFL franchise since who could stand with him.

To be placed on a pedestal that high in New York, an athlete has to be so much more than an on-field performer and that's exactly what Namath was. Whether he was throwing passes downfield or making passes at the city's trendiest nightclubs, people just couldn't take their eyes off him. He was that compelling a character, made all the more intriguing because he was also one of the city's all-time greatest players in the clutch.

I like Simms, and certainly he is the only quarterback we've seen since Namath that belongs in the same conversation. But when he quarterbacked the Giants to their Super Bowl XXI victory over Denver, it came at the end of a season when he wasn't even the team's biggest star. The Giants that year were Lawrence Taylor's team.

No one ever thought of the Jets as anything but Namath's.

I know I am pulling a fast one here, Dave, but I am not shy about it. I know the parameters for what we are doing here calls for us only to deal with New York sports from 1970 to the present. Namath played six of his twelve season with the Jets before that and those years were by far his best; they were when the legend of Broadway Joe was written. But even after taking the Jets to a sensational and stunning win over the Colts in 1969's Super Bowl III, he remained an icon. Namath was everybody's favorite football player until injuries made him mortal.

Namath—during all his years with the Jets—gave the team's following an identity and a reason to be proud where there really had been none before. Broadway has its rep because it is where the biggest and best shows can be seen, and Namath got his nickname because he was one of the biggest and best shows in town.

It's not enough to talk the talk in New York, though plenty of people do. To reach the kind of heights that we've recently seen Derek Jeter and Mark Messier and even Taylor ascend to, you also have to walk the walk. And we love it when someone does.

Namath was one of the originals. Yes, his team was a three-touchdown underdog against the Colts when he guaranteed the Super Bowl win. Then he made it happen, earning MVP honors for a game that many credit as the catalyst for the merger between the NFL and the AFL.

But he also made us feel good about ourselves in ways not unlike the young and charismatic John F. Kennedy did for the country when he was elected president.

Namath's era was a tough time in New York. There were political and racial divides here, Vietnam, and then financial chaos (anyone remember "Ford to City: Drop Dead"?). He could give the entire population—rich and poor, men and women, black and white—something to feel good about with his charismatic presence and impressive playing field exploits. His talk, his play, and his panty hose commercial were all things that made us laugh and smile.

Not too many athletes can pull something like that off. I'd say that's pretty great.

Lennon says: I don't know about you, Roger, but getting liquored up and propositioning ESPN sideline reporter Suzy Kolber on national television is not a weakness that many of us share with Joe Namath. In this debate, however, I'm not going to fault him for that. It wasn't one of his proudest moments, but acting like Dean Martin at halftime of a Jets-Patriots game fit in perfectly with his Broadway Joe persona and shouldn't detract from his on-field legacy established three decades earlier.

That's the problem with Namath. It's always been difficult to separate the man from the mouth, and the numbers from his nightcrawling notoriety. With Phil Simms, it's not that complicated. He played fifteen seasons for one team—the Giants—during an era when most players follow the money out of town, was the MVP of one Super Bowl and helped lead them to another before getting hurt.

Simms also holds just about every Giants passing record, and played the most efficient game in postseason history to beat the heavily favored Broncos in Super Bowl XXI. Of course, the Giants built their championships with defense, and relied heavily on the intimidation of Lawrence Taylor.

But they needed someone to outduel John Elway that evening in Pasadena, and Simms turned in a performance that no one—not Joe Montana, not Troy Aikman, not Tom Brady—has ever matched. Simms completed twenty-two of his twenty-five pass attempts (a record 88 percent) for 268 yards, and threw three touchdowns to win MVP honors as the Giants dumped Denver, 39–20. Simms also had ten straight completions—another record—to help the Giants earn their first NFL title since 1956.

No one realized it at the time, but immediately after that game, Simms cemented his place in history by becoming the first player to announce "I'm going to Disneyland." How's that for being a trend-setter, Roger? It's not panty hose and Bachelors III, but Simms did his part for pop culture, without soiling his squeaky-clean image in the process or donning a full-length fur.

Kidding aside, I have to disagree about the perception of Simms's place on the Giants. Despite the team's defensive might during those years, Simms was one of the most visible and vocal leaders, which is a strength that can't be found among the statistics.

In those days, quarterbacking in the NFC was not for the squeamish, and Simms was known for his courage to stand in the pocket and take a hit before delivering the ball. Also, few have handled the Meadowlands' swirling winds as well as Simms come December and January, which made him indispensable during the Giants' glory years. How good was Simms during those do-or-die Sundays? Before the 2005 NFL playoffs began, Simms was ranked third all-time for the fewest interceptions per attempt, with only six in 279 postseason chances, or 2.15 percent, behind the Patriots' Tom Brady and the Packers' Bart Starr.

Simms was forced to watch the Giants win their second Super Bowl in five years after an injury sidelined him late in the 1989–90 season—Jeff Hostetler took the reins for the stunning upset of the Bills—and he competed with Hostetler for the starting job the next two seasons. But Simms was reinstalled as the starter in 1993 and he led the Giants to the playoffs with a Pro Bowl season, only to be a salary-cap casualty the following year. Perhaps the best compliment ever paid to Simms was uttered by his former coach, Bill Parcells.

"Some quarterbacks can just drive Cadillacs," Parcells told the *New York Times*. "But I think Simms can drive a Ford, too. When the surrounding cast is sufficient, a lot of quarterbacks can drive the car. But there are only a few who can do it whether the support-ing cast is sufficient or not. And I think he can do that. When he's gone, people will say about the Giants' quarterback, 'He's good, but he's no Phil Simms.' "

Namath was good, Roger, but he's no Phil Simms.

Can the Nets Overthrow the Knicks for City Supremacy?

Lennon says: Flatly, no. Not as long as the Nets are called the Nets and you still need a tunnel or bridge to find them. Until Bruce Springsteen either suits up for the Nets or dons an Armani suit to coach them, there's no elevating the NBA's New Jersey franchise to the same level as the Knicks. Can't be done.

Of course, Bruce Ratner will try, first by building his dream arena on Flatbush Avenue in Brooklyn and then pushing the Knicks for TV airtime as well as attention on the back pages. But that's still years away, and the Knicks, who already have a sizable head start, could be rebuilt into contenders again under Larry Brown.

And as long as the Nets are stuck in the Meadowlands, they might as well be playing in Vancouver. That was a brilliant plan, sticking an NBA team in a location virtually unreachable by public transportation, in one of the worst traffic corridors of the civilized world. Once inside, the experience doesn't improve much, and after the game, it's another long walk through the parking lot and a slow drive back to the Jersey suburbs.

It's a shame, too, because the Nets have been more entertaining than the Knicks, and far more successful in recent years. Switch uniforms, and Madison Square Garden would have been rocking again with each of the Nets' trips to the NBA finals. The trio of Jason Kidd, Richard Jefferson, and Vince Carter is more deserving of

Garden exposure than the overpriced frauds under Brown's steward-ship, but they remain imprisoned in the swamps of Jersey, forever relegated to second-rate status.

Here's the difference. All the Knicks need to rekindle the title hopes of the Pat Riley-Patrick Ewing era is a spark, and their fans got that when Brown came on board last summer. Instantly, there was a buzz around the team again, and though they have a long way to go, the Knicks have begun a slow crawl back toward respectability.

Meanwhile, on the other side of the Hudson, the Nets keep Kidd and Jefferson, trade for Carter, and, despite winning seasons, can't get decent coverage in the New York newspapers unless they buy ad space. It's the New Jersey thing. The Giants and Jets both play in the Garden State, too, but their New York origins run so deep that it's almost like they never left. Do any of the Nets' younger fans even know that the franchise was born on Long Island?

It will be interesting to see how Ratner's Brooklyn gambit plays out for the Nets. Leaving New Jersey is definitely long overdue, but setting up shop in one of the so-called outer boroughs is no guar-antee of success. Sure it's worked for Peter Luger's steak house, but for the tourists venturing across the Fifty-ninth Street Bridge, that's part of the charm of eating there: telling your friends back in Iowa that you had dinner in Brooklyn!

When the Nets eventually move, and change their name, there is certain to be a spike in popularity. They'll sell more tickets, more replica uniform tops, and maybe even win a playoff series or two. But the Knicks are New York, as much of a part of this city's fabric as the Yankees or Giants, and they can't be replaced, especially not by the Nets however they are reincarnated on the other side of the East River.

The Garden may have lost some of its luster, and Brown won't have the Knicks championship-ready for who knows how long. But they have a history that has been passed from generation to generation, from fathers to sons. And while that loyalty can wither from neglect, as it has during the Dolan years, it never dies. For that, the Knicks should be grateful. And the Nets can take consolation in the fact that Brooklyn, while not Manhattan, is heaven compared to the Meadowlands.

Rubin says: There's something a little strange about this question and I think I've just figured out what it is. The Nets already are the city's top team. At least on the court they are. Whether they play in Continental Airlines Arena or at the Garden, the Nets would be the team you'd want to put your money on.

And the strangely annoying issue here is that this has been the case for a while. The Knicks have been dragging along the bottom for five long years now, under .500 and not within a breath of being called a contender. The Nets, on the other hand, were a playoff team in all five of those years and twice won the Eastern Conference championship.

On the hardwood, there's no doubt they've been the city's top NBA team for some time now. Credit where it is due: GM Rod Thorn did a superb job turning the team into an elite force in the league. They are also one of the league's most entertaining teams to see these days with Jason Kidd, Vince Carter, and Richard Jefferson leading the way.

But I also understand there is another component to being the dominant NBA force in New York and that has little to do with actual performance. It has to do with winning over the hearts and minds of people. It has to do with being the most followed team.

I've never truly understood why the Nets haven't been able to command a buzz from their location in New Jersey, and you may be right that the reason has to do with bridges and tunnels separating them from the passionate New York hoops fans. But the only buzz the Knicks have created lately had to do with the Larry Brown hiring/ firing and his feud with Stephon Marbury. If you use the back pages of the city tabloids as a barometer, the team that has really created the buzz during the last few NBA seasons would be either the Yankees or the Mets.

When it comes to a following, the only reason the Knicks have remained situated ahead of the Nets is because of their longevity. They have a fan base that's passed the adoration from generation to generation, even if they can't afford to buy tickets because of all the trendy posers who want to be like Spike and Woody.

It won't be long before the Nets and their newly accessible fans are going to give the 'Bockers a run for their money there, too.

Brooklyn is the reason. When new owner Bruce Ratner executes his master plan—building the arena on Flatbush Avenue and relo- cating the club—the Nets will grow a massive following. And it sure won't hurt that people will be able to come see the city's most exciting and successful NBA team without hauling their butts all the way into Midtown.

I have reasons for this belief and I invite you, Dave, to come with me and see it. Join me on an excursion to Bay Ridge, Benson- hurst, and Midwood. Swing through Bed-Stuy and Sheepshead Bay and maybe even Bushwick. There you will see on the tops of peo- ple's heads the reason for my confidence about this.

They're wearing Dodgers baseball caps. Not Los Angeles Dodgers baseball caps, but Brooklyn Dodgers baseball caps. This has been going on since before the era of the throwback jersey and it's fascinated me ever since I moved to New York. Brooklynites are loyal to a fault. When they take something into their hearts, they never let it go.

And that's exactly where the Nets are about to go.

Appreciate the scope of Brooklyn for a minute, the "outer bor- ough" that has produced more NBA talent than any of the other four. It is 2.4 million strong, big enough to be the fourth-largest city in the United States. And now they are about to get a pro team of their own, the first since the Dodgers packed and moved west.

That the team is already a winner will only make this snowball roll downhill faster. This isn't some lame expansion team that's going to have to take its lumps for a half dozen years. The Nets will instantly leave the people of Kings County feeling like winners. Because its new home will be right above the LIRR, the team will be able to easily reconnect with its Long Island roots. And before you know it, droves of NBA fans on that side of the East River will dump the stumbling Knicks for a successful team that is much closer to home.

This "outer borough as exile" notion you've been floating, Dave, hasn't exactly hurt the Yankees or Mets, now, has it?

Will the next generation of kids from Brooklyn grow up Nets fans? That's a lock. It's not so easy to find a Yankees fan in Queens or a Mets fan in the Bronx.

SETTLE THE SCORE/JOHN CALIPARI

(University of Memphis coach John Calipari was hired as Nets head coach after taking the University of Massachusetts to the Final Four in 1996. He spent three seasons with the Nets, during which he got a firsthand look at the New York sports landscape. We asked him to settle the score on whether the Nets can supplant the Knicks.)

I don't see any way the Nets surpassing the Knicks could ever happen. There's too much history there, too much tradition. The Willis Reed moment will never go away. The problem is the

Nets will never be the Knicks, just the same as the Jets will never be the Giants or overtake the Giants. Never ever.

They'll never do that, but that doesn't mean the Nets can't be successful. They have an unbelievable president in Brett Yormark; this guy could be at any company he'd want to run.

There's also where they are in New Jersey. I don't know if the move to Brooklyn will help them close a gap, but it will give them an identity. It will give them an area. It's going to give them a pizzazz they just don't have now.

What is the Meadowlands associated with? What area does it belong to? There's no flair to it. When they had a parade, it had to go around the parking lot. Then again, they had no choice. What were they going to do? Have it in downtown Secaucus? Have it across the street in East Rutherford? Where were you going to put it?

But even in Brooklyn, they're never going to overtake the Knicks. Then [again], I don't think that should be your goal.

Your goal should be to build with what you have and make it the best-run organization. And then make it an organization that is best for its fans. Make it an organization that is best for its players and the people that work there. It's all you can do.

They shouldn't worry about the Knicks. You've got no control over the Knicks. And I can tell you that the tradition is going nowhere. It's there. It's staying there. And it always will be, from Red Holtzman right on down the line.

I don't think they should try to convert the people they encounter in Brooklyn, and I don't think they are going to try. A Knicks fan—a true Knicks fan—is never going to be a Nets fan. Never gonna happen. It's the same the other way: A Nets fan will never be a Knicks fan. It's just that there aren't as many Nets fans, and I am talking dyed-in-the-wool types.

There had to be work that went into the decision to make a move like that. They had to conclude "this is better for us as an organization." I know Brett Yormark, and I have all the confidence in the world that he would not have joined on to be the president if he didn't look at this model and say, "This is really good for us—we could turn into one of the best organizations in the NBA."

They're not going to overtake the Knicks in the New York market. It's not what they should try to do or make their goal. They're just going to be the best organization they can and make their fans proud. They want and need to be thought of as a good organization that players want to come play for.

It's the same as the Clippers right now. They're never going to overtake the Lakers, but right now they're a better team. They play better and have a great leader in Sam Cassell. That's what the Nets can be, and that should be good enough.

It's amazing what's been done now. Rod Thorn has done an unbelievable job putting the team together. So now everything is in place for them to be great. They have the players. Their coach is doing a great job. As I've said, the president is first-rate. Management seems strong. Scouting seems strong. The players enjoy living and working in the metropolitan area.

But don't try to be the Knicks. You're never going to be the Knicks.

Do the Red Sox Now Have the Upper Hand over the Yankees?

Rubin says: Yankee fans aren't going to want to hear it, but during one week of October in 2004, the Red Sox tore down the walls of a prison the Yankees spent eight decades building around them. Boston's incredible postseason run—replete with staging the greatest series comeback of all time against the Yankees in the ALCS—altered the dynamics of sports' greatest rivalry.

That week saw the little kid who always used to get beat on when the folks weren't looking pop his older brother in the face.

Both teams know exactly what transpired there and neither is going to forget. The Sox will never go head to head with the Yankees—on a field or in a pennant race—surrounded by attitudes that their defeat is predestined. And the Yanks can no longer walk in with the self-confidence that they can't be beaten.

That was the Yankees' biggest edge in the rivalry and, make no mistake, it was huge. Psychological edges are difference-makers in sports and this one was so big, Atlas himself couldn't have lifted it.

The Red Sox and Yankees haven't had any reason to think any of their matchups would ever end up differently. The Sox swooned during the pennant races of the 1940s and 1950s and then raised falling short of the Bombers to an art form with a trio of postseason collapses: the one-game playoff in 1978 (Bucky Dent, anyone?), the 1999 AL Championship Series (a four games to one bludgeoning), and the 2003 AL Championship Series (courtesy of Aaron Boone).

New England baseball fans are very passionate, but they are not very optimistic. And, when it's come to the Yankees, why should they have been? It's that phenomenon where you keep doing the same thing over and over because it's all you know how to do. As far as the Yankees were concerned, the only thing the Sox knew how to do was lose.

Now imagine what it must have been like to be a player. You came to Boston with the idea of winning a World Series, and even your biggest supporters expect you to inevitably fail. That's not real positive. By contrast, New Yorkers always expected the best; and the players were surrounded by people who just knew they were going to win.

Ain't that way anymore. With Boston not only thinking, but also knowing, it can win, the psychological edge is gone and now it's just about baseball. If anything, the Yankees now have to contend with knowing they let sports' biggest advantage slip away.

Even though the Yankees have won five times as many pennants as the Red Sox, the playing field is now level. The assessment of who has the upper hand should be based on merit, and that may be where the balance begins to tip toward Boston.

Because Yankees owner George Steinbrenner loves collecting established stars like others collect coins, the Bombers are likely to remain an older team. As talented as the group is, how many of them this season are moving toward the back end of their careers? As for youth being in the pipeline, the Yankees farm system is practically bereft of serious prospects.

The Red Sox began a different philosophy when Theo Epstein became their general manager before 2003. The Boston farm system has talented young pitchers Jonathan? Papelbon and Craig Hansen.

And they are not spending their off-seasons going after veteran stars that are looking for the last big payday. They showed that much with their deal for Josh Beckett from the Marlins.

The Yankees are still going to get their share of wins against Boston, but it's never going to be quite the same. In one rivalry-altering week in October of 2004, Boston stripped the Yanks of their aura of invincibility.

The kid's not going to be afraid of big brother anymore.

Lennon says: Not even the baseball zealots that inhabit Red Sox Nation could agree with you on this one, Roger. Let's not treat Boston's 2004 World Series crown as some cosmic event that forever changed the way the planets are aligned in the American League. This was not the collapse of the Soviet Union, the end of Seinfeld's stranglehold on Thursday nights, or even Donald Trump's supposed bankruptcy.

The Red Sox winning the World Series that year was a lucky punch, the kind of freakish event that only happens once every eighty-six years. I seem to have forgotten Buster Douglas's reign of terror after knocking out Mike Tyson. I mean, were the Yankees even trying after they took a 3–0 lead in that American League Championship Series? They simply fell victim to human nature. Rather than go for the kill that October, the Yankees got complacent, and Big Papi caught them napping.

Check the scoreboard. The only thing that makes this a rivalry is geography. When it comes to world championships, the Yankees still have a comfortable twenty-six to six lead. The last time the Red Sox won back-to-back titles was 1915–16. The Yankees? You don't need a Google search for this one. The paint just dried on their three-peat run from 1998–2000 and the Yankees were a Luis Gonzalez blooper away from making it four straight.

This is what passes for a drought in George Steinbrenner's

world. The Yankees have gone five years without a title, despite two World Series appearances during that stretch, and already The Boss is getting itchy. And if you want to talk about psychological edges, Roger, what happened to Boston in 2005? Seemed like the same old Red Sox to me.

Rather than put the Yankees permanently in the rearview mirror when they had the chance, the Sox spit up their sizable lead and let their pin-striped nemesis swipe the AL East crown on the head-to-head tiebreaker. So what happened to that Kong-sized monkey Boston supposedly threw off its back in 2004? Apparently the gorilla returned to roost in 2005, and on-again, off-again GM Theo Epstein even borrowed his suit to sneak out of Fenway Park last winter during another episode of this Yawkey Way soap opera.

The Red Sox have one thing on their minds every minute of every day and that's keeping up with the Yankees. It's a mentality that manipulates the fans, the Boston media, and the hundreds of baseball executives the Red Sox currently have in their employ. How do you explain what happened up in Boston last winter? Sure, the Red Sox got off to a fast start by trading for Josh Beckett. But they followed that by watching Johnny Damon—the heart and soul of their ring-winning idiots—sign with the Yankees.

As long as the Red Sox keep crying about revenue streams, trimming payroll, and how few luxury seats they have at Fenway Park, they can't be considered in the same galaxy as the Yankees. Not only do the Yankees have unlimited resources and a billion-dollar stadium on the way, they have another significant edge when it comes to collecting all-stars: Every player, whether they admit or not, wants to wear the pinstripes.

The Yankees are the pinnacle of the sport, a bulletproof brand, like Microsoft or Nike. The stock price may dip on occasion, but those companies are indisputable winners, with an arrogance and a culture of success that is not easily shaken. So the Yankees are knocked for their corporate approach to a kids' game, criticized for their short haircuts and clean-shaven faces. But maybe that's just appropriate for a team that admits it's in the business of winning baseball games. As I see it, the gap between the Yankees and Red Sox will only continue to widen, and don't count on Boston getting close enough for another lucky punch any time soon. Maybe in another eighty-six years.

SETTLE THE
SCORE/KEVIN MILLAR

(Kevin Millar was a key member of the 2004 Red Sox team that not only beat the Yankees with a miraculous ALCS comeback that October, but also ended the eighty-six-year Curse of the Bambino as well. Here's what he had to say when asked if the Red Sox now own the upper hand in this rivalry.)

We had to win one championship for it to even become a rivalry. It was twenty-six to nothing. Do the Red Sox have the upper hand? Yeah, right now they do. The last World Series that Boston won was in '04. The Yankees haven't won one since 2000. So right now they do have the upper hand. But adding up the totals, it's still twenty-six to one.

In 2004, we had a group of guys that didn't worry about anything and didn't care what people said. The curse, this and that, all of the negative stuff that surrounds that club, a lot of that generates negativity, but we didn't allow that. We just kept playing baseball. People called us idiots. We just had a group of guys that wanted to be in that clubhouse. We played hard, and we had good players, and we eventually broke that eighty-six-year curse. So no matter what, forever and ever, that group of twenty-five men will be remembered. When you're down 0-3, and down in the ninth inning of Game 4, it's a situation where you're playing just one pitch at a time. You're not thinking, "Oh my God, we've got to beat the mighty Yankees four games in a row." If you're thinking that way, it's not going to happen. We just never gave up. We knew the pressure was always on them. It wasn't on us, because we weren't supposed to win. And then for Game 7, it still wasn't on us, because we had a chance to shock the world and they were a team that was about to lose a 3-0 advantage. We had a great group. We had a family. We had guys that cared about each other. If we didn't have that, it probably wouldn't have happened.

They had a great group of guys, too. They're very classy. I mean, you're talking about Derek Jeter, Mariano Rivera, Bernie Williams. Those guys are Yankees, man. We always had respect for them. The cities have fun with each other, but the players on the field respect each other. Rarely do you dislike or not respect them. They showed a ton of respect on opening day the next year by coming to the top of the steps—Joe Torre and his whole staff—as we received our rings. The fans had fun with Mariano Rivera. It was a great thing for baseball. Obviously, for the Red Sox, it was awesome. But it was good for baseball.

Those two teams are just awesome when they play each other. You don't know who's going to win, but you know something is going to happen. They've got great players, they've got big payrolls, a lot of big-name guys are on the field at the same time. That's what you get. There's tons of respect on both sides.

I loved it. I loved the passion. It was like the Super Bowl. Some guys don't like it, but I love it. That rivalry, for nineteen games a year, is an amazing thing.

18

Where's the Worst Place to Watch a Game?

Lennon says: When city officials were scouting parcels of land for Shea Stadium, according to urban legend, they visited the current site in Flushing Meadows during the winter, when the flight plans for LaGuardia did not carry directly overhead. Is that supposed to be an excuse? Didn't they see the airport about a half mile away, with planes taking off every five minutes? Was it too much to think that might be a problem someday?

Now, thanks to the infinite wisdom of those city planners, the Mets are serenaded by the deafening whine of jet engines during many of their home games. And if the wind is just right, the planes are so close you can practically wave to the passengers on their way up to cruising altitude. I'm surprised that the Mets, looking to squeeze every buck from their patrons, haven't figured out a way to charge those airborne spectators admission.

It's one thing for the players to be irritated by the constant air traffic, and believe me, they find it annoying. But at least they get millions of dollars to endure the noise and they get to be on the road for the other eighty-one games. As for the paying customers, the fans have to buy tickets for the privilege of abusing their eardrums. It's sort of like waiting for your flight at LaGuardia, but outside the terminal, sitting on a lawn chair.

Maybe this problem would have been solved if the builders followed through on their original plans and eventually put a dome on Shea, but that became too expensive a proposition in the 1970s. Instead, the stadium staff has chosen to combat the noise with—what else? More noise.

Attending a game at Shea is like tuning in your iPod to static and then cranking the volume up as loud as it will go. Enjoyable, right? Occasionally, they'll mix in some hip-hop tunes, but most of the entertainment involves inane sound effects or ads on the Diamond-Vision screen above the left-field picnic area.

But that's enough about the noise. As for the building itself, Shea was practically obsolete by the time it was finished, forget forty years later, now that it is universally known as the biggest eyesore in the major leagues. As a beat writer for the Mets, I've been to every stadium in baseball, new and old, and Shea is the only place that can have standing pools of water in the aisles—when it hasn't rained for a week.

Why is that? Is some worker breeding mosquitoes as a hobby to keep himself busy between home stands? And can someone explain why there's always some asbestos-looking goo leaking from the ceilings? I know the stadium is old, but the city still has building inspectors, right? Maybe the board of health would like to take some of that slop back to the office and run a few tests.

As for the seats themselves, New Yorkers must have been much smaller back in 1964, and it's no fun making room for your portly neighbor when he's trying to squeeze by you with an armful of $8 beers. An elbow here, a knee there, and things could get ugly.

But as long as you remain seated for four hours, wear earplugs, and stay away from open-toed shoes, Shea does have decent sight lines. The box seats are very close to the field, as they are in most ballparks, and as long as you're not too deep in the upper tier, you should be able to read the numbers on the backs of the uniforms.

The bottom line is that Shea is a dinosaur, the last of the two-sport concrete monoliths that sprung up in the late '60s and early

'70s. It was never supposed to be beautiful. Just a functional place where New York's expansion baseball team could share a home with football's Jets. That's the irony of the whole Shea situation. Is there a more appropriate place for a team called the Jets than at the end of a LaGuardia runway? How did they get to move to a new stadium and the Mets stay stuck at Shea?

Anyway, in 2008, the Mets will get their modern Ebbets Field and Shea will be reduced to a parking lot. There is no doubt a sentimental crowd will mourn that day. I will not be among them.

Rubin says: Nice call on the Blemish by Flushing Bay, Dave, although it was never the air traffic nor the pumped up volume on the sound system that got to me at Mets games. I, too, would have ranked Shea near the top in this category but for two very different reasons. Unlike Yankee Stadium or Madison Square Garden, most of the seats are pretty far from the playing surface, making binoculars a near necessity even when you've got a spot downstairs. And half the promotions the team runs are, quite simply, shlockfests.

There's more than one thing that makes a place a bad spot to catch a game, Len-o. Certainly it could just be a bad building, like Shea. But what I think makes any place less enjoyable—good venue or bad—is when the fans just aren't into it. And there's no place where the fans haven't embraced their teams like at Continental Airlines Arena at the Meadowlands.

And this applies to all the teams that play there: Devils, Nets, and Seton Hall. The place just doesn't generate much heat or emotion. Rather than fill you with excitement, catching a game at the former Brendan Byrne Arena leaves the true sports fan a little sad; both for the small group of truly impassioned spectators who are diluted by the stoic masses and for the players who don't get the real home-court or home-ice advantage.

I've been in Continental Arena when it's been loud and exciting and fun, but almost every time it was when I went there to see a concert. The Rolling Stones? Springsteen? U2? Absolutely awesome. In fact, the building might rate as my favorite place to see a show in the New York area.

Then you go to sporting event there and you're left wondering if they've lined the walls with sound-dampening foam.

I'm really not sure what it's all about. It could be that the people who show up for such games have had all their energy zapped from getting to the game—another big strike against the place. Only the Nassau Coliseum rivals it for inconvenience. If you don't own a car, chances are you took a subway to the Port Authority terminal to catch a bus. And we all know what a buzz-kill riding one of those buses can be; it's the last-place method of travel.

The unfathomable thing, though, is this strange fan apathy when it comes to the teams that call the Meadowlands home.

The Devils have been one of the city's most successful franchises, making the playoffs almost every single season and winning three Stanley Cups in a span of just nine years. Yet the place is consistently only two-thirds full when they take the ice. And don't tell me this is about how the grinding neutral zone trap has made their style dull to watch. THEY WIN! ALL THE TIME!

The Nets have come on like gangbusters in recent years, rising to become one of the elite teams in the NBA's Eastern Conference. They went to the NBA finals two straight seasons. And again, when it's time for tip-off at Continental Arena, only about three-quarters of the seats are filled. I don't want to hear that the cellar-dwelling Knicks are the real draw around here, either. THEY WIN! ALL THE TIME!

Seton Hall has been to eight NCAA Tournaments since 1988 and plays in the Big East, now the most exciting college basketball conference in the country. Teams ranked in the top twenty-five are coming to the Meadowlands practically every week now, and in recent years the Pirates have featured NBA-caliber talent like Eddie Griffin and Andre Barrett. Yet when the ball goes up, there are more empty seats than filled ones. Not one word now about there being no college-basketball market in New Jersey; Duke and Texas drew over nineteen thousand to the building in the third week of the 2005–06 season. Maybe The Hall doesn't win all the time, but people are missing out on some interesting stuff.

For my money, it really doesn't matter what structure the game is played in. What counts is that you're seeing a quality product and there's electricity about the event. I know that when Bruce brings the E Street Band home to play, Continental Airlines Arena is charged. I just don't know why the power goes out when the place hosts a sporting event.

Who Is the Most Underrated Athlete?

Rubin says: Want to know the best thing that comes with discussing the most underrated athletes? You get to jar people's memory and get to see that "Oh yeah, I remember" look on their face. It's a shame, but the underrated get relegated to a place in the back of the mind.

Here's someone most of us forgot about, but shouldn't have: Super John Williamson.

Is it coming back to you now? Are the chants of "Supe! Supe! Supe!" ringing in your ears again? Are the memories of him and Julius Erving teaming to decimate another Nets foe flashing back in your head? I hope so, because they were brilliant enough to have remained.

Williamson may have been the most valuable player on the Nets as they powered their way to the 1974 ABA championship. He wasn't the team's leading scorer or rebounder or assist man. He wasn't in any way their star. Here's what he was: the guy who turned them from an ordinary team into an extraordinary team.

Drafted in the sixth round of the 1973 NBA draft by the Atlanta Hawks, Williamson wasn't good enough to make their roster. In fact he was lucky to land a spot on the Nets and spent the first fourteen games of the 1973–74 season in the role of a reserve. There were games he didn't even play in while coach Kevin Loughery's club opened the campaign 4-10.

The Nets obviously had a problem and it turned out Super John was the answer. Erving was an atom bomb of an offensive weapon, but was the only real go-to guy the team had. It made them one-dimensional and easy to resolve for opposing teams. Williamson had been a prolific scorer at New Mexico State, finishing fifth in the nation as a senior, so Loughery took a chance on the rookie. He should have bought a lottery ticket that first night.

With Williamson in the starting lineup, the Nets went 51-19 the rest of the way that regular season and then lost only twice while winning twelve postseason games against the Virginia Squires, Kentucky Colonels, and Utah Stars.

Even though he was from New Haven, the guy had a game right out of a New York playground. He had deceptive moves, a sweet shot, and a nose for getting to the rim. He was awfully good at sticking that red-white-and-blue ball in the basket and he liked to put it up.

"He loved to take the big shot," Boston College coach and former Net Al Skinner told *Newsday*. "He played very aggressively, especially at the offensive end. As strong as he was, it was remarkable he could shoot the ball as well as he could."

"He was one hell of a player, a good player. He was tough. He never backed down from anything and he always wanted to take the big shot," then–Nets trainer Fritz Massman said after Williamson's untimely death from kidney disease in November of 1996. "He thrived on that."

In an eight-year career that included stops in Washington and Indianapolis, Williamson did two stints with the Nets. He spent his first three seasons with the New York Nets in the ABA and then two of five NBA seasons, in which he averaged 20.1 points, with the New Jersey Nets. There were many single-game performances he turned in that were worth remembering, including thirty-eight points against Philadelphia in a 1979 playoff game and back-to-back efforts of forty and fifty points when he played for the Pacers.

But if there is one night that he is revered for above all, it was Game 6 of the 1976 ABA finals against Denver, in which the Nets were an indisputable underdog. The Nets trailed the Nuggets by twenty-two in the third quarter and were looking at a trip back to Denver for Game 7. Williamson wasn't going to let that happen. In the fourth quarter, he scored sixteen points and the Nets won 112–106 for their second title in three seasons and the last captured in the ABA.

"John won us the championship," Massman said. "Everyone was keying on Doc, and John was popping them right in."

In my mind, Dave, that's certainly worth remembering.

Lennon says: I like the pick, Rog. But I also think you're confusing "underrated" with "obscure." Dredging up the New York Nets? Super John Williamson? You sure you couldn't find anybody on the Cosmos for this topic? How about the Long Island Lizards? (That's a pro lacrosse team, in case you were wondering).

I don't mean to rip Super John, but my candidate spent a little more time in the spotlight, on a bigger stage, and his name still triggers that "Oh yeah, I remember" look you're talking about. That's why I'm going with Jimmy Key, whose milquetoast demeanor and sneaky pitching style hid the fact that he was one of the game's best pitchers for most of his fifteen-year career, including four pivotal seasons in the Bronx.

That's not to say Key was invisible on the Toronto Blue Jays. He was the cornerstone of a championship rotation, averaging fourteen wins with a 3.35 ERA from 1985–92, and Key finished second for the Cy Young Award when he went 17-8 with a 2.76 ERA in 1987. The funny thing is, Key continued to shine once he put on the pinstripes. But if you ask people to rattle off the Yankees' top pitchers of the past two decades, Key easily is the one most overlooked.

Think about it. Even Jack McDowell—the Yankee Flipper himself—probably gets more recognition, just because he gave the bird to his own booing fans one night in the Bronx. But Key was never the most quotable person on the team like David Cone, nor the most imposing like Randy Johnson. Even Pascual Perez generated more of a buzz for being basically insane.

But there was Key, calmly and methodically racking up wins in his first two seasons. In 1993, he was fourth in the Cy Young voting after an 18-6 campaign with a 3.00 ERA, but the Yankees finished second that season, seven games behind the Blue Jays. The next year, Key climbed again to second place, with a superb 17-4 record and a 3.27 ERA, but a strike canceled the playoffs—with the Yankees atop the AL East.

Ironically, when the Yankees finally returned to the playoffs in 1995, Key was unable to help them. That year, Key made only five starts because of season-ending rotator-cuff surgery that put his career in jeopardy as well. But at age thirty-five, Key persevered through a difficult 1995 season to become an integral part of the Yankees' championship run, and even beat the Braves in the deciding Game 6 to complete the Bombers' stunning comeback.

The fact that Key even took the mound that night in the Bronx was amazing in itself. Back in April, it looked like Key was through. He labored to a 1-5 start with an ugly 7.14 ERA that prompted the Yankee brass to send him to Tampa for some fine-tuning. The reeducation of Key apparently worked. After returning at the end of May, Key finished the season 11-6 and rolled into October, where he had always been a reliable performer.

Key didn't do much in the first round against the Texas Rangers, a team that feasted on lefties anyway. But he allowed only three hits and two runs over eight innings in his ALCS victory over the

Orioles—his lone start—and then bounced back from a Game 2 beating against the Braves in the World Series.

Key, with the Blue Jays, had beaten Atlanta twice in the 1992 Fall Classic, once as a starter and later in relief. In the 1995 rematch, he was the loser in Game 2, this time as Greg Maddux threw a shutout in the Bronx, but Key got a shot at redemption once the Yankees won three straight to set up a possible deciding Game 6. Despite his shaky start early in the series, Key kept his composure for five innings, and turned a 3–1 lead over to the bullpen for the clinching victory. Before that game, manager Joe Torre said he had every confidence that Key would finish the job.

"Jimmy's a great pitcher because of what he has inside him," Torre said. "He has things you don't see in statistics."

When Key's name made it on the Hall of Fame ballot in 2004, he received a total of three votes, enough to get him immediately removed from consideration in future balloting. He seems to deserve better, but isn't that the definition of underrated?

20

Has the NHL Lockout Irreparably Damaged the Sport?

Lennon says: I'm no expert in labor issues, but here's a thought: When you have a product that people can live without, do not, under any circumstances, give them the opportunity to do so.

Somehow this simple concept escaped two pretty smart people in NHL commissioner Gary Bettman and NHLPA president Bob Goodenow when both conspired to detonate the 2004–05 hockey season.

I admit to not knowing much about Goodenow, but Bettman spends plenty of time in New York, where the NHL offices reside, and must read the newspapers or watch TV occasionally.

Even when the NHL was popular, riding a renaissance created by the Rangers' march to the Stanley Cup in 1994, it was never, ever, close to being on a par with the other Big Three professional sports, namely Major League Baseball, the NFL, and the NBA.

The New Jersey Devils could win the Cup every year—for a while there, it seemed like they did—and the best they could ever do was a measly reference box on the back page of the tabloids. Something like HELL YES. DEVS WIN (SEE PAGE 45). And that's only if the Yankees or Mets had an off day.

The point I'm trying to make here is that when you're No. 4 and sliding fast, don't put on a pair of concrete skates, which is precisely what Bettman did by locking out the players when the CBA expired on September 16, 2004.

With the owners spending 76 percent of their gross revenue on player's salaries, Bettman declared it was time for "cost certainty," which is a fancy way of saying, "We don't feel like paying this much to the guys chasing the black rubber thingy anymore."

And just like that—poof!—hockey pulled a disappearing act that David Blaine would have been proud of. But unlike baseball's labor struggles, hockey's negotiations were virtually ignored, and the fans who cared about their MIA sport were left to gripe to their family members at the dinner table. During the 310-day lockout, I probably heard WFAN talk about it once or twice, and only when Bettman refused to come on the air and talk about it.

The NHL did make history by becoming the first major sports league to cancel an entire season, and it was the first time since 1919 that Lord Stanley's Cup was not carried around a rink in celebration.

So what did Bettman and Goodenow get for their trouble? Well, the commish got exactly what he wanted—a $39-million salary cap for his pals and a bunch of new gimmicky rules, like an overtime shootout and smaller goalie pads that have all the effect of rearranging deck chairs on the Titanic.

And Goodenow? He was handed a pink slip, even though Goodenow officially "resigned" after failing to accomplish any of his goals, caving to a salary cap and costing the players millions of dollars in lost salary. Nice job, Bob.

So Bettman wins, Goodenow loses big, and hockey remains as much of a mess as it ever was, only now people can't watch it on TV, either. ESPN, the sport's biggest ally, refused to pick up its $60-million option for 2006, deciding instead to broadcast money-making events like poker tournaments and lumberjack competitions.

Obviously, this was a huge embarrassment for the NHL. Their response? Don't fret. Tune into the Outdoor Life Network for our marquee matchups. Talk about your unintentional comedic moment. Going from ESPN to Channel 873 on the dial, and that's if your cable provider even carries OLN or ODLNet or whatever the abbreviation is for it.

The bright spot is that NBC agreed to televise a handful of games, but isn't paying the NHL a dime to do it, offering only to split any proceeds. The league would be better off having a bake sale organized by the players' wives. Who wouldn't buy cookies from supermodels like Carol Alt or Kim Alexis? Only in the NHL are the wives more famous than the players. I can't necessarily blame the lockout for that, but you get the idea.

Rubin says: What we have here, Dave, is a textbook case of perception versus reality. On this one, you have gone with perception.

There is a reality, though, that is being ignored. The last thing I would want to do is fog a good debate with facts, but if we're measuring the health of the NHL, we would be remiss not to start with attendance. I always find that to be a pretty good barometer. Would it surprise you to know that more than half the league's arenas were back to 95 percent full by mid-season of the first year back from the lockout?

I'd say that alone is an indicator that the NHL's popularity will return to prelabor dispute levels even faster than Major League Baseball came back from the strike that canceled the 1994 World Series. In fairness, however, it has to be pointed out that accomplishing this is easier for hockey, which has never been as popular in the U.S. cities.

This comeback is in no way a testament to the efforts of the clods who run the NHL; I refuse to defend either NHL commissioner Gary Bettman and the owners or former players' association chief Bob Goodenow.

This is about not being able to keep a great sport down. With its combination of speed and strength, hockey has always been a delight to watch. Also, if you've ever seen a Game 7 of an NHL playoff series, you have seen the highest form of "playing with reckless abandon."

And oddly, as a result of the labor dispute and the lost season, the NHL game has been distilled to an even more entertaining competition.

So many things that were downers in the sport have been removed. We no longer watch a great contest and walk away without a winner; now we have the shootout. We no longer have the constant stoppages of play, because the two-line pass has been made legal. And goaltenders' equipment has been shaved down to make the affairs more high-scoring. All of these were changes the majority of players wanted to see.

Perhaps the best innovation—and the one that has the highest impact on us in New York—is the way the schedule was changed to put a greater emphasis on contests within the division. Divisional foes used to play only six times a season, and now that number is eight.

That means 33 percent more opportunities to see the Rangers and Islanders wage a bloodletting. It means 33 percent more days when the Devils can try to prove that they actually own the New York hockey scene. It means that the burgeoning Islanders-Devils rivalry—which could become one of the league's best—will grow 33 percent faster.

I've always been one who finds the concept of a salary cap pretty abhorrent. It seems completely contrary to the free-market economy we Americans love to espouse (not to mention I wouldn't want someone to tell me I am only allowed to make so much no matter how well I perform). But the new cap in the NHL could do two things that spark even greater enthusiasm. First, it could encourage the kind of parity we see in the NFL, where it seems almost every team has a contending season every couple of years. And second, it could narrow the divide between players and fans because there will be less resentment toward a guy who earns an exorbitant salary.

Things aren't perfect by any means. I'm not sure that ESPN would have picked up the $60-million option on the national contract, and I agree that OLN is a significant step down.

But is it really fair to use ESPN's decision as a true barometer of whether people still love hockey? I again think this will turn out to be a "perception vs. reality" issue.

The television execs in Bristol are a savvy group, but they don't make the right call every single time. Anyone remember their running two hours of *Cold Pizza* twice a day for about a year?

I'm not so sure that Coyotes vs. Bluejackets wouldn't pull better ratings.

SETTLE THE SCORE/JOHN DAVIDSON

(John Davidson was an NHL goaltender for eleven years before becoming one of the game's most respected television commentators, as well as the lead analyst for the New York Rangers. We asked him to settle the score on the lockout's effect on the NHL.)

In my mind, the only damage it did was that it affected people who make their livings around the National Hockey League. In other words, people who are ushers, people who serve the food, people who do a lot of that secondary work. They were affected deeply by it. That was a giant negative that very few people talk about.

Regarding the game itself, I think it's better. They had the summit last December to try to say, okay, how can we make the game better, instead of sitting around and waiting for the lockout to continue. They decided that they'd better wake up, open their eyes, and open their ears, and it really progressed into a series of meetings that evolved into discussions and ideas, and the transition was made. The game is a much better game on the ice than it's been for the last decade.

Had there not been a lockout, there probably wouldn't have been many changes. I watched the playoffs the last time there were playoffs, and there just wasn't enough lead changes. There wasn't enough scoring. There wasn't enough scoring chances. It was passionate. It was tough. It was nasty. But it wasn't exciting enough. And I was right in the middle of that. I totally agreed with the concept of, "You know what? Let's figure out how to make it better." But I don't think it would have happened if there hadn't been a lockout.

In a way, it was a blessing. We've also been somewhat fortunate that a lot of the greats have had to retire. Mark Messier, Al McGinnis, Brett Hull, Ron Francis. Those types of players. They've retired. A bunch of them. And we've been blessed by the kids that have come back, that have joined the league now, like [Alexander] Ovechkin, [Henrik] Lundqvist, [Sidney] Crosby. We've been blessed by what's been two years of rookies, really. That's been a salvation, too.

Without question, it's healthier economically. The owners should make money and the players should make money. The pie's being cut differently and everybody has a better chance of competing now. People who are fans in a lot of these cities have a genuine sense they have a chance—if their team is run well—to have a good team.

There were some people who were steamed about the lockout. But once they had a chance to see how the game was being played early in the season, there's nothing negative. They all love it.

Something interesting happened. The league front-loaded the schedule. There were a lot of rivalry games early, and the reason they did that was to insure that the crowds would come out because the Islanders were playing the Rangers, or the Rangers were playing the Flyers, or Calgary was playing Edmonton, etcetera. But in hindsight, they didn't need to. People are excited about the game.

Teams can't let down. There're too many teams that are in the hunt for playoff positions. You can't take a week off.

I think players were angry with what went on within their own association as opposed to being angry with the NHL itself. That's now calming down. The NHL needed a correction. It got a correction. It was hard to get there. But I think the game on the ice speaks for itself. And if everything goes according to the way it should go, they should be able to make this pie grow. I think so far, so good. And the fans, they're the ones coming to the buildings. They're the ones that seem to be happy with the style of play. So far, it's been very, very good. We haven't had to go through a slow growth process to get it where it once was. It's there and it can only get better.

Keith Hernandez or Don Mattingly?

Rubin says: This was *the* question in New York during the '80s and it's a great one. The debates raged from playgrounds to street corners to barrooms and everywhere in between. If you were a baseball fan in the area, you had to be embroiled in a few heated discussions on this very topic.

How could you not? The Mets' Keith Hernandez and the Yankees' Don Mattingly were two of the best first basemen in the game and here they were playing on opposite ends of this fair city. Both were Gold Glovers. Both won MVP awards. Both were extraordinary hitters. Both had kind of cheesy mustaches.

The question today is as hard to settle as it was twenty years ago when each was in his prime and tearing up his respective league. Mattingly was the leading stud in the Yankees' stable. Hernandez may not have been more of a star than Dwight Gooden, Gary Carter, or even Darryl Strawberry, but he was seen as one of the big-time leaders on the 1986 championship team. There are dozens of reasons to go for either one, Len-o, and I feel like I could argue for Mattingly today and Hernandez tomorrow, but . . .

Right here and right now I have to cast my lot with Donnie Baseball.

My argument for Mattingly is based on the numbers—and I

know that's not always the best way to judge—but there also are some intangibles to it, as you will see.

Hernandez played seventeen seasons and Mattingly fourteen, and the Yankee has some decided edges in his work with the bat. In three fewer seasons he hit sixty more home runs and logged twenty-eight more RBI. In terms of season averages Mattingly led in batting .307 to .296 and in slugging .471 to .436.

Hernandez may not have had Mattingly's pop but he was far better at getting on base, drawing nearly five hundred more walks and outpacing him in on-base percentage .384 to .358.

That's the lumber; now about the leather. Each of them was considered the very best first baseman in his league. Mattingly won nine Gold Gloves to Hernandez's eleven and might not have been as fleet afoot when charging a bunt, but he couldn't be beat when it came to snaring a smash down the line.

There's an essential tie in terms of leadership, too. Neither the Yankees nor the Mets are very giving about the title of team captain. In more than one hundred years, the Bombers have had eleven, including Mattingly from 1990 to 1995. In forty-four years, the Mets have had three, including Hernandez, who shared the honor with Carter from 1987 to 1989.

The thing that most people like to point out when making an argument for Hernandez is the World Series rings. He won one on the 1982 Cardinals and the other with the Mets in 1986. But if you look at the playoffs as baseball's biggest stage, Mattingly may have to get the edge as the better performer on it. His Yankees made only one postseason appearance—losing a five-game series to the Mariners in 1995—and the guy hit .417 and drove in six runs. Sure, he left the bases loaded one inning in the Game 3 loss, but he knocked in a pair in each of the last two games (also losses).

Hernandez was in five playoff series and hit .265, though his 21 RBI in thirty postseason games is more than respectable.

The numbers dispatched, I see other things that sway me onto Mattingly's side of this engagement.

During the mid-'80s the Mets were far more popular in this town than the Yankees. They were the team that won, had the dynamic stars, and produced all the buzz. Mattingly played on some awful editions of the Yankees and still was the more popular player around these parts.

Believe it or not, in 1988 *Newsday* (that's your paper, Dave) commissioned Gallup to do a poll of New York area residents on several baseball topics. They talked to more than one thousand people and Mattingly was overwhelmingly the most popular player. The Mets, by the way, were the preferred team by "nearly 3-to-1," the paper reported.

There is a final thing, and I hesitate to go there because some will say it's just not fair, but it has to do with image. I don't know whether he deserved it or not, but Mattingly's was squeaky clean; he was a tremendous role model. Hernandez had the whole cocaine thing going on. His substance issue wasn't nearly the scope of Gooden's or Strawberry's, but let's just say that after that came out in 1985, fathers weren't telling their sons to model their game after him.

The Mattingly-Hernandez thing is a horse race that goes to a photo finish. From my perspective, it's Mattingly by a nose.

Lennon says: Solid argument, Rog, but here's a question for you. Did I miss the Don Mattingly episode on *Seinfeld*? I don't think so.

Which brings up another question. You ever wonder why there never was a Don Mattingly episode? Because the Yankees' captain has the charisma of a Gatorade bucket, that's why, and if I recall, the same number of World Series rings.

Which is why Elaine dated Keith Hernandez—not Mattingly—and pretty much decided this particular debate for us. Say what you will about Hernandez's well-documented cocaine troubles, but that's an unfair shot, Rog.

If you want to start discrediting players who tried cocaine in the drug-infested '80s, we're talking about the handful of users who were unlucky enough to be exposed and the majority who were fortunate enough to avoid detection.

To rip Hernandez for a mistake he made before coming to the Mets just doesn't float in comparing him to Mattingly. The Mets may be the second team in this town, but between these two, they had the better first baseman.

I'm not going to go too crazy with the statistics, Rube, because you've already taken care of the numerical analysis. Thanks for the research. I'd rather focus on how each player figured into the winning equation, and Hernandez buries Mattingly in the category that matters most.

The Mets caught a huge break when the Cardinals—suspicious of Hernandez's drug habit—shipped him to Flushing for Neil Allen and Rick Ownbey on June 15, 1983. The deal was so lopsided that Cardinals fans actually are beginning to believe that a Hernandez Curse has been preventing them from winning another World Series title since 1982, the year he helped them get the ring.

The angry Cardinals believed they were exiling Hernandez to baseball oblivion by sending him to the awful Mets, but he became part of their resurgence instead. A very big part, in fact. Who better to help give a growing team confidence than a slick-fielding first baseman with a clutch bat and something to prove? It was a second chance for Hernandez, and his newfound intensity became contagious throughout the Mets, who fed off the man nicknamed Mex.

Hernandez wasn't just an eleven-time Gold Glove winner. He never made more than thirteen errors in a season, which is the lowest total to ever lead the National League. Hernandez singlehandedly defused rallies, charging to turn bunts into force-outs at second base or flawlessly engineering 3–6–3 double plays.

We're arguing whether he was better than Mattingly? Many consider Hernandez the best to ever play the position, in New York or anywhere else on the planet. Former St. Louis catcher and later Mets broadcaster Tim McCarver said he had never seen anyone do more to help his team win than Hernandez.

And the Mets did win with Hernandez. They showed a twenty-four-game improvement from the time of Hernandez's trade to the end of the 1984 season, and they finished first or second in the standings until his release in 1990. In case you forgot, Rog, the Mets also won the World Series in 1986, and Hernandez played as big a part in that title as anyone.

Maybe it's unfair to elevate Hernandez, because he had a superior supporting cast to Mattingly's subpar pin-striped crew. But Hernandez's grind-it-out attitude rubbed off on the entire roster, and he did plenty more than simply provide flashy defense. Only someone with the street cred of Hernandez could brawl with Darryl Strawberry during a spring training photo shoot one day and play catch with him the next.

Hernandez was a patient hitter long before A's GM Billy Beane turned on-base percentage into an art form, and no one came through more in clutch situations. Mattingly had numbers, too, but who was watching? Everyone in New York was too busy taking the No. 7 train to Shea Stadium, where they got to see Hernandez ply his trade on a nightly basis.

Face it, Rog. The only TV show you'll ever see Mattingly on is *Yankeeography*. And only on YES is he considered a better first baseman than Hernandez. Maybe Hernandez isn't in the Hall of Fame, but he should be. At least he's immortalized in *Seinfeld* reruns, and that's an honor that means more to some New Yorkers than Cooperstown.

22

The New York City Marathon:
Love It or Hate It?

Lennon says: I understand why this question made the list, but hating the marathon is like saying Central Park is a waste of prime real estate. Or the Empire State Building is a nuisance because it attracts too many tourists to midtown Manhattan.

But these are some of the things that make New York what it is: the greatest city on the planet. And if there is one event that blends all of these unique ingredients together, putting them on display for one early November afternoon, it is the five-borough extravaganza known as the New York City Marathon.

In the interest of full disclosure, I've run the marathon three times, cracking four hours on each occasion, so I'm biased. But there are tens of thousands of people who enjoy the marathon and have never laced on a pair of running shoes. It's not just about the running.

At the elite level, the marathon is a professional sporting event, with prize money and a new car awarded to the victors, just like in many other sports. But those dozen or so world-class runners who cover the 26.2-mile course in a little over two hours finish too quickly in my estimation.

Soaking up the atmosphere through all five boroughs is the true pleasure of the race: Crossing the Verrazano Bridge at the start and seeing the Statue of Liberty barely visible in the distance. Veering into Brooklyn, where the sights and sounds of the very first spectators hit you like a wall. Up through Queens, across the Fifty-ninth Street Bridge and into the mass of humanity camped on First Avenue, with the bar crowds spilled onto the sidewalks.

Where else can drunken partiers, Bloody Marys in raised fists, cheer madly for their friends and neighbors, who are grunting and sweating like plow horses? During this stretch, the pain actually fades to euphoria, and the bond between New Yorkers never seems more real. It's a rare phenomenon in a metropolis of close to ten million people, and a sensation that I've not experienced at any other time during the year.

The marathon is even good at duplicating parts of the big-city experience that out-of-towners aren't familiar with. For example, the penned-in farm-animal-feel at the Staten Island starting line is like riding the No. 6 train at rush hour. With less groping, of course, but you won't see hundreds of people urinating in the subway, either, unless you're on the way home from a Mets game.

I compare running through this mass of humanity as kind of like being a member of the Yankees during a ticker-tape parade through the Canyon of Heroes. The level of adoration obviously is scaled back a bit, but the affection is there, and no one holds out cups of water and oranges for Derek Jeter and Joe Torre.

That's what separates the marathon from any other sporting event—the fans get to participate rather than sit in their seats and drink $8 beers. It's also more fun to cheer on one of your best friends instead of a $252-million athlete who doesn't hear you anyway and wouldn't cross the street for a cup of water from a fan if he were on fire. Makes you rethink about paying $80 for a ticket, doesn't it?

The runners are the focal point of the day, obviously. But in the big picture, everyone wins. New York's economy gets a huge boost in hotel business and restaurant patronage, with marathon weekend becoming sort of a dress rehearsal for the upcoming holiday season.

Mayor Bloomberg gets his photo op, crowning the winner with a laurel wreath. And the rest of the average, ordinary New Yorkers either run the race of a lifetime or have a guilt-free excuse to drink on the sidewalk like it's New Year's Eve in November.

What's not to love?

Rubin says: I've never been afraid to voice the unpopular opinion, but in this case I don't think I am. The best kept secret in New York is that most of us who live here find the New York City Marathon a complete inconvenience, not a wondrous event that makes the city great.

We know there are a thousand other things that make our city tops. The problem is that on marathon day, there's no getting across town to experience them because you and your silly friends have the place in a total snarl.

The one thing, Dave, I do agree with you on here is that Central Park is a treasure. Too bad no one but you and your cult get to use it on that day. You guys couldn't have picked a weekday? By the time the place empties out to the point where the rest of us can partake, it's littered like Fresh Kills and inhabited by mutants in space blankets.

There are lots of occasions during the calendar year when America decides to descend on New York. They come for New Year's Eve to watch the ball drop. They come on Thanksgiving Day to see the Macy's parade. They come on St. Patrick's Day to get all the booze they can and, perhaps, catch a blurry glimpse of a great parade.

You know what those of us who live here do on those days? We get the hell out of town. Know why? Because New York already is overcrowded and the last thing we want is to be a part of a miniature population explosion.

Weekends are occasion for the true New Yorker to cut loose.

We're hitting a musical or a drama on Broadway. We're getting reservations for dinner at Smith and Wollensky or Spice Market. We're going for a cocktail at the Bread Bar at Tabla. But on marathon weekend it gets a lot harder than it usually is. The event adds some twenty-five thousand racing tourists and their family and friends to the mix. And none of them are cooking at home.

The other thing I don't get is this idea that the marathon is such a great sight for all of us to see. If you took away the family and friends, I really wonder how big the crowds would be. Would it even be enough to fill Giants Stadium? I'm not so sure. There's hardly anyone turning out in the Bronx and I can speak from personal experience that northern Manhattan isn't exactly showing it a lot of love.

I am not a hard-hearted person and I do not think that running a marathon is a waste of time. It's a tremendous achievement, which is why, when I have a friend like you running in it, I go out to show my support. I always go to Fifth Avenue at about 112th Street—approximately Mile 22. I know I can show up and stand right next to the course because no one who lives around there has any interest at all.

I couldn't help but notice, my friend, that in your argument for loving this 26.2 mile log-jamming fiasco you pointed out that you've run it three times in less than four hours (impressive, but as Derrick Coleman might say, "whoop-dee-damn-doo!").

It seems like four hours is the magic number on marathon day. It's the same amount of time is takes to get to the fantastic Asian Garden in Staten Island or to catch a cab to the theater district at around 5:30 P.M.

SETTLE THE SCORE/MARY WITTENBERG

(Mary Wittenberg, race director of the NYC Marathon, knows better than anyone the thrills and pitfalls of staging this world-class event, so we asked her to settle the score.)

The New York City Marathon is in a league of its own. With new projects, like the half-marathon, we have to introduce it and work with all the city agencies to accept it and then we have to work with the various communities. But the marathon is so embraced by everyone. The NYPD loves it. As much as it's a workday for everybody, I think it's a favorite workday for all of the agencies, and they're like partners. They're every bit a part of the race as we are. I think they have a real ownership of it and a pride in representing New York.

We always continue to work with the communities that are impacted, but I think over the years, New Yorkers have come to feel like it's their very own event. They want their street in Brooklyn to be the best street in terms of the most cheering, and the most activity and the most entertainment, and the most music. Our challenges are so few with the marathon because New Yorkers feel it's part of what defines the city and themselves.

I think it's the city's best day of the year. Whether you're a lifelong New Yorker or just visiting the city, the beauty of the marathon is that everybody is a part of it, well beyond the thirty-seven thousand that run the race. Every spectator counts.

It's our best advertisement, or postcard, to the entire world. Over 260 million people worldwide watched it last year. We're on national TV; we're on for five hours on local television. And most importantly, everybody that's touched by it—the two million spectators and the thirty-seven thousand runners—all walk away thinking that New York City is the friendliest city they've ever been to because everyone's out cheering for them and supporting them. They wear their medal out that night, everyone congratulates them, and then congratulates them again the day after the race. I think it's just a fabulous promotion about how incredible New York City is.

And I think it shows a side of New York City that the world doesn't always see. The world knows Wall Street. The world knows about the World Trade Center. The world knows about New Yorkers being brash and arrogant and sophisticated. But what they also see is the friendly, community side of New Yorkers as residents and people who are so proud to be living here.

The city agencies all play key roles and they thrive on that. From NYPD Deputy Commissioner [George] Grasso, who runs the race, to Chief [Joseph] Esposito to Commissioner [Raymond] Kelly. They have very serious jobs, from a security perspective. I mean, our stadium is 26.2 miles and it's safe and secure and well maintained because the NYPD is out there.

The departments of transportation and sanitation insure the streets are ready and the sidewalks are in good shape for the runners and spectators. The Parks Department, not only at the finish but throughout the course, takes extra measures to make sure we're all ready to go. It's critical for the EMS and FDNY to be at their best, and they always are.

There's no race like the New York City Marathon. It's an experience of a lifetime and I really believe it's the best tour of New York City you'll ever find. You get to see all five boroughs, you get to see the different communities and all the different neighborhoods, and it puts a whole different light on what we know as the city. I think, compared to other races, our city is alive for every step of the 26.2 miles. There's no one else that can touch that. From the moment you step off the plane, or walk into the hotel, there's a feeling that this is the big time. And every one of those thirty-seven thousand athletes is part of a big-time event. This is the major leagues. Our goal—and I think many people feel this way—is that this is your Broadway stage, your chance of a lifetime.

Do the Jets Need to Leave Giants Stadium?

Rubin says: Dave, there's a secret I've been keeping and this seems like the time to share it with everybody.

Here's my favorite route to drive from the Jets' practice facility in Uniondale, Long Island, to Giants Stadium in East Rutherford, N.J. I like to start by getting on the Meadowbrook Parkway heading north, switch over to the Northern State going west and then scramble out onto the Cross Island to head for the Whitestone Bridge . . .

I honestly have no clue what the Jets are doing playing their games at Giants Stadium besides making most of their fans pay some hefty tolls and fostering their image as the second-class NFL team in this town.

To all the Jets executives, a couple words of advice: Get your own stadium!

It's not like I'm suggesting the Jets do something they don't already have an inclination to do. Before the effort failed dismally, they wanted to play at the new facility that would have been built on the West Side of Manhattan. Well, now that it's not an option, it's time to come up with a new and better idea, something that serves their fans, something that gives them an identity all their own.

One team playing in another's arena is not something that hasn't happened before. Anyone remember how the Mets ended up playing a season in Yankee Stadium? Obviously, it seemed and sounded pretty stupid, but it was temporary! Now imagine doing that permanently and you have exactly what the Jets are a part of.

The Jets' home schedule is predicated on the Giants', and they don't have the advantage that comes with access to working in close proximity to their own facility. The Giants leave the practice field every day and make their way to the same locker room they will be using on game day. For the Jets to do the same, they'd need a half tank of gas and $4.50 for a toll.

This is obviously not a team that is doing everything in its power to help its players succeed, and I think we can all see it reflected in the franchises' comparative record for success. Since they moved to Giants Stadium in 1984, the Jets have been to one conference championship game. The Giants have been to three Super Bowls and won two of them.

The main issue here has to be identity. What kind of personality does a team have when it plays its games at another team's home field? The Giants took plenty of flack in the years after their move to the facility and the criticism had to do with a team that has "New York" in its name playing in Jersey (we all remember the jokes about a Super Bowl victory parade in the Lincoln Tunnel, right?). But at least the new facility was their own; the Jets can't even say that.

Things have improved a great deal since the Jets first moved their games to Giants Stadium; the place used to be half empty for their games and there was little in the way of markings to indicate it was anything but the Giants' home field. They have gained a New Jersey following and regularly sell out these days.

But lost in the move were many of their true fans, people in Nassau and Suffolk counties who always came to their games at Shea Stadium. Plenty still go the distance to the Meadowlands, but plenty of others find the haul ludicrous.

There are plans on the books to scrap the current Giants Stadium. New York's two NFL franchises would team up in creating a new stadium that we might see several years from now. That's a step in the right direction, because the new building will surely not bear the name of only one of the teams. But it's a far sight from the distinction and character that would come from having a facility they could truly call home.

Kid, it's time you moved out of mom and dad's house and got a place of your own.

Lennon says: Location is not the Jets' problem, Roger. Personnel is, from the owner's box to the front office and right down through the coaching ranks to the locker room. If the team is lousy, as the Jets have been more often than not recently, why does it matter where they play?

The last time I checked, the Giants have NY on their helmets, too, and they seem to do just fine in the Meadowlands, aside from Eli's meltdown last January against the Panthers. Obviously it should feel more like home to the Giants, considering the building carries their name, but as far as the stadium causing an identity crisis for the Jets . . . please.

Do you think the Jets would be a playoff team if they moved back to Shea? On Sundays, the only place where it even says Giants Stadium is on the outside, so I fail to see how that affects their psyche. The grounds crew does a fine job stringing up the green banners that line the walls, they zipper-in the Jets end-zone logos and Fireman Ed does his job leading the J-E-T-S chants. You don't see the Giants complaining that they should paint the artificial turf blue, do you?

I'm sure fans from Long Island, where the Jets draw most of their supporters from, want the team in their backyard, or at least in one of the five boroughs. That makes sense for the sake of convenience. Would the same Gang Green crowd be upset if Giants Stadium was located in Suffolk County? I doubt it would be as big of an issue. This is all about driving two hours or more, over a couple of bridges and through tunnels, to see a football game. And if the Jets were a perennial playoff contender, those same fans would be sitting in bumper-to-bumper traffic with ear-to-ear grins on their green-painted faces.

Team owner Woody Johnson stumped relentlessly for a shiny new billion-dollar retractable domed stadium on Manhattan's West Side, and we heard all about how the Jets need a home of their own to join the NFL's elite franchises. But the PR ploy had little to do with improving the Jets' on-field fortunes and everything to do with making a fortune for Johnson, who probably regrets the day he signed the check to buy the team.

If it's such a bad idea for the Jets to play in Giants Stadium, then why the hell is Johnson in such a rush to share another home with his NFC brethren as soon as the paint is dry on the new building? It's still going to be in New Jersey. It's still going to take a couple of bridges and tunnels to get there. And I have a hunch that plenty of fans are still going to refer to the new arena as Giants Stadium, even if it's called Google Park at Secaucus Yards.

Here's my suggestion to the Jets: Deal with it. There's no use pretending they are on equal footing with the Giants, just like the Mets can never stand shoulder to shoulder with the Yankees, even if they have climbed back to respectability. And that's more that can be said for the Jets these days. They should consider themselves lucky the Giants haven't kicked them out of the Meadowlands on principle.

And from a taxpayer's perspective, there's no reason to have two football stadiums. Each team plays only ten home dates a year, including the exhibition games, unless you count the postseason, and the Jets don't need to worry about that just yet.

Instead, the Jets should spend their time worrying about the other team on the field with them, and I don't mean the Giants. As long as people are still paying to see their games, the Jets should be happy they have someone to split the mortgage with. And if the Jets finally pull their act together and win the Super Bowl, they can have their parade through the Canyon of Heroes, just like every other New York team. When that dream becomes a reality, they won't have to be concerned about scheduling conflicts with the Giants in reserving lower Manhattan for a few hours.

Bobby Valentine's Firing:
Wise Move or Huge Mistake?

Lennon says: Japan or not, baseball is baseball, and when Bobby Valentine led the Chiba Lotte Marines to their first championship since 1974, nothing could top the feeling of vindication for the Flushing exile.

Valentine probably had voice-mail messages from the Dodgers and Devil Rays waiting for him before the final out of the Japan Series. But for a proud man burned by his last go-round with the Mets, Valentine savored his moment on center stage, even if it did not receive much media attention in the States.

And when he explained why he would not return to the majors in 2006, anyone familiar with his rough exit from Shea could easily read between the lines of his comments.

"I'm doing a job that I'm extremely happy doing," Valentine said. "I have an owner that showed me an incredible amount of loyalty, giving me total control of the organization. There would be no reason to leave, other than hypocrisy and disloyalty."

Those were the twin daggers plunged into Valentine's back immediately following his 2002 campaign with the Mets. For a franchise in perpetual need of a fall guy, Valentine fit the suit at the end of that tumultuous season—and it took only ten months for the Mets to realize their mistake when they ultimately canned GM Steve Phillips the following June.

What exactly was Valentine guilty of? Aside from maybe caring too much, and an ill-timed impression of a stoned batter dodging a ninety-five-mph fastball, he should have built up enough good will to survive another assassination attempt from Phillips.

Valentine, after all, somehow got the Mets to the World Series in 2000, outfoxing the Giants' Dusty Baker and the Cardinals' Tony LaRussa in the process. In 2001, during the 9/11 tragedy, nobody in the sporting world did more to aid in the city's grief-stricken recovery efforts. Love him or hate him, Valentine made the Mets matter, either creating headlines or mocking them, and that's no small feat in a city ruled by the Yankees.

Widely recognized as a brilliant tactician of the game, if not the most diplomatic of managers, Valentine grew frustrated with the flawed team under his command in 2002 and eventually took the bait from a GM who had wanted him gone years earlier.

It was during that 2002 season, after the Mets had suffered their twelfth straight loss in Colorado, that Valentine stunningly broke down in the manager's office, tearfully saying that someone in the front office claimed he was trying to get himself fired. That was the start of Valentine's rapid decline in the owner's eyes, and with his players already mailing it in, it was only a matter of time.

Valentine was not at fault for the marijuana-smoking accusations that rocked his clubhouse, though he did little to defuse them. And with the public calling for someone's head, owner Fred Wilpon gave them Valentine's, inexplicably sparing Phillips, the mastermind who assembled the $102-million failure with overpaid and underachieving veterans.

When Valentine arrived at Shea that October morning, he was led to believe it was for a staff meeting. Called in to see Wilpon, Valentine couldn't contain his anger when told of his fate, blurting out, "What? And Steve stays?"

Valentine's firing was never about whether he was a good manager or not. Even his critics can't deny that. Last year, Valentine piloted Chiba Lotte, a perennial loser, to the Japan title with a lineup that featured Benny Agbayani and Matt Franco, two of his former expats from Flushing.

An entire country adores Valentine now—just not his own—for a management style that is referred to as "Bobby Magic." He is signed to a multiyear contract that more than triples what his annual salary was with the Mets. Valentine even has his own best-selling beer.

But the only job Valentine ever wanted was ripped away from him by circumstances beyond his control, and the scheming of a hated rival in Phillips. Who was more of an embarrassment to the Mets—Valentine or Art Howe? Is Willie Randolph, in his second year, comparable to Valentine? Those are easy questions.

The Mets realized their mistake with Valentine too late. Maybe one of these days, if Valentine chooses to let them, they will correct it.

Rubin says: There's no denying that Bobby Valentine is a good manager. He always has been. It was never more apparent than when he orchestrated the Mets into that 2000 World Series. He is a master of the subtleties of the game, and in that case showed himself capable of getting as much out of a group of players as possible.

You've been doing this for more than fifteen years, Dave, so forgive me if I am stunned at how naïve you're being. Wake up! Being good at your job isn't always enough, no matter what the profession. Good people—even those who have won a pennant—get fired for lots of reasons. A bond trader who makes his company $40 million in a year earns a big bonus; if he or she loses money the next, they're getting a pink slip. Managing a baseball team isn't that different.

By the time the 2002 season began to decay, Valentine had problems brewing on two major fronts: in the front office and in the clubhouse. That means about the only place where things were working smoothly was in his huddles with the media before and after every game.

Every workplace has its politics. The Mets' front office is no different. I always considered Valentine good at playing the political games, but he obviously wasn't as good as general manager Steve Phillips, who could just as easily have been held responsible.

Valentine was never all that good at keeping all his passion or his sense of humor in check, and that cut in two directions for him. He was truly candid, a rare treat for people who cover a team. As a result we, and in turn the fans, got very close to him. The issue was that Bobby V. never kept the huge rift between him and the GM out of the public eye. Perhaps he was trying to orchestrate Phillips's ouster, but the image-conscious Wilpons weren't crazy about having that be a part of the daily coverage of the their team.

You mentioned the press conference after the marijuana scandal broke, replete with V's hilarious and embarrassing imitation of a stoned hitter swinging at a fastball. That one's never going to be a winner with the bosses. They're trying to put out a fire and he's using a can of lighter fluid to make it all the more entertaining.

Political mistakes could have been overcome, in Valentine's case with quality performances on the field. That wasn't happening as the Mets nosedived to a last-place finish. Dave, you pointed out the players were "mailing it in." That Valentine couldn't get this group to play hard—no matter what their deficiencies—was evidence that he'd lost control of his clubhouse.

There was a faction of players that regularly sniped against Valentine. The manager had pitted some teammates against one another. And he maneuvered himself into a spat with then-captain John Franco—a bad political move in the clubhouse.

The other thing to remember about the marijuana scandal is that it happened on his watch. Was he ignoring a problem? Or did he just not know? Neither one of them is an acceptable answer; either reflects badly on him.

I was glad to see that Valentine had won the 2005 championship in Japan with Chiba Lotte. Doing that with an undermanned club was a vivid reminder of how good he is at his job. I know he likes it there, but a guy with his talents belongs back in the majors and I hope that happens soon.

I think that bringing in stoic Art Howe to replace Valentine might have been the mistake we should be ruing, because that was a disaster. But at the conclusion of 2002 there was no way Bobby V. would be able to make the team better. He didn't have the support of the embarrassed ownership or even that of the players.

I thought that the Wilpons should also have jettisoned Phillips, too, because he was at least as responsible as the manager. But there was no question Valentine's time was up. Any smart move the Wilpons were going to make had to include his dismissal.

25

What Was the Most Sensational Scandal?

Rubin says: Scandal is about two sides of a single coin. On one you have the shocking entertainment value: The bigger the stunner, the more delectable it is for New York's voyeuristic public. On the other there's the tragic reality: Some person or institution is being exposed and sullied before everyone's eyes.

In sticking with the coin theme, I offer the silver dollar of sports scandals in New York: the St. John's sex scandal of 2004. It was a salacious spectacle from the moment it started with an outlandish night on the outskirts of Pittsburgh just hours after a humiliating twenty-point loss. And it just got more and more sensational as it unfurled. Of course, the more delicious it got for New York's scandal-loving citizens, the worse it got for a storied basketball program and highly regarded university.

Dubbed by the tabloids the "Sexcapade in Pittsburgh," this is the scandal that had it all, from the tragic to the comically stupid. Let me count the ways:

Sex—If there's one thing that makes a scandal compelling, it's sex; the more sordid the details, the more gripping. After the players were supposed to have gone to bed, six of them met up for a night out. They picked a strip joint called Club Erotica. There, they met a patron, a furloughed flight attendant, and propositioned her for a night of group sex. She agreed to a price and went back with the group to have the romp in the university-purchased hotel room.

Some players had sex with her and others preferred to just watch, but when it was over, none had the money.

Crime—No scandal would be complete without it. The woman served the players, all African-American, an ultimatum: Pay up or be accused of raping a white woman. They didn't and she went to the cops, but in the end the tables got turned. One player recorded her shakedown with a cell phone and she ended up facing charges for levying the false claims. She uttered the scandal's signature line upon leaving police custody: "I am not the hooker of Pittsburgh."

Race—Adding this to the mix always has an explosive effect. With his institution dishonored, St. John's president, Rev. Donald J. Harrington, chose to take little responsibility. He blamed the players' poor judgment, fostered by the "culture" of the basketball program. The remark was intended to be a jab at Mike Jarvis, whom he'd fired less than two months earlier, but instead touched off a firestorm that left him apologizing to a student body that construed it as having racial overtones.

Punishment—It always brings out the rubbernecking effect on those who follow a scandal. Actions were taken against the six players in the form of expulsions, suspensions from school, and suspensions from the team (one player was allowed to withdraw); but even that didn't put an end to it.

Cheating and Payback—They're icing on the cake in any scandal. One of the disciplined players exacted his revenge by revealing that a member of the coaching staff had been giving him regular under-the-table cash payment for years.

If anything seems clear it is this: Had the relationship between Jarvis and Harrington not grown so contentious just weeks earlier, none of it probably would have happened. But Harrington wanted no more of the man—perhaps with good reason, as the Red Storm got worse and worse—and dismissed him six games into the season. Then he handed the team to unprepared associate head coach Kevin Clark; talk about getting dealt a bad hand.

As for the allegations of under-the-table cash payments, St. John's had already served a one-year postseason ban and lost two scholarships and was still dealing with the prospect of further penalties as recently as the 2005–06 season.

Scandals have a way of consuming us. This one sent a regaled basketball program to its lowest point. Our dirty little secret is how entertained we were watching its descent.

Lennon says: C'mon, Roger. The St. John's incident in Pittsburgh was no scandal. That was an after-school special. College basketball players, strippers, a hotel room . . . talk to me when people start shooting each other. What else is there to do in Pittsburgh past midnight? You expect them to go skinny-dipping in the Ohio River?

I understand that student-athletes are not supposed to be having sex with, um, exotic dancers. And paying for it—or not paying for it, in their case—is asking for trouble, especially when you got your scholarship from a Catholic university.

Maybe I'd be on board with your choice, Rube, if these randy schoolboys cost the Red Storm a national championship. But I'm not going to get upset over seeding in the Big East tournament.

If you want a bona fide "oh no, he didn't" scandal, I present Jason Giambi, aka the Shrunken Slugger, the BALCO Bomber, the Deca-Durabolin DH. The only thing missing from the Giambi saga of 2004 was sex, but these days, there's an even more disgraceful S-word: steroids.

Unlike sex, there is no forgive-and-forget with steroids. It is a scarlet letter that brings dishonor to a professional athlete, and until Giambi, no active baseball player had been outed so publicly for using performance-enhancing drugs. There always had been whispers of suspicion about certain players, but Giambi removed all doubt when his testimony to a grand jury was leaked to the *San Francisco Chronicle*.

I'll give Giambi credit for coming clean (no pun intended) and telling the truth after swearing to do so, because the same can not be said of everyone who takes the stand. But 2003 was not a good time to be admitting to steroid use. Not with Congress itchy to open a can of whoop-ass on Major League Baseball for its inadequate drug policy and the public salivating for its first high-profile fall guy.

And here was Giambi, unwittingly serving himself up to be eaten alive by the relentless New York media machine. His grand jury testimony in the BALCO case was supposed to be sealed, invisible to the prying eyes of reporters. But once the *Chronicle*'s intrepid staff revealed it to the world, I can't even imagine what Giambi's reaction must have been like. He was probably looking to book a ticket on the next space-shuttle flight.

I mean, take a look at the stuff that just kept appearing in the newspapers over and over and over again. Then on every TV channel. Over and over and over again, for what seemed like eternity. It was an endless news cycle. Here's a sample:

Prosecutor: "So, you would put it in your arm?"
Giambi: "No, you wouldn't. You'd put it in your ass."
Prosecutor: "Excuse me? I couldn't hear you, Mr. Giambi. Where did it go?"

Okay, I made that last part up, but there really was no need for embellishment. As soon as Giambi was exposed, there was talk of the Yankees trying to void the remainder of his $120-million contract, and speculation that he would never play baseball in this town again.

Reporters were dispatched to Giambi's Las Vegas home to look for him. The Yankees had no choice but to adopt a bunker mentality as the tabloids pounded away with new revelations on their front and back pages.

It didn't help that Giambi had repeatedly lied about his steroid use when asked by reporters at different points during the 2003 season. That's the kind of stuff we don't forget. When a slimmed-down Giambi showed up for spring training that year, looking more like Jason Priestley, he said his stunning weight loss was from giving up In-N-Out burgers. Don't think that interview didn't reappear a few thousand times.

Every scandal, no matter how heinous, usually ends with a public apology, and Giambi eventually said he was sorry. He just didn't say what he was apologizing for. Some mea culpa. In retrospect, Major League Baseball can thank Giambi for shining a flashlight into the dark corners of clubhouses everywhere and exposing the sport's dirty little secret. Not only was Giambi's life forever changed, his steroids revelations rocked this city and shook a hornet's nest up on Capitol Hill. Now that's a scandal.

THE TEN MOST SENSATIONAL SCANDALS

1. The Giambi steroids confession: Testimony from the BALCO trial was leaked to the *San Francisco Chronicle*, including Jason Giambi's admission that he used steroids. It contradicted denials he'd been making for years and cast a pall over all his accomplishments. He issued a public apology without saying what he was apologizing for, and the Yankees sought to terminate his contract.

144 • Roger Rubin and David Lennon

2. The St. John's prostitution scandal: Six basketball players went out to a Pittsburgh strip club after a twenty-point loss, struck a deal to pay a woman to have sex with them, and then brought her back to the team hotel for the romp. When they refused to pay, she told police she'd been raped, but a player's cell phone recording of her shakedown exonerated them. One player was expelled and two others suspended, one of whom went public with NCAA violations; it was the low point in nearly a century of great basketball.

3. Danny Almonte's lie: The left-handed pitcher led his team, the Rolando Paulino All-Stars of the Bronx, to the Little League World Series. There, he threw a perfect game as the club finished third. When it came out that he was actually fourteen—and not twelve—the squad was stripped of its district, state, and regional titles. Worse, it embarrassed an American institution in front of the world.

4. The Howie Spira fiasco: Yankees owner George Steinbrenner was banned from baseball for the second time in 1990 after it was revealed that he'd paid gambler Howie Spira approximately $40,000 to dig up dirt on outfielder Dave Winfield. Commissioner Fay Vincent didn't lift the ban for three years.

5. The wife swap: Fritz Peterson and Mike Kekich, a pair of Yankees left-handed pitchers, decided to swap wives between the 1972 and 1973 seasons. They also exchanged houses, children, and pets. The Yankees became embroiled in a morality scandal and commissioner Bowie Kuhn found himself having to answer questions about the conduct of the players in his sport. He called himself "appalled" by the incident.

6. The Mets' marijuana revelation: At the end of the miserable 2002 season, it was revealed that seven Mets had used marijuana, and a photo of one using a water bong was published. A comical press conference was held at Shea Stadium to respond to the report, where manager Bobby Valentine did a hilarious imitation of a player on drugs trying to hit a ball. The Mets fired Valentine when their last-place season ended less than two weeks later.

7. The Marv Albert accusation: In the summer of 1997, the iconic broadcaster was accused of sexual assault. During a sensational trial, the sordid details and his sexual proclivities became public. Albert ends the trial with a plea to a misdemeanor assault-and-battery charge for biting his former lover. NBC fired him and he was forced to resign at MSG Network.

8. "I'm not gay.": One of the first insane moments in a 2002 Mets season filled with them came in Philadelphia when Mike Piazza called an impromptu press conference on the Veterans Stadium to announce that he wasn't gay. It brought to an end weeks of speculation that followed the publishing of an article in which manager Bobby Valentine said baseball ought to be able to handle an openly gay player.

9. The Isiah Thomas accusation: The Knicks president and general manager was already was under fire during the 2005–06 season for the team's poor performance and high payroll when recently fired team VP Anucha Browne Sanders files a lawsuit alleging that Thomas approached her for sex, called her a "bitch" and a "ho" in front of other team staff, and had her terminated when she complained about his antics. During the fallout, it is revealed that Thomas fathered a child weeks before his wedding to another woman and had no contact with the child.

10. The Proposition: On hand for a celebration of the Jets' All-Time team, an inebriated Joe Namath consents to a television interview with Suzy Kolber. When asked about the team's tribulations during the 2003 season, he responded, "I want to kiss you. I couldn't care less about the team struggling. What we know is we can improve. . . . We're looking to next season. We're looking to make noise now and I want to kiss you." In the wake of it, the New York icon goes public about his battle with alcohol abuse.

26

Which New York Athlete Would Be the Most Fun to Hang With?

Lennon says: Just suppose for a second that Derek Jeter has actually dated half of the women he's been linked to in the media. I'll even settle for a third of them. Or maybe only one, say Jessica Alba. Doesn't that make him the hands-down winner? Can anyone else even touch that? No shot.

But for the sake of argument—after all, this is supposed to be a debate—I'll attempt to state the obvious. It's Friday night, and your accountant friend, Bob, wants to hit a few bars with the crew. Bob is a funny guy, isn't going to sucker punch the bouncer after six Heinekens, and won't suddenly come down with malaria when it's time to settle the tab. Overall, a solid citizen and a good wingman for the club scene.

Everyone has a friend like Bob, and trust me, hanging out with him would be more entertaining than chillin' with 80 percent of professional athletes. The cult of celebrity is simply too much to deal with in this day and age. The relentless attention and constant stream of autograph hounds has made them feel like hunted prey, which pretty much explains their reclusive behavior outside of stadiums.

But here's why you can't go wrong with Jeter (and again, this is not rocket science). True, the Yankees' captain comes off a bit restrained in interviews, and reporters will tell you he's not as gregarious as some of the players across town, like Cliff Floyd or even David Wright. But let Jeter loose in Manhattan—or South Beach or Las Vegas—and people can't open doors fast enough. Jeter, with four World Series rings at age thirty-two, already is The Mick for this generation, and owns New York in a way that Donald Trump can be envious of. Trump's got the real estate and a TV ratings-winner, but he doesn't play shortstop for the Yankees. Sorry, Donald.

But let's get back to those aforementioned Hollywood hotties. When you're an A-lister, you can expect the occasional Page Six item that has you canoodling with whoever's in town that month. Tough life, I know, and Jeter has done his part to elevate ballplayers to rock-star status, if you read the newspapers, anyway. This was a guy who broke into the bigs with Mariah Carey back in 1996— before she slipped in the standings—and then rebounded with the reigning Miss Universe at the time, Lara Dutta. That's money.

Evidently, Jeter has plenty of game after the final out, and that's the guy you want to hit the town with. Not only do you breeze past the velvet rope at Marquee and Lotus, but when you show up at the VIP room, there's a good chance you'll be sharing a banquette with Scarlett Johansson or Vanessa Minnillo or some up-and-coming actress who will be on the cover of *People* in three months.

I can't verify that Jeter does, in fact, hang with either of those women—though the *New York Post* did have pictures of him cavorting Hawaii with the MTV VJ Minnillo—but you definitely get the sense that he has their phone numbers. Or could easily get the digits if he wanted them.

So where does the Average Joe fit in here? The truth is, we don't. That's why this is a hypothetical question, with little empirical evidence to support it. But given the choice of watching an Eagles game with Philly native Joe McEwing—a very good guy, by the way—or maybe having a beer with Aaron Small, you have to shoot for the moon and go with Jeter.

Getting the chance to roll with Jeter is like stepping off that sea-plane when it touches down at Fantasy Island. Here comes Mr. Rourke and Tattoo; they've arranged your bungalow down by the beach, and all you ask is that you get some quality time with the Yankees' shortstop. When that night's over, and you're dragging yourself back down the pier to that seaplane, you know you made the right choice.

Rubin says: Here's my big piece of advice for you, Dave, before you go out for your big night with the Yankees' captain: Don't forget your Visa card.

Dave, I can see you in one of Derek Jeter's now-famed television ads. You're hitting the hot spots, getting great seats at the best restaurants, enjoying the company of beautiful women. Then at the commercial's conclusion, it's you behind George Steinbrenner in the conga line. That's a thirty-second spot I'd just love to see.

Your argument is sound, pal. Spend a night hanging out with Jeter and you probably will see and talk to more beautiful women than you have in any year of your life. And you would be able to dine where and when you please. And you would gain entry into all sorts of exclusive nightspots that even Page Six reporters have never heard of.

It sounds like a good time. But if you look at any of the chosen few people who have been labeled "New York's most popular ath-lete," I think the experience would be similar. Going back, I'd bet that a night out with Mickey Mantle or Joe Namath would get you all the same things and maybe more in terms of entertainment. Hey, Broadway Joe is the kind of guy who could pick out the pret-tiest woman in any place and tell her "I want to kiss you." And I bet it works a lot better in a darkened night club than it does on live television.

And you'd have a hard time convincing me that a night out with

Mark Messier a few years ago wouldn't have brought you the same kind of fun. We're talking about a guy who was every bit as cosmopolitan and charismatic as Jeter and, hey, we all know that hockey players might be the nicest group of guys in sports.

But if all you want is a nice table, a good meal, and a nice view, then you and I have different tastes. I'm looking for something a little more cutting edge. I want hilarity. I want danger. I want to drag my tired behind home with the sun coming up on the athlete's game day and feel like I just rode Space Mountain all night long.

That's why the choice right here would be to hang one night with Lawrence Taylor when he was at the apex of his popularity (in truth, I think it would still be a damn good time right now).

LT got into all the great night spots. He got the superstar treatment in the best restaurants. And, as Wilt Chamberlain would say, he never longed for "the company of women." Were they Jessica Alba? Maybe and maybe not, but they weren't far off. Plus think of some of the other things you might get to be a part of.

You could get a sampling of the off-field fun that plays a part of the competition in the NFL. I'd want to go out with Taylor on game night. Maybe we could send some "professional women" to the hotel rooms of our competitors in tomorrow's game. That was one way Taylor liked to keep the on-field edge. In many of his accounts, he said that was a favorite move of his. I think it would be fun to be there when he executed one of these moves.

You could get a sampling of his living-on-the edge lifestyle. Taylor liked to drive fast and he had a penchant for overindulging in things that other people do "recreationally." A night spent with Taylor could take you anywhere: to meet a dealer, into a crack party, to an orgy. I don't know about you, Dave, but I might like to get a look at what that's all about. (I promise not to inhale.)

And think of the firsthand experiences you might get interacting with law enforcement. I've never talked my way out of a speeding ticket, but I can bet you LT has. We're talking about a guy who loved to drive fast and had a number of "meetings" with police. You know that for every one of those that made the newspapers, there had to be four where his big smile and sweet charm got him off the hook.

I am not suggesting that Derek Jeter is Goody Two-shoes, here. We've all read the articles in the gossip columns. He goes out and has his fun. But there's something irresistible about the idea of walking on the wild side with LT.

You can have your *Fantasy Island* experience. I'd rather keep it real and see the highs and lows of the edgy world of the superstar athlete.

Who Is the Most Talented City-born Basketball Player?

Lennon says: Ask fifty people hanging around the West Fourth Street cage, or Gaucho Gym in the Bronx, or the Rucker Playground, and you could get fifty different answers to this question. It's really a matter of taste, like choosing between a Matisse and a Picasso. But looking at the big picture, from his early development to the finished product, I believe that Chris Mullin gets the nod.

Mullin, raised in the Flatlands section of Brooklyn, was destined for greatness by the time he got to St. Thomas Aquinas Elementary School, where he already was courted by legendary St. John's coach Lou Carnesecca. That's not so uncommon these days, but back in the early '80s, getting recruiting calls in the sixth grade was not considered routine.

"We had the early book on him," Carnesecca would say years later. "You knew he was going to be something special."

Carnesecca's fashion sense was a little off, but as a talent evaluator, Lou was dead on. Mullin toyed with kids his age in CYO leagues, started his high school career at Power Memorial before switching to Xaverian as a junior transfer, and then led the Clippers to the State Federation title in 1981, when he was voted the tournament MVP, naturally. Mullin was selected to the McDonald's All-America team as a junior and senior at Xaverian, and after graduation, was named to nearly every All-America team at St. John's.

He also received the John Wooden Award as the collegiate player of the year in 1985, when Mullin led the Redmen—long before they became the hokey Red Storm—to their second Final Four appearance.

It was during that stage of his career that Mullin evolved from Brooklyn schoolboy phenom to national stardom, but those were still his formative years. How appropriate that Mullin wore number 17 to emulate his childhood idol, Celtics great John Havlicek, and he was destined for the NBA almost from the moment he first picked up a basketball.

Once Mullin got there, he lived up to the hype, despite a small but significant detour as a recovering alcoholic at the age of twenty-four. Mullin's story is an uplifting one for his personal triumph over alcohol addiction, though the résumé he built as one of the best NBA players of his generation stands on its own.

Mullin was picked seventh overall by the Warriors in the '85 draft, and in his rookie season averaged fourteen points and shot 89.6 percent from the free-throw line, the second-best mark by a rookie since Ernie DiGregorio's 90.2 percent in 1973–74. Again, that was only the tip of the iceberg.

Mullin's breakthrough season came in 1988–89, when he teamed up with Mitch Richmond to form the most potent 1-2 punch in the NBA, combining for 48.6 points per game. Mullin himself averaged a career-best 26.5 points, 5.9 rebounds, and 5.1 assists. He also became only the third player in Warriors history—along with Wilt Chamberlain and Rick Barry—to have two thousand points, four hundred rebounds, and four hundred assists in a season.

Together with Mitch Richmond and Tim Hardaway, Mullin was the C in the Warriors' Run-TMC—a takeoff on the rap pioneers—and the nickname was a by-product of Golden State's fast-paced style. But it would get even better for Mullin. In 1991–92, he finished sixth in the MVP voting, and was named to the All-NBA first team. Mullin also joined Chamberlain as the only players in franchise history to average twenty-five or more points in a game, and was ranked among Golden State's all-time top ten in sixteen different categories. He consistently was at the top of the league in minutes played, and always among the leaders in field-goal and three-point shooting percentage.

That all-around greatness, in every facet of the game, is what really distinguishes Mullin in this debate. Not to mention the fact that he was selected to the original "Dream Team" for the 1992 Olympics, a squad that also included Michael Jordan, Magic Johnson, and Larry Bird.

The one thing that eluded Mullin as a player is a championship ring. But as the GM to a new generation of Warriors, his NBA career is not over, and switching to the front office is further testament to Mullin's basketball savvy, which had as much to do with his intelligence as his lethal left-handed jumper. Mullin's Hall of Fame plaque is yet to hang in Springfield, but he's already done plenty to establish himself as the reigning king of the city game.

Rubin says: I think you're right about how many different opinions this one can elicit. I spent some time running back through the great players of the last thirty-five years and there were more than a dozen you could make an argument for. Your choice of Chris Mullin is very respectable.

I, however, am going to go old school on you. My pick is Bernard King. It doesn't matter which era of his career you look at—from his All-City play at Fort Hamilton High in Brooklyn to his All-American seasons at Tennessee to his all-star years in the NBA—King was always a player to marvel at.

He was a lunch-pail-and-hard-hat worker who was amazingly consistent in his performances. He still ranks No. 22 all-time in scoring average in the NBA.

One of the things that I find so amusing about King's career arc is that, unlike Mullin and three-quarters of the other candidates, he wasn't considered the best player in the city as a high schooler. That accolade went to Butch Lee from Clinton High in the Bronx, probably because Lee's team was the Public Schools Athletic League champion.

"He was the Rodney Dangerfield of city basketball in the seventies," is how the noted talent evaluator and city basketball historian Tom Konchalski described King. He might not have gotten the respect he deserved in high school but it was a different story after that.

Here's what Larry Bird said of the 6'7" King: "I don't understand how Bernard does it. He's in heavy traffic—guys all over banging him and waving their arms—and he gets the shot off, not just any shot, but the shot he wants, and he cans it. Time after time. He's the best scorer I've ever seen or played against."

That's pretty high praise from a very credible source.

Another thing I love about King is that he was a New York product that New Yorkers loved to follow and root for, even as he reinvented himself and his game at two pivotal junctures in his career.

When he left the city to attend Tennessee he paired with another city great, Ernie Grunfeld from Forest Hills High in Queens, to make one of the great dynamic duos in college basketball. People in the city just loved to follow the exploits of "The Bernie and Ernie Show" as they tore it up in the Southeastern Conference.

King averaged 25.8 points and 13.2 rebounds in his three seasons with the Volunteers, helping them to make NCAA Tournament appearances the last two. On the strength of being one of the country's great scorers, the Nets picked him in the first round (seventh overall) of the 1977 draft. He was a star for the locals for two seasons, but was plagued by off-court demons that led to a trade to the Jazz.

King played only nineteen games for the Jazz before seeking help for alcohol and substance abuse. He realized that without reforming himself, he would damage a promising career.

The reinvented King starred the following two seasons with the

Warriors—and was Comeback Player of the Year the first of them—before returning home to join the Knicks, where he had his best seasons, twice being named to the all-star team and finishing second to Bird in the 1984 MVP voting after averaging 26.3 points in the regular season. He averaged 34.8 in twelve playoff games that year as the Knicks reached the conference finals.

Without a doubt, though, the 1984–85 season was both his best and his worst. He led the NBA in scoring at 32.9 points a game and had five fifty-point games in a six-week stretch, but saw his season end with a gruesome knee injury. The torn ACL he suffered in Kansas City cost him almost two seasons.

For most players with lesser wills, that would have been the end. Not King. This is where we saw him transform himself so that his career could go on. The preinjury King was one of the league's most explosive players, a low-post force with eye-popping moves to the basket. King changed his game to that of a face-the-basket slasher and again became a twenty-point scorer. He was back on the all-star team in 1991, when he averaged 28.4 points for the Bullets.

Another knee injury and a second surgery (in 1992) spelled the end of his career in 1993, but he went out in a way that every New Yorker would be proud of.

When he was a high school player, King scored the first two points in the first Wheelchair Classic, a charity game to help the severely disabled at an area hospital. By 1993 there was an NBA version of the game and he played in that one, too. There, at the end of a career in which he scored 19,655 points, King announced his retirement.

When he was asked whether he regretted not reaching the twenty-thousand-point mark, King said he was going to go home and score the last 345 at the hoop in his backyard.

He was entertaining to the very end.

SETTLE THE
SCORE/BOB OLIVA

(Bob Oliva has been a part of the New York basketball scene since the 1960s and has been head coach at Christ the King High in Queens since 1981. His teams there have reached nine Catholic city championship games, won four of them, and featured eight players who went on to the NBA. This is his opinion on the matter.)

Chris Mullin and Bernard King definitely belong in this conversation, but I have to go with Jamal Mashburn. It's funny that all these guys are forwards, but maybe New York is a little underrated in the forwards department. It certainly is underrated in the center department, because it produced maybe the greatest of all time in Kareem Abdul-Jabbar.

New York got its reputation as a city of great guards many years before any of them played. Around the country, the position of point guard wasn't played very well. In other places it was played methodically, and the New York guys were flashier and more flamboyant. When guys like Bob Cousy came out of New York, the reputation started and it's grown and grown ever since.

The first time I saw Jamal Mashburn play, he was a sophomore at Cardinal Hayes and we scrimmaged them up in the Bronx. I didn't know anything about him. He was a 6' 8" kid and that was about all I knew. [East coast recruiting guru] Tom Konchalski was at the game.

When you think of a big kid, you think of someone they're going to throw in the hole and play him close to the basket. This guy was inside, he was outside, he touched the ball at just about every position on the floor. He could score from everywhere, plus there were his rebounds and assists.

Now, I had Jamal Faulkner, and Tom kept good statistics even on a scrimmage and he told me Faulkner had scored thirty-four points. Mashburn had, like forty-five. At that point, the cat was out of the bag.

What impressed me then is what has always impressed me about Mashburn. There's his strength. There's his size. There's the way he can handle the ball and also shoot it. He can take it to the basket. There really is not much offensively that he doesn't do. At his size, there really isn't anybody I can compare him to. Lamar Odom is as good a 6'8" or 6'9" guy as there is, but you really can't compare them because their games are so different. Mashburn's offensive skills have always been incredibly well-rounded.

Once Mashburn got rolling in the league, there was no stopping him. When he was a senior, his Cardinal Hayes team won it all in a season when they really weren't expected to go that far. I couldn't even tell you who was playing on the team around him—that's how good he was. Then he went to Kentucky, and playing for Rick Pitino was a big thing for him. It helped his game there. He could take games over at every level: in high school, during college at Kentucky, and in the pros.

One of the craziest things about his final year of high school was, when the McDonald's All-America team got picked, there were four other kids from the city who were chosen and he didn't even get picked. There were Khalid Reeves and Derrick Phelps from Christ the King, and Brian Reese and Adrian Autry from Tolentine. They left Mashburn [who was New York's Mr. Basketball] off. In hindsight, that was not the right call.

Jamal always had certain something about the way he played. He always looked like he wasn't exerting himself, which is a quality that many of the great ones have. They glide through a game, make it look effortless, and then they have thirty points at the end. He was like that. He had a rhythm to his play, and like so many of the great players, he made everyone else in the game play his rhythm.

Winning also kind of followed him around, and I guess that's part of his mystique. It was that way with Jabbar in the generation before him—everywhere he went, the teams won. With Mashburn it's been the same thing. I don't think that all the greats always win, but when they do, it adds to their [mystique]. The one thing they all have in common is that passion to win, and Mashburn definitely had that.

28

Does Mr. Met Actually Serve a Purpose?

Rubin says: There's a rumor going around that when Dan Aykroyd and Harold Ramis were writing *Ghostbusters*, they ran into a serious conundrum about the climactic showdown scene at the film's conclusion. After much debate they picked the Stay Puft Marshmallow Man over Mr. Met to be the instrument of Armageddon that Bill Murray and Co. had to defeat. I think that while Mr. Met was the scarier image, they couldn't resist the humor of shooting the entire cast covered in marshmallow.

Seriously, I know this character is supposed to be some kind of cheerleader/entertainment during a Mets game at Shea, but does he really do anything for the young fans besides give them something to have a nightmare about?

Plenty of Major League Baseball franchises have more dignity than to showcase a mascot. Those that do at least put something entertaining and memorable on the field for their fans.

The San Diego Chicken was so charismatic it became part of baseball's fabric during thirty years of performing at Padres games. The Phillie Phanatic, with his silly tongue and his four-wheel motor scooter, was a part of the experience of catching a game at Veterans Stadium. The cuddly Youppi!—the only mascot ever ejected from a game—was more popular (and enjoyable to watch) than the Expos team he was there to support.

Heck, even the Angels' Rally Monkey was the inspiration for Southern California's favorite plush toy.

Mr. Met? He is none of these things.

Not only is his overblown baseball cranium frightening, I quake every time some little kid's head gets near the thing's mouth. He has no routine that people look forward to, no creativity that makes him part of the entertainment, and no charm whatsoever. Are any kids asking for a Mr. Met doll for Christmas this year?

The saddest thing about Mr. Met may be that he is actually the embodiment of how small-time the Mets can be sometimes. The team constantly is providing between-inning sideshows that seem more appropriate for a minor league team than for a big-league club with a massive following.

We're talking about the Mets here. This is a team that in recent years has been to the playoffs twice, the World Series once, and now is one of the most exciting to follow in- and out-of-season. They've got Pedro pitching every fifth game. They've made deals to get guys like slugger Carlos Delgado. They've signed compelling players you can't wait to see, like one-hundred-mph fireballer Billy Wagner.

Then you go to a game and find out its Polish night or Jewish night or a day when a bad Beatles tribute band is going to play a thirty-minute show between batting practice and first pitch. Does the marketing department over there believe things like this are going to raise ticket sales? These things might actually repel fans.

Isn't the team that's been assembled good enough to draw?

If the Mets must insist on having this monstrosity on the field and in the stands, they should consider constructing an act that people would enjoy seeing.

The suggestion here is that after "Take me out to the ballgame," five kids from the stands are given thirty seconds with wooden bats to beat his giant noggin in.

Or maybe the Mets should just take a page from some of the

other stately clubs around the league like the Yankees, Cubs, and White Sox: Drop this clown like a bad habit.

Every move the front office makes is about being a big-time team. Now it's time to start acting like it.

Lennon says: Roger, I loved *Ghostbusters*. Great movie. But you know what would have made it even better? Ditching the Stay Puft Marshmallow Man for Mr. Met. Who or what is more New York than Mr. Met? It would have been an inspired choice, and I have to disagree with you—Mr. Met is even goofier than a giant marshmallow creature.

But therein lies his charm. Mascots are supposed to be funny-looking, Roger. We're talking about minimum-wage workers in a furry costume for crying out loud. Okay, so Mr. Met is not the San Diego Chicken or the Phillie Phanatic. Last time I checked, neither one is featured in TV commercials as much as Mr. Met is these days, which means the Flushing Fathead is more famous than either one at the moment.

And what does a chicken or some kind of green bug-eyed creature have to do with their respective teams, anyway? So they can ride four-runners and mock umpires? Whoopee. How original. In the case of Mr. Met, he embodies the everyman quality the franchise has stood for since its birth in 1962.

Aside from the giant baseball head, there's nothing remarkable about Mr. Met. He's just a happy-go-lucky guy enjoying a baseball game at Shea. He shakes hands with the fans, grabs a T-shirt gun to fire some souvenirs into the stands, poses for some pictures. Nothing outrageous. And the people love him anyway.

Mr. Met is one of the few things the organization has done right over the years. He's the perfect blend of cuddly and kitsch. The oversized cranium makes him a great bobble-head giveaway and he also can be a hot seller as a plush toy in the team's gift store. Sure, Mr. Met doesn't dance around or smash opponents' helmets, but who needs that at a baseball game.

And I have news for you, Roger. Mr. Met isn't going anywhere. Back in 2003, Tony Clark learned that the team's beloved mascot was not someone to be messed with. Clark wore No. 00 in his first few months with the Mets until he came to the realization that the number already had a place in the hearts and minds of the team's fans. Maybe the 6'7" Clark wasn't actually threatened by mobs of elementary school kids, but let's just say Shea wasn't big enough for the two of them.

"It was time to change," Clark said then. "The kids kept reminding me that Mr. Met and I couldn't have the same number. All the kids on photo day were telling me the same thing. Mr. Met is a hero to a lot of young kids, so now Mr. Met is free and clear."

Don't let the smile fool you. This guy is an icon who is afforded rock-star status in Flushing. When the Mets traveled to Japan to open the season against the Cubs in Tokyo, they took Mr. Met with them for the historic series, and he signed more autographs than anyone except Mike Piazza and Sammy Sosa. Clown? I don't think so.

Granted, Mr. Met isn't much to look at. He's basically a stick figure come to life. He doesn't have the cool costume of Florida's Billy or the notoriety of Baltimore's Bird or the cool beer slide of Bernie Brewer. But he's not offensive, either. Boston's Wally the Green Monster is nothing more than a transparent attempt to cash in on the stuffed mascot market. He's an eyesore at an otherwise beautiful ballpark.

To his credit, Mr. Met never makes some lame attempt to steal the spotlight. Like you said, Roger, the Mets are good enough now to sell the product between the baselines. They don't need a skyscraper in sneakers or a some oversized Big Apple dancing to hip-hop tunes. Mr. Met adds a nice nostalgic touch to ugly Shea, a reminder of Joan Payson, Casey Stengel, and the simpler times of the team's early days. He's always been smiling, too, and it never hurts to have an eternal optimist hanging around when your team can be so miserable.

Who Is the Best Executive?

Lennon says: Unfortunately, I have to give this honor posthumously to the late, great George Young, who is universally credited with resurrecting the New York Giants from the darkest era in the team's once proud history.

Maybe you're among the armchair GM crowd still upset over Ernie Accorsi's draft-day trade for Eli Manning rather than waiting for Ben Roethlisberger. But watching Manning come up small in that playoff loss to the Panthers is nothing compared to the misery the Giants served up every Sunday before Young was named the team's first GM after the 1978 season.

You want despair? How about fifteen years without a playoff appearance prior to Young's arrival? And who could forget The Fumble that gloomy afternoon against the Eagles, the play that ultimately sabotaged the Giants' chance to end their postseason drought and later cost head coach John McVay his job.

In retrospect, that pathetic chain of events was the best thing that could have happened to the hopeless Giants, who could not have predicted the dramatic turnaround under Young. That brutal '78 season was a wake-up call that convinced co-owners Wellington and Tim Mara to hire a GM, even if the feuding family members couldn't agree on a candidate to clean up the mess in the Meadowlands.

The Maras needed the intervention of commissioner Pete Rozelle to settle the argument, and he selected Young, the former high school teacher from Baltimore who cut his NFL teeth as a coach with the Colts and Dolphins. As far as building champions, Young did win six straight Maryland high school titles as the coach at Calvert Hall and City College High School.

Young, who was sort of an offbeat character to begin with, didn't endear himself to New York by using the Giants' seventh overall pick in 1979 on Phil Simms, out of Morehead State. Aside from the fact that Giants fans still have no idea where the school is—it's located in foothills of the Daniel Boone National Forest in Kentucky—they wanted running back Ottis Anderson that year.

As it turned out, Young eventually got both. Simms developed into one of the best quarterbacks to wear the uniform—winning the MVP of Super Bowl XXI—and Anderson, acquired by Young as backfield insurance in 1986, earned MVP honors for Super Bowl XXV when the injured Simms was replaced by Jeff Hostetler.

Not many front-office suits can say they're responsible for getting their hands on two Super Bowl MVPs—other than the guy who drafted Tom Brady—but Young did much more than that as the architect of the Giants' return to prominence.

Young's draft ledger is remarkable. In 1981, after the Saints selected running back George Rogers with the No. 1 overall pick, Young gladly took Lawrence Taylor at No. 2, leaving the Jets with Freeman McNeil. That just turned out to be the most influential draft pick in Giants history, even if Young publicly pretended like he didn't put much stock in the process.

"I never draft anyone too smart," Young said. "If he's smart, he can find something else to do other than play this dumb game."

Young, who taught history and political science, earned two masters degrees at Johns Hopkins and Loyola College. When it comes to football knowledge, however, Young had a Ph.D.

In addition to Simms and Taylor, he drafted Joe Morris in the second round in 1982 and selected Mark Bavaro in the fourth round in 1985. In 1984, Young got Carl Banks in the first round and offensive tackle William Roberts in the second round. The GM also snatched Michael Strahan—from Texas Southern—in the second round of the 1993 draft and stole Jessie Armstead, a future Pro Bowler, in the eighth round.

Not a bad résumé. But in assessing Young's impressive nineteen-year run with the Giants, it's just as important to understand how terrible the team was before his arrival. This man was not only a GM, he was a savior—and in New York, there's no better job title than that.

Rubin says: Couldn't agree with you more, Dave, about savior being the best job title in New York. George Young did a tremendous job of turning the Giants around and consistently being a better talent evaluator than 90 percent of his NFL counterparts. Moreover, the guy was a total class act and a big part of why the Giants organization is one of the most respected in the league.

But if there were one thing that would make you more revered in this town than being the guy who saved the Giants, Dave, it's being the guy who saved the Yankees. That's exactly what Gene Michael did and yet, somehow, he's never gotten all the credit he deserves.

Every time we see Derek Jeter make one of those great stops in the hole, or Bernie Williams deliver a clutch hit, or Mariano Rivera rescue the Yankees from peril, we should throw a little "thank you" Michael's way. These guys, and half a dozen other essentials from the franchise's recent championship seasons, are here because of the man they call "Stick."

Sport's greatest franchise was in need of some serious saving as the '80s ebbed into the '90s. The Yankees had been dragging along the bottom in the AL East and the back-to-back titles in 1977 and

1978 were fading from memory. Boss Steinbrenner was in trouble with the law over the Howie Spira affair and was about to go on a forced leave from baseball for three seasons.

Michael, who'd already served the club as a player, scout, and manager, was tabbed to be the guy who'd mind the store in Steinbrenner's absence and was anointed general manager in 1990. Right there and then, he began reshaping the Yankees' way of doing business, moving it away from the big-name-at-any-cost mind-set that interestingly has returned in recent years.

It was Michael's idea to focus on evaluating talent to restock the Yankees' farm system; he and then-manager Buck Showalter then proceeded to give the club's brightest young talents—like Jeter—opportunities to play early in their career. Within two years of becoming the GM, Michael drafted Jorge Posada, called Williams up from the minors, signed Rivera out of Panama, signed the undrafted left-hander Andy Pettitte, and then used the team's first-round pick in 1992 on Jeter.

Talk about a strong showing.

Assessing young talent was not Michael's only strength. He, often in consultation with Showalter, was very good at ascertaining the right kind of players to meet the club's needs, and after George Steinbrenner was reinstated by baseball, he was not afraid to stand up for what he believed. On a number of occasions, The Boss would have impulsively dealt players we now consider mainstays of the team's best years; Michael wouldn't let it happen.

The signing of Jimmy Key before the 1992 season gave the Yankees a bulldog who would prove to be essential in their return to the top in 1996. He infused competitive spirit with the brilliant 1993 deal of Roberto Kelly to the Reds for Paul O'Neill, what will go down as one of the best deals the Yankees ever made, along with the purchase of Babe Ruth from the Red Sox.

Even though the Yankees finished with the best record in the AL East during the aborted 1994 season that ended without playoffs because of a labor dispute, Steinbrenner was looking to tinker in 1995. When the Boss wanted to ship Williams out for Darren Lewis of the Giants, Michael fibbed and said there was little or no interest. And with Big Stein salivating at the prospect of bringing David Wells into the fold with the Tigers asking only for a sore-armed prospect named Rivera, Stick dragged his feet long enough for Rivera to come back stronger from the injury than when he got hurt.

Not making deals wasn't the only thing Michael did that season. There were a few extremely shrewd trades that directly led to the championship run. He grabbed closer John Wetteland from the Expos for Fernando Seguignol. He plucked David Cone off the Blue Jays for a pair of minor leaguers who never panned out. And he scooped Tino Martinez and Jeff Nelson from the Mariners in exchange for Russ Davis and Sterling Hitchcock.

"Somehow, Gene knew to keep Rivera and Bernie, but it was okay to trade Russ Davis and Roberto Kelly," current Yankees GM Brian Cashman told the *Bergen Record*.

It was a shame that Steinbrenner went for a regime change after the Yankees won the 1995 AL wild card and fell in the first round to the Mariners. Michael walked when offered a 33 percent pay cut and Showalter was shoved out the back door. In came Joe Torre and Bob Watson, who oversaw the final stages of the reconstruction and celebrated with champagne when it was over.

Even though he never got the credit, Michael remained a huge asset as the Bombers won three more titles from 1998 to 2000. His knowledge of players' strengths and weaknesses made him the perfect advance scout—or "superscout" as some have called him—and it was his scouting reports that Torre touted so highly during those Octobers.

30

Which Is the Greatest New York Sports Movie of the Last Thirty-five Years?

Rubin says: We do our best work when it's something we're passionate about, and it isn't often that we get an assignment or project that brings together several of the things that stir us most deeply. This is why Spike Lee's 1998 ode to basketball, *He Got Game*, is such an enthralling film to behold. He applied his considerable talents to his love of Brooklyn, his interest in controversial issues, and his enthusiasm for roundball. What he came out with was a beautifully shot interlude that, while flawed, stands as the best city basketball movie that's been made.

And let's face facts, Dave, basketball had better be a major component in the best New York sports movie. It's the city game, right, my man?

There are lots of reasons why we should hail this work, but none is more significant than the way it captures several aspects of the rich basketball culture in our town. We've been producing some of the sport's finest talents since Naismith hung up his little peach basket, so when a story is told about the nation's best recruit growing up on our hardscrabble streets, it's no leap for us. The story of Jesus Shuttlesworth was supposedly loosely based on Stephon Marbury's, but there are things about it New Yorkers have seen over and over again. Lew Alcindor, Pearl Washington, Brian

Reese, Felipe Lopez, Marbury, Sebastian Telfair, and soon Lance Stephenson have all offered glimpses of this tale.

And kudos to Lee for going with the name Jesus, which not only allows the not-so-subtle images of a tortured protagonist but also gives us the chance to savor our tabloid obsession with that JESUS SAVES back page headline. Stuff like that can make even the most jaded of us feel good about being a New Yorker.

You and I both cut our teeth writing about high school sports here, Dave, and *He Got Game* isn't afraid to bring to life the seedier side that you and I know too well.

A relative with his hand out? An imprisoned parent in need (played by New Yorker Denzel Washington)? A coach looking to peddle influence? Runners for agents offering cash? Recruiting visits that offer booze and sex? An adoring throng of classmates obsessed with knowing where the blue-chipper's going to go to college? All these things are not dreamt up. We've seen 'em. They're based on reality.

NBA star Ray Allen does a superb job of articulating the often sad truth: that a kid should never be forced to deal with all this, that these are some of the reasons our homegrown basketball stars grow up much too early.

The thing is, this film doesn't just teach by giving a window in on this life. It glorifies our New York in spectacular ways.

Lee has captured beautiful images of Coney Island—the boardwalk, Nathan's, Astroland Amusement Park's Ferris wheel, the playground nicknamed "The Garden." While they may not be the cornfields from *The Natural*, he's shown them to be downright Rockwellian. Too many people think of Coney as more ghetto than anything else and this is a wonderful reminder that it is so much more.

Even if you are only a hoops junkie, and that stuff flies right by you, there are elements to covet in *He Got Game*. There is tremendous basketball footage and it's set to a sound track that includes classical and hip-hop, which underscores the game as art. Plus there are wonderful cameos by the folks from ESPN *SportsCenter* and coaches like Dean Smith, John Thompson, John Chaney, Rick Pitino, Jim Boeheim, and Bobby Cremins. Don't think this movie is significant? Lee's got a veritable who's who from the ranks of college basketball.

Some of the best stuff, though, I think has to do with the concept of the Jesus Shuttlesworth character as a high school teammate. He plays for Lincoln, one of the city's most storied programs, and there are a couple of great scenes shot in the bare-bones gym where the Railsplitters actually play. And the interaction between the star and his teammates, none of whom are depicted as being on a star track, is actually what its like in high school. You still care about your teammates like family at that level.

I know it would be easier to make everyone agree on a comedy. *He Got Game* doesn't have a particularly happy resolution. But for the way it celebrates New York basketball—the good and the bad— I say it can't be beat.

Lennon says: While I'm a big fan of Spike Lee, and *He Got Game* did a decent job capturing the Brooklyn hoops scene, the winner in this debate, by technical knockout, has got to be *Raging Bull*.

This movie is an all-time great, but pure New York, from Jake La Motta's gritty Pelham Parkway neighborhood to his bloody fights inside Madison Square Garden. Shot in black-and-white because director Martin Scorsese wanted to distinguish it from the handful of boxing movies at the time, *Raging Bull* comes off like a cross between *Rocky* and *The Godfather*, with Robert De Niro acting like Sonny Corleone on steroids.

The scary part about the film is that this stuff really happened, and you could almost see someone like La Motta living in the apartment next door to you. Who hasn't heard the neighbor screaming at his wife for an overcooked steak, then threatening to kill your dog? That's every Saturday night for some New Yorkers.

The hook for me is the tumultuous relationship between La Motta and his brother Joey, played by an up-and-coming Joe Pesci. After watching these two interact, you come to the realization that no other duo could have done a better job. De Niro and Pesci practically invent the concept of slightly psychotic Italians here, and later went on to reprise these roles over and over again, specifically in the mobster classic *Goodfellas*.

Check out the scene in Jake's kitchen when the boxer is challenging Joey to hit him. Joey, at first reluctant, wraps a dish towel around his right fist and then starts teeing off on his brother's face. When Jake tells him to get rid of the towel, he does, then opens up fresh cuts on his face.

But that's only the warmup for the violence that follows. It's no surprise that De Niro wears a prosthetic nose that looks like a butternut squash in the center of his face—the trademark of a brawler like La Motta—and he dishes out plenty of punishment, too. La Motta is despicable in many ways, especially to women, but he's the kind of flawed hero that New Yorkers love. A product of the mean streets that gets to the top on his own two feet, or in La Motta's case, with his two fists.

And the dialogue for this film is unique to New York, too. When La Motta gets angry at his wife for saying that his next opponent, the younger Tony Janiro, is good looking, Jake spouts off, "She was talking about a pretty kid." To which Joey replies, "So you make him ugly."

Jake does, of course, going into a jealousy-fueled rage in the ring that nearly kills Janiro. It's the first scene where the blood—or in this case, Hershey's syrup—really starts flying, as Jake pounds

Janiro's face into a fleshy mess. You're rooting for Jake then, as he climbs toward a title shot, but the wheels are about to come off, and when he takes a dive to satisfy some local mobsters, he hits rock bottom.

On the side, we get to see Pesci perfect his wigged-out tough-guy routine, demonstrating how to smash a bottle against a guy's face and then repeatedly slam a car door on his shoulder. Hey, everybody has to start somewhere, and this is when Pesci honed his craft and made his career.

As for De Niro, his role required a little more depth, and it's no wonder he took home the Oscar for Best Actor. La Motta absorbs a brutal beating at the hands of Sugar Ray Robinson when he loses his middleweight championship, and after landing a monstrous right hand on La Motta's face, a gusher of blood sprays across the reporters sitting at ringside. Having covered a handful of boxing matches in my time, that's the real deal. Getting covered with blood and spit is part of the job description for boxing writers.

You've got to love the cameo by Nicholas Colasanto as gangster Tommy Como—this was right before he hooked up with Sam and Diane on *Cheers*—and De Niro is on top of his game in showing La Motta's ugly descent into retirement. De Niro gained sixty pounds to play the older La Motta, a record at the time, and the scenes of him reciting lines as part of his nightclub act are priceless.

"Though I'm no Olivier, if he fought Sugar Ray, he would say, that the thing ain't the ring, it's the play, so give me a stage, where this bull here can rage, and I can fight, I'd rather hear myself re-cite . . . That's entertainment."

With two Oscar trophies, and six other nominations, *Raging Bull* is top-flight entertainment, and a classic New York story that wouldn't have the same impact if it took place anywhere else on the planet.

THE TOP FIVE NEW YORK SPORTS MOVIES

1. *Raging Bull* (1980): Shot almost entirely in black-and-white, director Martin Scorsese gives us a window into the brutal and sometimes corrupt world of boxing in this account of fighter Jake La Motta's rise to middleweight champion and subsequent fall. Robert De Niro won the Academy Award for best actor, portraying the ultraviolent and self-destructive protagonist. Joe Pesci, also nominated for an Oscar, plays the fighter's caring brother whose relationship with him deteriorates over the course of the film. It has some great scenes of gritty New York and tenements. *Raging Bull* is considered more of an artistic endeavor, but it also is one of the best sports films ever made.

2. *He Got Game* (1998): It tells the story of a New York basketball player who has emerged as the nation's top college prospect and how he must handle the wonderful opportunities that presents, along with a myriad of pressures no teenager is ready for. The telling of the story is not without flaws, but it very realistically depicts many of the seedier sides of the basketball scene that character Jesus Shuttlesworth (Ray Allen) experiences. Director Spike Lee makes tough parts of Brooklyn beautiful to look at. And the parts shot in the gymnasium at Abraham Lincoln High are authentic stuff. It's a must-see if you like New York basketball.

3. *The Natural* (1984): A captivating fable about the resurrection of a once-burgeoning baseball star, who at thirty-five becomes the catalyst for the fictional New York Knights' ascent from last place to first. Robert Redford is Roy Hobbs, a great pitcher whose career comes tragically untracked before it blossoms. He reappears more than a decade later as an unknown who becomes one of baseball's great sluggers. Director Barry Levinson shows Hobbs battling his inner demons as he tries to make hard choices in his only shot at baseball stardom. The ending is a little cheesy, but it tells a nice story.

4. *61* (2001):* It's one of New York's great sports stories, about how Roger Maris broke Babe Ruth's thirty-four-year-old home run record during the splendid 1961 season. The demure Maris is played wonderfully by Barry Pepper, who even bares a remarkable resemblance to the former Bronx Bomber. The film gives a wonderful accounting of the adversity Maris faced in eclipsing a mark that no one wanted to see broken. Thomas Jane portrays Mickey Mantle as he pushed Maris with a great season of his own. The brashness of the interplay between the Yankees players is toned down, but the sentiment is captured well. Even though Mark McGwire is featured in a framing device, it's nice to see a story about someone whose feats aren't being questioned as so many are today.

5. *Fast Break* (1979): A rollicking comedy about a Brooklyn guy who gets his dream shot to coach college basketball. Gabe Kaplan is about as New York as they come as he agrees to take the position at a rinky-dink Nevada college and then drums up five veritable unknowns from New York to be his team. If you like Bernard King, the former Knick who came out of Brooklyn, you'll want to see him in a featured role. The film also has former UCLA point guard Michael Warren as one of the quintet that goes west to a place where New Yorkers are not understood.

31

Is Madison Square Garden Special Anymore?

Lennon says: I don't want to say no. I really don't. I'm a nostalgic guy with classic tastes when it comes to uniforms and ballparks. But the old building on Seventh Avenue and Thirty-third Street no longer feels like "The World's Most Famous Arena."

Why should it? What's so great about going to see the Knicks lose by twenty to the Memphis Grizzlies? Or watching St. John's embarrass themselves against Marist? Whatever happened to Willis Reed? Bernard King? Patrick Ewing? Hell, I'd settle for John Starks or Latrell Sprewell. And what in the name of Louie Carnesecca is going on with the Redmen, um, Red Storm?

Please. It's not the teal seats and laser light shows that make an arena special, although I have to admit the Knicks City Dancers do have a certain charm. It's what happens on the floor, or ice, that makes memories. And other than a U2 concert, is there much reason to pay your way into the Garden these days?

But don't take my word for it. Ask Spike Lee or Bill Bradley about their favorite Garden moments, and they'll mention Willis Reed limping onto the court to inspire the Knicks to the NBA title. That was 1970! This current incarnation of Madison Square Garden—number four for those keeping score—was built in 1968, so that makes the past thirty-five years pretty much a pleasant diversion rather than a modern-day Roman Colosseum.

Don't get me wrong. There have been moments. Going to the Big East tournament used to be a major thrill. Back in the stone age, before every NCAA game was shown on ESPN, the Big East championship used to be a huge television event. And if you were lucky enough to get tickets for that afternoon, you remember screaming like crazy when the announcers said it was time for the Garden to be broadcast coast-to-coast.

That's when basketball fans from Boise to Bismarck dreamt of the day they might be lucky enough to watch a game at the Garden. It was everything New York City was supposed to be. Bright lights. Big stage. If you can make it there, you can make it anywhere. Yada, yada, yada.

Now, the best the Garden can hope for is a thrilling NIT final between Wisconsin and Bucknell. A second-rate championship for a second-rate arena. Even the Meadowlands gets an NCAA regional once in a while. Same with the Nassau Coliseum. The Garden gets the consolation prize.

Once upon a time, the Garden hosted Ali-Frazier I and II. But the biggest events in recent memory have nothing to with sports, unless you count Wrestlemania, which staged its very first mind-numbing spectacle under that very roof. The only segment of the population who finds that special is ten-year-olds who idolize steroid freaks.

There was the 2004 Republican National Convention, which caused a political firestorm in the middle of liberal Manhattan, and the 9/11 benefit concert featured an unprecedented collection of musical talent. But the Garden merely served as a high-priced auditorium for those events.

In truth, the magic is gone. The aura has left the building. Its Cablevision owners desperately blocked the construction of a West Side stadium because they wanted to keep their monopoly on every dog and pony show that steers its way into Manhattan, and the gambit succeeded.

You want Muppets on Ice or the Wiggles, then the Garden is your place. Both attract more paying customers these days than the Knicks and Rangers, the arena's two main tenants, who share the hallowed ground with the WNBA's Liberty.

Maybe the Garden is the same as it ever was—simply a place for New York's teams to call home, as well as a nice arena to rent for a visiting tournament or concert. Of course, Cablevision is pushing for yet another Garden, to be built across the street, and that is sure to include loads more luxury boxes and advertising space.

When that day comes, the current Garden will be demolished, its championship banners and retired numbers hoisted to the new rafters on the other side of Eighth Avenue. But what of the memories? Is this Garden doomed to be remembered as an arena half-full of disenchanted fans booing the miserable Knicks?

It sure looks that way. Turn out the lights, and bring on the wrecking ball.

Rubin says: Is it possible, Dave, that you just don't realize what you're saying here. Saying that The Garden isn't special anymore is like saying that the Empire State Building used to be a nice skyscraper or that the Cathedral of Notre Dame in Paris was a pretty fair church in its day.

The Garden is so many things—a monument, a cathedral, a concept, a destination. It doesn't cease to be those things just because the teams that play there aren't winning at the moment. When the Yankees were no better than a fifth-place team from 1988 to 1991, the Stadium didn't stop being a wonderful place. It still holds the magical sod where Ruth and DiMaggio and Mantle all played.

The Garden has lived an incredible life, from Willis Reed to Ali-Frazier and from the Rangers winning the Cup to St. John's capturing the 2000 Big East championship. Hosting those spectacular

events—plus the litany of others that date back through the Garden's other three incarnations—have made it a living, breathing en-
tity. And it has an impact on everyone who walks through those
doors, from players to coaches to fans.

Rick Pitino spent two seasons as head coach of the Knicks, practically living in the building. But during 2005–06, when his
Louisville team joined the Big East and he returned to the building,
the guy couldn't contain himself.

"I think any time you go to Madison Square Garden . . . you're
going to one of the special places to go in the history of
basketball—period," he said. "Whether its college or the NBA. I
think the pro guys look at it as a special place. I think the college
guys, high school guys, everybody looks at it as a special place."

Much of basketball has its roots in New York—it's the city game
after all—and the Garden is *the* basketball arena here. It's why players and coaches call it the Mecca. What is basketball's most famous
and important destination now? T.D. BankNorth Garden? Staples
Center? Arco Arena?

From coast to coast, there are kids shooting baskets in their
driveway or at the local park and I can assure you that none of them
is pretending to take the last shot at US Airways Center.

The Garden also has a stateliness and dignity about it. If you
look throughout sports, there are places where the venue is itself an
enormous part of the fan experience. None of them has a first name
that also is a publicly traded stock. Fenway Park, Chavez Ravine,
Lambeau Field—this is the kind of thing I am talking about.

Going to a game at an historic venue is a thrill. You spend a
childhood enamored of a team and its players and you finally get to
go see them at a game. It's not just about whether your team won or
lost. It's about parents and children talking about the past and the
present. In the Garden it's about the things that are said and felt
when you look skyward to see Mark Messier's banner hanging from
the rafters or Chris Mullin's name on the façade of the upper deck.

That's the reason the place is electric: It's a shrine to some truly amazing stuff.

Since Lou Carnesecca retired, city kids have still been coming to St. John's. Inevitably they always say that one of the things that attracted them is the chance to play on the same floor as their childhood heroes. And now that St. John's is going to honor its finest players with banners to commemorate their achievements, city kids will surely want their names to hang in the World's Most Famous Arena with Mullin's and Walter Berry's and Malik Sealy's.

In that way, the Garden remains conceptually the biggest stage in maybe all of sports. Kids who play ball dream about competing at the Garden in the same way that kids who act want to perform on Broadway. When you're a hit there you are something important in the country's most important city.

Dave, I can't believe you're ready to call for the destruction of a great monument. If you ask me, the only thing ready for the wrecking ball is your attitude.

32

Does Goose Gossage Deserve to Be in the Hall of Fame?

Rubin says: The first dulcet tones come over the sound system at Yankee Stadium and the crowd erupts with glee. The song is "Enter Sandman" by Metallica and whether you're seated in the upper deck or the visitor's dugout you know what it means: The game is over. Mariano Rivera is coming in to pitch.

Few things leave a Yankees fan feeling more confident than seeing number 42 trotting in from the bullpen, but for those who have been around long enough, the feeling is not altogether new. Back before closers had entrance music and 95 percent of baseball's saves required three or fewer outs, Bomber buffs could take the same kind of comfort late in games. It was the late '70s and early '80s and Rich "Goose" Gossage was baseball's most-feared pitcher.

The Goose was as close to an automatic as there was in those days, ranking right there with Hall of Famer Rollie Fingers. The two of them were pioneers in relief pitching, something that used to be the purview of ex-starters who couldn't hack it anymore. The fact that Fingers has been enshrined—as well as closers Hoyt Wilhem, Dennis Eckersley, and now Bruce Sutter—and Gossage has not is a complete outrage.

"Put it this way: I had Rollie Fingers. He was good. He's in the Hall of Fame," former big-league manager Chuck Tanner once told the *Denver Post*. "I had Bruce Sutter. . . . He was one of the best. I had Kent Tekulve. He was one of the best. But no one was better than Goose. No one.

"If you put all those guys together and I had to pick one—and I probably shouldn't say this because I don't mean to slight any of my [former] players—I'd pick Goose. It offends me he's not in the Hall of Fame. Those who don't vote for him, it's a disgrace."

Gossage was perhaps the biggest mound intimidator to the game since Bob Gibson. He was a daunting 6'3" and 225 pounds. His windup was all arms and legs right up until he uncorked the ball sidearm. And his fastball? With a velocity up to one hundred mph and great movement, hitters would rather have their eyelashes plucked out one-by-one than stand in and try to hit it.

"I'm a son-of-a-gun out there and I hate anyone with a bat in his hands," he once told UPI.

When the Yankees signed Gossage as a free agent before the 1978 season, their closer was Sparky Lyle, who was coming off a Cy Young Award season. The Goose's arrival immediately sent Lyle to middle relief. That's how significant an acquisition he was. And Gossage almost always delivered the goods with a brash attitude typified by the fact that he wouldn't shave his trademark Fu Manchu, even for owner George Steinbrenner. He instantly made an impact with twenty-seven saves in the regular season, a win and a save in an ALCS defeat of the Royals, and six scoreless innings of relief against the Dodgers as the Yanks won the World Series.

I don't really see what more Gossage could have done. The statistics—something leaned on far too hard in assessing a player's HOF credentials—are more than solid. He had 310 saves, a 3.01 ERA, five Top 10 finishes in Cy Young Award voting, nine all-star selections, and succeeded on the World Series stage.

Even so, the stats can't tell the whole story, because today's re-lievers ply their trade so differently from the Fingers-Gossage era. There weren't as many save opportunities, because complete games were far more common. In Rivera's nine full seasons as closer,

Yankees pitchers have thrown eighty-one complete games; that's one less than they threw in Gossage's first two seasons in pinstripes.

Also, the saves were a lot tougher to earn. In Gossage's time, closers were regularly summoned in the seventh inning—something you'd never catch Joe Torre doing with Rivera—and almost never to start an inning the way today's closers often are.

As Eckersley recently pointed out: "What Goose did in his era was a lot tougher than what I had to do by the time I became a closer. Those guys had to pitch two or three innings. That would have worn me out at [that] stage of my career. Goose did it and did it with gas."

Lennon says: Everybody wants to compare Goose Gossage to Mariano Rivera when it's time to discuss the Hall of Fame. They always start off by saying, "His job was harder than Mo's, he pitched more innings, hitters were tougher back then, his mustache was cooler." It goes on and on.

Well, I have a news flash for you, Rog. If Gossage was Rivera, then how come the current Yankees' closer has all the records that matter? And I don't care how fearsome Goose was back in his day, Rivera is the unanimous pick when everyone talks about the best-ever in that role.

So let's just drop the whole "Rivera before there was a Rivera" argument. If we're going to discuss Gossage as a Hall of Fame candidate, it should be on his own merit, and I can't find fault with your body of evidence, Rog. You make a very compelling case.

But there has to be a reason why Goose keeps falling short on votes, and he narrowly missed in the last election, closing to within 54 of the 390 needed to punch his ticket for Cooperstown. In the interest of full disclosure, I'm a member of the BBWAA, I've had a Hall of Fame vote for two years now, and I've left Gossage off my ballot each time.

Heck, the two guys I wanted in—Jim Rice and Jack Morris—

didn't make it, either, and I didn't vote for Bruce Sutter, who was the only player enshrined by the BBWAA last year. Honestly, I think Gossage will get in the Hall of Fame, and I'd wager that it will happen sooner rather than later, probably in January 2007. But I don't think it's some outrage that he hasn't gotten to Cooperstown yet.

And Gossage should calm down about being passed over. Screaming about how flawed the system is and portraying yourself as the victim of some baseball injustice is not conduct befitting a player of his stature, and I'm not referring to his bulky 6'3" frame. Ripping Sutter, as he did to the *New York Post* after the 2006 election, was not a classy move, either.

"I just can't believe Sutter got in before me," Gossage said. "He deserved it. I was hoping Sutter and I could go in together . . . I don't know if I ever will make it."

Then Gossage added, "You know what, I never hear from those guys who didn't vote for me. But I'll take on any writer, anywhere, on any show, and I will bury him."

Like it or not, Goose, you could hit the campaign trail tomorrow and it probably wouldn't make a difference. Granted, I happen to agree with him on Sutter. If Sutter deserves to be in the Hall of Fame, then so does Gossage. But the main thing that keeps tripping him up is the inherent bias against relief pitchers.

Maybe some guys felt that voting for both Sutter and Gossage in an otherwise lean year was excessive. Relievers still have a hard time getting the credit they deserve, which explains why Rivera has yet to win a Cy Young or MVP. Gossage also may have to overcome some anti-Yankee sentiment, but I'm only guessing on that one. Could be.

While I'm willing to concede that Gossage may someday get his plaque, I'm not going to bury the BBWAA for the fact that he's still waiting. The system may not be perfect, but it's the best that baseball has, and there is no better way to guard the gates of Cooperstown. No one is more qualified to vote for the Hall of Fame than baseball writers with ten consecutive years of service. In my case, that's about 150 games a season that I witness in person, and I've been doing it for a dozen years.

There may be blind spots when it comes to certain candidates, but over time, those slights usually are remedied. Gossage isn't helping himself by griping about the process, and personally, I'm more outraged that Rice and Morris are still waiting.

SETTLE THE
SCORE/TOM GLAVINE

(Tom Glavine is a two-time Cy Young Award winner who was closing in on three hundred wins when we asked him about Goose Gossage's candidacy for the Hall of Fame. Here's how he felt about Goose and the process in general.)

For relief pitchers, it's different. If you're a starting pitcher with three hundred wins, to me, you're a lock. I used to think anybody that hit five hundred home runs was a lock, but that's changed a little bit. I think the trouble for Goose is that that role is still kind of being defined. They're still trying to figure it out. I don't think there's any question, in terms of the game, that he's one the best there ever was. And now that door is being opened a little bit. I think that, eventually, his time is going to come.

But there are certain numbers, in the history of this game that, if you achieve those numbers, the way you're judged is so much different than everybody else. But for relievers, that's still being defined a little bit.

The game keeps changing. Getting to three hundred wins is going to get harder and harder. It's almost like, for a starting pitcher, that number is going to go down to 279 or 250. Five hundred home runs is a pretty hefty number, but I don't think it's looked at as awe-inspiring as it was back in the day when Frank Robinson and those guys were doing it.

So I think those numbers are going to evolve, but I still think that wherever those numbers shake out, if you achieved those as a player, you've done something special in this game. And because of that, you should be a lock. Then again, there are other guys that don't that are still great players. I mean, Sandy Koufax is probably the best that ever played the game, but he didn't come close to three hundred wins for number of reasons. So there are going to be guys that you have to judge just on their talent and ability.

I always use to hear the complaint about [Don] Sutton on why it took him so long. I don't care. If you pitched that long and won three hundred games, then you've done something. To me, that's a no-brainer.

As for the Hall of Fame voting process, I'm not sure that it's the best way, but I don't know how else to do it. I think the thing that bothers me is when you hear that certain guys aren't going to get voted in on the first try just because [the writers] don't want to. If the guy has the numbers to get in, I don't care if you liked him or didn't like him, or if, just for the principle of the matter, you're not going to vote him in. If he deserves to get in, then he should get in.

I think of lot it has become more and more about what the player's relationship with the media was. Does that mean more than what he's done on the field? Obviously not. But there's no question that it plays a big factor. I don't know. I don't know that there's a perfect way to do it, and we've been doing it this way for so long, I don't know if you can change it. There's no question there's some flaws in the system, but in the end, I guess you just hope that everybody that deserves to get in there gets in there.

33

Who Is the Top NHL Goaltender?

Lennon says: I'm going outside the box on this debate and looking beyond the numbers in my nomination of Billy Smith, the man between the pipes for the Islanders' dynasty of the early '80s.

Some would argue that Smith merely benefited by his association with those great teams, an expansion pick from the Los Angeles Kings that was lucky enough to be in the right place at the right time. But I prefer to think of him as a cantankerous brick in the Islanders' championship foundation, and his eighteen-year résumé, which includes both the Vezina and Jennings trophies, the highest awards for a goaltender, earned him a spot in the Hall of Fame.

Plus, Smith was in the hockey business to win—not make friends—and that was a point he stressed on a nightly basis. If you loved the Islanders, then you loved Billy. But if you were sporting another sweater, and dared stray into his crease, Smith had no problem giving you a not-so-gentle reminder, like a stick to the knee or a blocker to the face.

Hey, this was the NHL of '70s and '80s, not the figure skating lovefest hockey has become since the turn of the century. Smith played during a time when bloodstains and missing teeth were badges of honor. He treated opposing players like they were trying to steal his last nickel, and became infamous for refusing to shake hands after playoff games.

"I learned that from Gerry Cheevers, whom I respect," Smith told the *New York Times* back then. "I saw that he never shook hands, and he was right. It's hypocritical, after all that battling on the ice to go over and say: 'Good game. Have a nice summer.' I know how I felt when someone said it to me after we'd lost the big game. It made me feel even worse.

"If we're playing golf or tennis and it's for fun, I'll shake your hand if you win. But this is different. These are the playoffs, and there's a lot of money and your livelihood at stake."

That's the guy I want as my goaltender. The one who doesn't need water, because he's already filled to his wisdom teeth with hatred for the other team. And Smith wasn't all talk, either, which is why he excelled in the playoffs. Smith won the Conn Smythe Trophy as the postseason MVP in 1983 for shutting down the powerful Edmonton Oilers in the Islanders' four-game sweep for the Stanley Cup.

That Oilers' team featured Wayne Gretzky, Mark Messier, Paul Coffey, and Jari Kurri. But Smith pitched a 2–0 shutout in the opening game and surrendered a total of six goals in those finals. With Smith in goal, the Islanders won a record nineteen consecutive playoff series, and he would go on to break Ken Dryden's record of postseason victories with eighty-eight.

Of course, that didn't mean Smith was a nice guy. He also set a single-season record for goaltenders with forty-two penalty minutes during the 1972–73 season, and infuriated opposing skaters by flopping all over the ice with phantom injuries. Smith wasn't called "Battlin' Billy" for nothing, and as intense as he was on the ice, it was no act. Nobody liked to be around him on game days, and that included his family.

"The main thing is I don't talk to anybody all day, not even my wife," Smith said. "The players understand this and leave me alone.

At the rink, I sit in front of my locker and think about the game. Nobody bothers me. I do call my wife just to check up on things, but that's it. I concentrate one hundred percent on what I'm going to do in the game."

Smith finished with 305 regular-season wins, placing him ninth on the all-time list, and owns the distinction of being the first goaltender to actually score a goal. That happened on November 28, 1979, when Smith was the last Islander to touch the puck before the Colorado Rockies' Rob Ramage passed it into his own net.

Of course, Smith had his number 31 retired by the Islanders for his gift of stopping pucks, and it is only fitting that it hangs alongside all of the championship banners he helped hoist to the rafters. That's always been the bottom line with Smith. His No. 1 priority was winning, and there's no better quality I want in a goaltender.

Rubin says: Nice job, Dave. You actually made it look like Billy Smith's best asset was his curmudgeonly personality and not his ability to stop a puck, which is what always impressed me. Feigned injuries? Vigilante cheap shots at skaters near the crease? A guy who doesn't have enough respect to shake an opponent's hand after the series is over?

He sounds like a real treat. I guess it's a good thing he was playing goal behind those powerhouse Islanders.

Tell you what, Dave: You can keep Billy Smith as well as his tactics and attitude. I'm going to take New Jersey Devils net-minder Martin Brodeur and his superior skills and work ethic.

Truth of the matter is that Brodeur doesn't really belong in this conversation at all. Among the greats who have tended the pipes in New York, he stands above Mike Richter and Eddie Giacomin of the Rangers, as well as your beloved Billy Smith.

Brodeur is more fit for a debate entitled "best goaltender in

NHL history." He's only a little more than halfway through his career and already he has surpassed all of them in terms of accomplishments. When you look at the way he'd performed going into this past season—a standout on three Stanley Cup champions, a pair of Vezina trophies, four Jennings trophies—it becomes obvious that he belongs in a discussion with all-time greats like Patrick Roy and Ken Dryden.

He's the only goaltender with five forty-win seasons and he also holds a record with ten straight thirty-win campaigns. And he is on a pace to become hockey's all-time victories leader—Roy logged 551—before the end of the decade. Numbers like these scream: "Billy Who?"

The way I see it, there are two things that make Brodeur off-the-charts good: the way he turns up his performance in the biggest games and the way he never wants a night off.

Big-game play is the No. 1 thing when it comes to a goaltender and it's a great place to go in any conversation about Brodeur. In the regular season his goals-against average was a jaw-dropping 2.21 going into this past season—that would be exactly a full goal per game less than "Battlin' Billy"—which is why his Devils teams have been to the postseason in twelve of thirteen years with him in the net. And in the playoffs Brodeur finds a way to take his game to an even higher level, allowing only 1.96 goals per contest.

"I understood my [playoff] responsibilities," Brodeur told *Sports Illustrated*. "That goes with trying to be one of the best goalies in the league. I take that pressure with a lot of pride. If you want to be the best, you have to perform like it."

That's what it should be like. None of this "don't talk to me before a playoff game" crap. Just strap it on and get the job done. That's what you really want in a goalie.

The 6"1" Brodeur is the perfect centerpiece for the grinding Devils defense because he is relentless. Lots of goaltenders are great at stopping a first shot, but Brodeur stands apart when it comes to the second and third shots that come on the rare occasions he doesn't snare the puck and there's a rebound.

"You don't expect Brodeur's game to fall off," says Flyers coach Ken Hitchcock. "For all the great talent he has, he's a really tough guy to outwork. He never gives up on a puck or shot. That can be tough to deal with over the course of a game."

Even though Brodeur plays an incredibly taxing position, he insists on playing almost every game. This is uncommon in the NHL and testimony to how dedicated he is to doing his part for the defense-oriented Devils.

"The pressure of playing a defensive game puts the spotlight on me, but I don't think about it," he said. "I just have to play my game."

One of the interesting things that may come from the new innovations in the hockey rule book is that Brodeur may become an offensive threat. The changes allow goalkeepers to get out and intercept the long two-line passes that used to stop play. For a goalie like Brodeur, who is considered among the best with a stick, it could give him a chance to initiate offense.

Strangely, this is something he wants. Even though he grew up in Quebec, the new hotbed of hockey net-minders, Brodeur always wanted to play facing the net and not with his back to it.

"As a kid, I always wanted to be a forward, so playing the puck is a way for me to be a part of the offense," he says. "I love making that long pass, hitting a guy right on the tape."

It's that kind of passion that has put him atop the heap.

Does New York Care About College Football?

Rubin says: Where the hell did this notion get floated? I mean, I am more than willing to admit that the question bears asking here because there are people who actually believe this malarkey. But the answer is that this is just another urban legend from the streets of New York, Dave.

No one was killed by a penny dropped from the top of the Empire State Building. There are no alligators in the sewer system. No mob bosses are buried beneath the Yankee Stadium sod. And people in the Big Apple do like their college football.

I suspect the notion for this derives from the fact there is a dearth of good college football in the area. The only program in the city proper is Columbia, which unfortunately has a tradition of losing like few others. The only big-time programs in the area—and I hesitate to use that combination of words here—are Rutgers and Army, which have been losing more than they've won for most of the last twenty years. Hofstra's program's been decent and Iona's irrelevant.

It's clear that if you want to see good college football, you're not headed for an area stadium—you're headed for a television set. And that's what plenty of people here do, for the most part, in the city's many sports bars.

The thing about college football is that while some programs have a national following—Notre Dame and Penn State are the favorites in this town for obvious reasons, and Alabama, Texas, and Southern Cal have their coast-to-coast contingents—most people want to root for the team from their alma mater.

New York is a great melting pot in many ways and that includes the blending of graduates from many of the schools that boast high-powered programs. Because the city is the financial and legal center of the universe, lots of people have lots of reasons to come from all over the country. And they don't check their allegiances to their college teams, Dave, when they come over the George Washington Bridge.

You of all people should be aware of the huge mass of college football fans in this town. Every autumn Saturday they are packing the many bars in your Upper East Side neighborhood. At Dorrian's they're rooting for Virginia and Purdue. At Ship of Fools, it's Auburn and Washington. At the Blondie's near you, they're into LSU and Ohio State.

Across town at the Blondie's near me, you can find alumni from five schools—Michigan State, Illinois, Iowa State, Northwestern, and Iowa—all packing the joint to see their team play. The Florida fans are at Gin Mill and Arizona Staties patronize Timeout.

There are local alumni associations holding events in just about every area watering hole that deigns to hang a few television sets on every single college football Saturday, including nine from the Big Ten, seven from the Big XII, six from the ACC, and five from the SEC.

I know that neither of us went to schools that compete in those conferences, but football games meant good times for the grads of those schools and the good times didn't end when they donned the cap and gown.

Notre Dame generates more heat around here than any other school, possibly because it is the sort of unofficial team of Catholic America and Irish America and both groups are strongly represented in these parts. Many may not realize that the now-ubiquitous term "subway alumni" was coined to describe the Irish's massive following in Greater New York. Notre Dame officials have fostered the relationship by scheduling a game in the area about every other year. When the Irish were last in town, in 2004, to play Navy at Giants Stadium, they drew 76,000. And they didn't all drive in from South Bend.

People can think what they want, but anyone who thinks there are no college football fans in New York has an open invitation from me to go alligator hunting beneath our fair streets.

Lennon says: Here's what I got from your argument, Rog. You know a few Manhattan bars and plan on drinking free at every one of them as soon as this book comes out. In the shameless plug department, you win hands down. Just remember when you bring in that signed copy to collect that free round, tell them about your thirsty coauthor. I'll make it a point to stop in.

Where were we . . . Oh yeah, college football. I'm sorry, Rog. It's going to be tough to spend much time on this debate when every newspaper in this city barely acknowledges that college football exists. And shouldn't you reveal that you spend every January jet-setting between bowl games for your job? That makes you more than just a casual observer.

I'll tell you who else has more than a passing interest in those Saturday afternoons, and it doesn't have much to do with what campus they're from. It's all the "fans" who are betting on the games.

I don't care if you're watching at the Hard Rock in Vegas or the ESPN Zone in Times Square, there's a lot of money riding on these student athletes. And if it wasn't for the ubiquitous sports books—legit or otherwise—I'm not sure anyone would even know who Auburn is playing, never mind gather in a bar to watch them.

You really expect me to believe there is some sort of Purdue following here that meets for the games? That's in Indiana, right? If those kids made it to Manhattan, they're so happy to be out of Indiana they're not wasting time watching a perennial Big 10 doormat. They're sleeping off Friday's hangover, getting ready to hit the bars again Saturday night and then waking up in time for the NFL games.

Things would be different if the metropolitan area had big-time football—as you pointed out—instead of glorified intramural teams. That's just part of New York's built-in snobbery. If we don't have it here, then we don't want it, and it must not be any good anyway. Obviously, Columbia is a top-flight academic institution. But when it comes to playing football, any number of high school teams from Texas or Florida would probably beat those brainiacs senseless.

It's like that *New Yorker* cartoon, with a New Yorker's view of the world. Anything west of the Hudson River, between here and California, is pretty much overlooked. That includes just about every major college football program, and the only school that seems get an exemption is Notre Dame.

I can understand the fascination with the Fighting Irish because ND has more than just the subway alumni on its side. With its hallowed tradition—Rockne, Rudy, et al—Notre Dame is really America's Team, not just New York's favorite. But if you check the TV ratings every Saturday, that doesn't mean ND is an automatic draw. While the Fighting Irish do better than most in the nation's top market, it's not even close to the number that the local pro teams generate, and those ratings are not in the same universe as the Mets and Yankees.

New York likes its pro sports, and even college basketball, which is stocked with this city's top players from coast to coast, has been experiencing a lull here because of the struggling local programs. But New York also enjoys a big event, and that's why everyone finally tunes in for the New Year's bowl games, followed by the national championship.

Still, that's only three days out of 365, so I don't count that as any sort of sustained interest. And that's okay. There are plenty of people from Gainesville to Ann Arbor, from Austin to South Bend, that are rabid fans of their respective teams. Just don't tell me that New Yorkers deserve mentioning in that group.

Maybe it's because there's no place to tailgate around here, but when it comes to college football, no one cares.

35

Which World Series Title Meant the Most to New York?

Lennon says: It seems impossible to comprehend now, only a decade later, but there was a time when the Yankees didn't punch their playoff ticket on opening day. A year when they had to do more than spend millions during the winter, throw their gloves on the field over the summer, then wait atop the AL East to find out who was coming to the Bronx in the fall.

These Dark Ages, boys and girls, stretched from 1981, when the Yankees lost the World Series to the Dodgers, until 1995, when they ended a fourteen-year playoff drought by clinching, of all things, baseball's first wild-card berth.

Not exactly a return to greatness for the Yankees, who were eliminated by the Mariners in a thrilling five-game Division Series. But that was merely a stepping-stone to the one of the most magical chapters in New York baseball history, which was the crowning of the 1996 Yankees as World Series champions.

Think about it. Imagine the House that Ruth Built silent and empty for all of those Octobers. It was like Christmas had stopped playing in December.

And then the Yankees—not the expensive juggernaut of today, but a flawed and inspired bunch under new manager Joe Torre—cap a roller-coaster regular season by coming back to turn on the lights in the Bronx. New York was gripped by a pin-striped hysteria not witnessed in recent memory, and the cast of characters was straight from a Hollywood screenplay.

Need proof? Dwight Gooden, the derailed Mets phenom who fired his first career no-hitter in May of that season, had his own troubled tale optioned by a movie company. As did Torre, whose story was made into an HBO feature, though not a very good one.

Just the fact the Yankees made it to the World Series would have been enough to sustain this baseball-starved city. But the way in which they won their twenty-third championship, with guts, perseverance and the help of a twelve-year-old New Jersey kid named Jeffrey Maier, is a script that will never be duplicated, or outdone for that matter.

Not only did the Yankees add Gooden that season, they dusted off another Mets icon, Darryl Strawberry, in signing him from the St. Paul Saints of the Independent League. And while we're on the subject of former Met stars, don't forget that David Cone returned from a life-threatening aneurysm in his right shoulder to again be an integral part of the rotation, conning Torre to stick with him for the pivotal Game 3 victory over the Braves in Atlanta.

Which leads us to the World Series, one that the Yankees began by spotting the Braves the first two games—in the Bronx no less. John Smoltz and Greg Maddux dumped the Bombers in that 0-2 hole, sucking the life out of an entire city. But not the Yankees. When owner George Steinbrenner visited Torre in the aftermath of that 4–0 loss in Game 2, the manager coolly told The Boss that his team would go to Atlanta, win the next three, and then return to clinch it in the Bronx.

Did they ever. The Yankees rallied back from a 6–0 deficit in Game 4, tying the score on Jim Leyrtiz's three-run homer off Mark Wohlers in the eighth inning and then getting the winning run in the tenth when Wade Boggs, as a pinch hitter, drew a bases-loaded walk. In Game 5, there was Andy Pettitte, before he was Andy Pettitte, outdueling Smoltz for eight innings in the 1–0 victory. Jimmy

Key finished off the Braves in Game 6, fittingly back in the Bronx, when he combined with four relievers.

Oh, and watching on TV that night, from his hospital room, was Torre's brother, Frank, who had received a new heart only twelve hours earlier. These Yankees captured a city's imagination like no other team, plastered over both the front and back pages of its tabloids for weeks, and set a dynasty in motion, even drawing praise from its perpetually cranky owner.

"This is a team New York can be proud of," Steinbrenner said.

Rubin says: Got a news flash for you, Dave. There's another baseball team in New York besides the Yankees. They play over in Queens. Maybe you've seen the stadium on a flight into La-Guardia?

Just because the Yankees have won twenty-six World Series titles doesn't mean they automatically captured the city's most important one of the last thirty-five years. Anyone who remembers the Mets' magical season of 1986 will beg to differ as I do right now.

I don't believe that the city was starved for playoff baseball between 1981 and 1995. I think even Yankee fans could appreciate what the Mets had working in 1986, from their brashness, their invention of the rally cap, and the way they extended Boston's Curse of the Bambino after a play that no one will ever forget.

Mets fans suffered thirteen years without seeing their team in the playoffs while the Yanks made four trips. But all that frustration melted away with one of the great playoff runs in baseball history, one that saw the Mets cheat elimination in both rounds.

The Yankees' triumph in 1996 was a phenomenal sight, but the Mets' in 1986 couldn't be beat for drama, back-to-the-wall heroics, and the way it united a city. The Astros had them right where they wanted. The Red Sox were reading them last rites. And both times the Mets wriggled out.

The Mets put together a brash and cocky group that season. On their way to 108 regular season wins they got into several bench-clearing brawls and grew to be disdained in baseball circles for an attitude New Yorkers adored. We like a little self-assured bravado here in the Big Apple.

The postseason was unreal. Seeing the Mets peer over the edge into the abyss twice and find a way back each time like going on a five-ticket carnival ride all night every night.

The 1986 Mets were New York's team because they were just like the city: a melting pot. Hall of Fame talent like Gary Carter played alongside journeymen like Rafael Santana. There were blossoming stars like Dwight Gooden and Darryl Strawberry. There were zany characters like Lenny "Nails" Dykstra and Mookie Wilson and Roger McDowell. And also everyman heroes like hulking Sid Fernandez and crafty Jesse Orosco.

And when you put them together it just worked, exactly like the Big Apple.

The playoff games were so compelling; you couldn't wait to see your friends or coworkers the next day to start talking about what had happened the night before. The drama was must-see for all baseball fans. And if the Mets were your team, you had to watch through your fingers as you covered your eyes.

In the NLCS, the Mets looked like dead ducks heading into the ninth inning of Game 6 at the Astrodome. Even though they brought a 3-2 series lead into the game, they were down 3–0 with three outs to go and were looking at a Game 7 no one wanted. They'd have to face Houston's Mike Scott a third time and he'd already shredded them twice. The Mets couldn't do anything with Scott; he even beat Gooden in Game 1 on a night when the Mets' ace allowed only one run.

After Scott stifled them again in Game 4, the Mets knew they'd have to win the next two to avoid a third confrontation with the Astros' ace. They scored three in that ninth inning to tie the game, scored three more in the sixteenth, and then hung on as Houston scored two and got the tying run on base in the bottom.

The situation was more dire in the World Series against Boston, when the Mets were down to their last out and Shea Stadium's scoreboard had anointed Red Sox second baseman Marty Barrett as the Series MVP. They snatched that one away from Boston when Bill Buckner muffed Mookie Wilson's ground ball. It was a play for the annals and made Wilson a household name.

That was the moment when it became clear the Mets were just meant to win. Boston did lead in Game 7, but the Mets came roaring back to take it.

The 1986 Mets are even more significant because of the aftermath. Baseball fans in this town thought they could become a dynasty, but human frailty was that dream's undoing. There was a great lesson in that, but if you add that to the way they enthralled the entire city, this World Series title was clearly the city's most important.

SETTLE THE SCORE/DARRYL STRAWBERRY

(Darryl Strawberry and Dwight Gooden were the only two players on both the rosters of the '86 Mets and '96 Yankees, so we asked Straw to settle the score on which title was more important to New York):

It would definitely have to be the '86 Mets. I think we set the city on fire. I'm just being honest. Those were crazy times and the team we had was one of true destiny. We had hunger in us from day one, and when we rolled out, we were as crazy as ever.

I mean, we got into all kinds of fights. The '96 team, and all the Yankees teams I played with, we weren't like that.

Those Mets were old-school throwbacks. We didn't only get in fights on the field. We got into fights off the field, with each other, in bars. And for us to still have the chemistry to go out and put it together on the field, that takes a lot. I think a lot of people overlooked that about us. That was part of what we all went through on that team. We had a group of guys where everybody had a different personality, but when it came to that one common thing, we all had that same goal: to win.

It was so different [in '86] because it was time for a change for Mets fans. I mean, when I came up in '83, we weren't nothing, but we were nowhere in the picture of being great until we got to the point of Davey Johnson coming in and taking over. They built that ball club basically with young players from the farm system with a couple of veteran players, which was different from when I joined the Yankees in '96.

Basically, a lot of us came up together through the farm system, and I think we had a real confidence in ourselves, a real swagger about ourselves. And we fed off our fans. I think they saw that we were pretty much homegrown and there weren't that many free agents. You talk about Keith [Hernandez] and [Gary] Carter were the main guys we got through trades. They were the last pieces to puzzle. You had myself, Kevin Mitchell, Doc, Lenny, Wally.

I was homegrown with the Mets, and to win a championship with them was like "Wow." It was big. Coming back to New York [in '96] and winning with the Yankees was very special because of the opportunity and the group of guys that fell in line over there, first and foremost with Joe Torre. To play for Joe was great. I have nothing but respect for him after playing over there.

With the '96 Yankees, I kind of parachuted in, snuck in the back door. It was a little easier to get into the playoffs, too, because of the wild card. We didn't have that in '86.

We couldn't lose. We knew that. There was no question about it. It takes years to find a team like that. When I played with the '98 Yankees, it was the same way. People always ask me about that team, how do I compare that '98 team to the '86 Mets, and I say they would have never beat the '86 Mets.

36

Johnny Damon or Carlos Beltran?

Rubin says: You know that phrase about killing two birds with one stone, Dave? Well the Yankees killed three when they inked Johnny Damon to a new four-year contract in December of 2005. And I'm not talking about the Dave Winfield kind of bird killing.

The Yankees wanted to get a new leadoff hitter? Check. The Yankees wanted a quality center fielder to replace Bernie Williams after a decade and a half? Check. The Yankees wanted—as they always do—to be a thorn in the side of the rival Red Sox? Check again.

With that one ingenious move, Bombers' general manager Brian Cashman resolved the two biggest issues the Yankees were facing after their first-round exit from the 2005 playoffs and also separated Boston from their identity. The shaggy, rambunctious Damon was chief idiot in the Sox' clubhouse. He and catcher Jason Varitek were the two biggest leaders on that team.

That may be the number one reason that I have to go with Damon in this choice between New York's two present and future center fielders. Compared to Damon, Beltran is a wallflower. And I seriously doubt that anyone in the Mets clubhouse is looking to follow his lead; they're just hoping he'll keep hitting and not revert to what he did (or didn't do) in 2005.

Don't underestimate what it's taken to be a part of the Red Sox the past three years. They've stood up to the bullying of the Yankees. They picked themselves back up after the heart-wrenching 2003 ALCS that ended in the eleventh inning of Game 7 on Aaron Boone's home run. And they had the intestinal fortitude to scratch and claw and cajole themselves back from a three-games-to-none deficit in the 2004 ALCS to finally oust the Bombers.

People don't realize it because of his rock-star image and the adulation that was showered on him, but he might have been the gutsiest guy on that team. "He's one of the toughest guys I've ever been around," Boston manager Terry Francona says.

That quality translates into a lot of areas. It's there when you see him crashing into walls to make plays. It's there when you see him refuse to take more than a couple of days off to deal with an injury or when he plays most of a season with a sore shoulder and still hits .316 and scores 108 runs like he did in 2005. And it's there when you see him shorten a pitcher's game by an inning with one of his ten-pitch turns at bat; you can bet the Yankees will be thrilled not to be on the business end of those anymore.

Damon averaged 115 runs scored and twenty-five stolen bases during his four seasons in Boston and hit over .300 the last two. With Derek Jeter hitting behind him in his preferred number two spot in the batting order, Damon shapes up as the perfect table-setter in one of the greatest batting orders ever assembled. Beltran is clearly the better defensive player, but the Mets got him to be the perfect run producer in the order, and he was anything but that in his first season.

There are two big clinchers to my point here, Dave. Let me serve them up.

First, Damon is costing the Yankees $4 million less per year than Beltran is costing the Mets; perhaps Beltran will prove to be the better player, but to be worth $4 million more per year, he'd have to carry the Mets farther than the Yankees. And second, Beltran wanted to come to the Yankees before the 2005 season and the

Bombers took a pass; right before he signed the $119 million deal with the Mets, he told the Yankees he'd wear pinstripes for only $100 million and they didn't even want him at that price.

I don't know where we're going to be on this one in a few years. The Red Sox obviously felt that Damon was at or nearing his peak after 2005, so concerns of physical breakdown loom, especially his throwing arm. In Beltran's first season with the Mets, his play wasn't worth half what he got paid (technically a little more than $11 million) and he was not exactly enthralled with the produce-or-be-booed mind-set of the Shea faithful.

We only have the here and now to judge between them. No one in New York wants to hear this, but Boston's Coco Crisp probably is a better dollar-for-dollar player than either of them. But in a choice between the New York guys, the performance, leadership, and value all favor the guy in the Bronx.

Lennon says: Funny that you should mention Dave Winfield in this particular debate, Roger. As soon I was reminded of Winfield gunning down that poor seagull in Toronto, I thought of the Yankees' newest big-ticket prize, Johnny Damon, trying the same thing with that weak excuse for a right arm.

Let's just say, for the sake of argument, that Damon was able to actually hit a seagull with one of his throws, though the odds of that happening are somewhere around the likelihood of George Steinbrenner buying a condo on Yawkey Way. Would the seagull even be dazed? He's probably been hit harder by raindrops than one of Damon's lollipop tosses.

So Carlos Beltran had a rough first season with the Mets. Really, who doesn't? But if you want to do a straight-up comparison between two of the favorite clients of superagent Scott Boras, I'm afraid you're going to lose with your cleaned-up Captain Caveman. On physical tools alone, Beltran has him beat, and a solid throwing arm is nothing to sneeze at for a center fielder. Look what happened to Bernie Williams during the 2005 season. His decline wasn't pretty.

And seriously, Roger. Do you really think the Yankees took a pass on Beltran for any reason other than out of respect for Williams, who helped them win four World Series rings with clutch performances and pure class? That was a tough one. You can bet the Yankees didn't balk at the money—$100 million was a bargain for Beltran—and he'll live up to his seven-year, $119-million contract with the Mets before he's through in Flushing.

A metrosexual like Damon is a perfect fit for New York, where there's plenty of places for him to get his hair styled and his nails done. I can't really question his toughness, either, not after seeing his scary collision with teammate Damian Jackson during the 2004 playoffs and knowing that he played with a hurt shoulder through most of 2005.

But again, Beltran has the edge here, too, considering he returned from a near-death experience to finish the 2005 season. Beltran suffered no less than a fractured face when he collided with Mike Cameron on that horrific headfirst crash in San Diego, then passed on surgery to help his team during what eventually became a meaningless stretch of games. Maybe the final weeks of the season didn't amount to much in the standings, but it meant something for Beltran, who felt a responsibility to be out there with his teammates.

That's leadership, Rog, and I can tell you that everyone in the Mets' clubhouse appreciated Beltran's display of courage. It would have been easy for Beltran to sit at that point after what had been a personally frustrating year, but he didn't take the easy way out—the way Damon bolted Boston because of pride and a bigger payday in the Bronx.

There's no disputing the fact that Beltran didn't do so hot statistically in his first season with the Mets. His .266 batting average was almost twenty points below his career mark, and his seventeen stolen bases were definitely a disappointment after he swiped a combined total of eighty-three during the previous two seasons.

But you have to believe that Beltran's best days are ahead of him, while Damon, who at thirty-two is four years older, could very well be on the decline. The Red Sox certainly thought that was the case in lowballing him during negotiations, and if the team he helped break an eighty-six-year curse didn't want him, that's a telling sign.

Beltran, to a much lesser degree, did the same thing to Houston after carrying the Astros to the brink of the World Series in 2004. That October, Beltran did things at the plate that no one short of Barry Bonds had accomplished, and it was that ridiculous power surge that got him his big payday from the Mets.

You won't see Damon's name ever mentioned in the same sentence as Bonds, that's for sure. And given the choice, I'll take the switch-hitting, slick-fielding, five-tool Beltran over the pretty-boy, all-hair, no-arm Damon any day of the week.

Who Is the Best New York–born Point Guard?

Lennon says: By the purest definition of the term, this should be no contest. There is no greater responsibility for a point guard than to distribute the basketball, and only one person in the history of the NBA did it with more success than Mark Jackson.

But John Stockton was born in Spokane, Washington, and that puts him about 3,000 miles outside of our neighborhood. For local products, the Brooklyn-bred Jackson is without peer when it comes to point guards, and in New York, the city known for producing them, that's the highest of praise.

Jackson, at a lumpy 6'3", was never the most athletic player on the court. He was a high school star at Brooklyn's Bishop Loughlin High School—neck and neck with Molloy's Kenny Smith for the city's top point-guard honors—but didn't even start for St. John's when the Redmen advanced to the Final Four in 1985. And by the time he was a senior, later becoming the school's all-time assist leader, many still believed Jackson was too slow to make it in the NBA.

For that reason, Jackson slipped all the way to No. 18 in the 1987 draft, below fellow New Yorker Smith, Kevin Johnson, and even the 5'3" curiosity Tyrone "Muggsy" Bogues. But the Knicks were thrilled to grab the hometown hero in that spot, eliciting cheers from the fans inside the Garden's Felt Forum, and Jackson did not disappoint once he got upstairs on the court.

Jackson had a style honed on the city's playgrounds, but it translated just fine to the NBA, where he earned Rookie of the Year honors by averaging 10.6 assists per game. Overall, Jackson piled up 868 assists that season, far eclipsing the previous rookie record set by Oscar Robertson (690) during 1960–61.

In today's NBA, where passing the ball is a lost art, Jackson would probably be less appreciated. Everyone wants to score—including point guards—and that was never Jackson's game. But if you wanted a catalyst for your offense, Jackson was the guy, and it was no coincidence that his teams won. He made the playoffs fourteen times in seventeen seasons, and finished twelfth all-time in postseason assists with 904.

Jackson also figures to end the recent drought of New Yorkers getting voted into the Hall of Fame. His numbers make him a virtual lock for Springfield. He's second all-time with 10,334 assists, tenth with 1,296 career games, and twentieth with 1,608 steals. Jackson also was among the top ten in assists for eleven of his seventeen seasons and finished with seventeen triple-doubles, no easy feat for a guy who lived to pass the ball.

To put Jackson in perspective, only three players in NBA history have ever surpassed the 10,000 plateau in assists; not bad for a point guard once considered a risky draft pick. The only puzzling part about Jackson's prestigious career was how much he bounced around the league. He played for seven teams, including two different stints with the Knicks and Pacers, and his hometown team traded him twice.

In addition to his floor skills, Jackson deserves credit for his resiliency, too. Starting his NBA career in his own backyard was not easy, despite surprising early success under Knicks coach Rick Pitino, and Jackson even outlasted Smith, his schoolboy rival. The only thing Jackson didn't accomplish during his seventeen seasons in the NBA was winning a ring, and that wasn't his fault.

All Jackson ever wanted to do was make everyone else better, and that's exactly what he did whenever he took the floor. Jackson loved to be in control on the court, but once the ball left his hands, what happened after that was somebody else's responsibility. More often than not, Jackson got it to them, and only Stockton did it more often in the history of the NBA.

Rubin says: Let me just make sure I've got this straight, Dave. Mark Jackson proved his greatness by getting his team to the playoffs in fourteen of seventeen seasons, but his failure to pilot any of them to a championship was not his fault?

I'm not sure any New York point guard—including a future Hall of Famer like Jackson—would buy what you're selling. This is appalling talk in a town like this one, the eternal spring of great playmakers and source of origin for the pipeline of point guards to NBA. Any floor leader worth his weight knows that, in the end, the credit or blame for winning or not winning a championship rests with him and him alone.

Your poor Socratic skills pointed out, allow me to just soften the blow by saying that at least you picked someone worthy of your kind of enthusiasm. Jackson was a tremendous player from high school to the pros and has to rank high on any list of top New York point guards.

The feeling here though is that he can be done one "tiny" bit better. Specifically I am referring to Nate "Tiny" Archibald, born and raised in the Bronx. He had a humble and impoverished upbringing that only served to toughen his desire to cut the NBA to ribbons during a fourteen-year Hall of Fame career.

No player in history combined his playmaking skills and scoring ability, and to this day, he is the only player ever to lead the NBA in scoring and assists during the same season. During the 1972–73 campaign, after his Cincinnati Royals had become the Kansas City/

Omaha Kings, Archibald averaged 34.0 points and 11.4 assists and the *Sporting News* anointed him the league's MVP.

Standing only 6'1"—"tiny" by NBA standards—Archibald spent more than a decade proving that a small player could still be one of a dominating force at the sport's highest level.

"I thought he would be an impact player," Don Haskins, his coach at Texas Western (now UTEP), told the *Boston Globe*. "But I had a hard time selling him [with NBA teams] because nobody had small players in those days.

"Archibald was the greatest player I ever watched in the NBA. What couldn't he do? He would do amazing things—shoot, set up players, run the fast break. One summer he came back [to school] to take some classes and said he was going to lead the league in scoring and assists. Sort of like Babe Ruth calling his shot."

Archibald came out of a basketball hotbed in the South Bronx and played at the Paterson housing projects gym. It may not have shown up on most maps, but in the basketball world it was a landmark that drew many of the city's biggest talents. Guys like Charlie Scott and Len Elmore and even Lew Alcindor ran ball there, but Archibald was the guy everyone talked about.

"The area was better than some, but it wasn't a place I'd let my grandmother walk through at night," former NBA guard Ricky Sobers said in one interview. "It was an experience I couldn't replace. It's why I'm so physical now. [That area] was tough and it rubs off."

Archibald was already on the radar of basketball fans when he was playing high school ball. He was the point guard and team leader for some of DeWitt Clinton's powerhouse teams. And in 1966, he guided the Governors all the way to the city public school championship.

At Texas Western, he was a twenty-point-per-game scorer for three seasons. In his senior year he took the school to the NCAA Tournament and was named honorable mention All-American.

Interestingly enough, Dave, Archibald was like Jackson in that his physical attributes pushed him down in the draft. His size allowed him to tumble to nineteenth overall, the second-round pick of the Royals. Cincinnati coach Bob Cousy—perhaps the greatest New York point guard ever (but of course, outside our debate)—knew a thing or two about floor captains from the Big Apple.

And ultimately, Archibald piloted a team to an NBA championship. He was acquired by the Celtics to be a sixth man, but proved his value as a starter and was the point guard on The Green's 1981 title team.

When his career ended after the 1983–84 season, Archibald ranked among the top ten all-time in assists and his career scoring average was 18.8 points (nearly double Jackson's). The fans might have loved his moves and nicknamed him "Nate the Skate," but in my book he goes down as "Nate the Great."

SETTLE THE SCORE/JIM LARRANAGA

(Coach Jim Larranaga led George Mason to the 2006 Final Four during one of the great Cinderella runs in NCAA tournament history. He grew up in the Bronx, played high school ball at Molloy in Queens, and has recruited in the city as an assistant at Virginia and head coach at Bowling Green and GMU. This is his take on New York–born point guards and how they developed as pros.)

There are two areas where a point guard must excel to be considered great. One is physical and one is mental. Physically it's in terms of speed, quickness, jumping ability, and basketball skills such as dribbling, passing, shooting, and defense. Mentally—and this is probably more important—it includes leadership, decision-making ability, and basketball IQ, like knowing when to push the pace and when not to and who to get the ball to for the best chance of success. A great point guard knows who to get the ball to when he is in a certain position on the court. That's leadership on the court, but there is also leadership off the court. That's about being looked up to and being counted on.

I'd have to go back to my generation and pick out Tiny Archibald as probably the best. He was great when he was playing in high school, around the same time I was, but every time he went up a level, he would develop his game further and again rise to the top.

He was not a shooter in high school. He didn't shoot jump shots at [Clinton High]; he was only a layup-maker, but a great layup-maker. He used speed and quickness to get to the basket. He could penetrate like few people and he could also then drop off passes to others, putting them in a position to score.

He continued to improve his game, first in college and then again in the NBA. At those levels he became a great scorer as well as a passer. He developed into an excellent jump shooter. He got to the point where he led the NBA in both scoring and assists, which is quite a feat.

If you want to talk about guys who were great in high school, great in college, and then great in the professional leagues, he's probably No. 1 in my mind. Tiny Archibald was the best at being able to continue to do what he did in high school in college and then adjusting his game—adding to it—to be great in the NBA. He was able to do that and that's really something.

I remember seeing him with Kansas City and thinking that it was amazing how his game had changed. He was shooting jump shots when he'd never done so in high school, and he made good distance shots.

Of course, there have been great point guards from each generation and, even though they played very different styles and had very different strengths, all were among the best. In one generation there was Dean Meminger, a tremendous athlete and defensive player and a great slasher. Jim O'Brien was a cerebral passer and great playmaker who made everyone around him better. John Roche was a scoring point guard who could shoot like an off guard and handle like a point guard.

The next generation had Kevin Joyce and Brian Winters—neither was a traditional point guard, but their games translated to greatness at every level they played. Winters may never have been called a "true point guard" because he was such a great shooter, but he ran his team and handled the ball and was good enough for the Milwaukee Bucks to retire his jersey.

Pearl Washington, Kenny Smith, and Mark Jackson were in the next group and, again, you can see where the styles could be so different but the players each still tremendous in their own right. Pearl Washington was an unbelievable penetrator and it made him great in high school and in college at Syracuse, but his lack of an outside game caught up with him in the NBA. Kenny Smith was a jet—Kenny the Jet—and his quickness and athletic ability made him an unmatched open court player. He also had the outside game that allowed his greatness to translate and for him to win NBA championship rings. Smith was a great example of being able to blossom and develop more at each level. He might be second in terms of changing his game to be successful at every level.

Mark Jackson was the prototype power point guard. He didn't have Kenny Smith's great open court speed and he didn't have Pearl's penetrating ability, but he was able to use size, strength, savvy, and body control to be successful. He could back guys down to where he could score or draw other defenders and use his great passing ability to find an open man. He had a great pro career because of how smart he was.

Kenny Anderson is the only guy from the following generation who fits in this conversation. Players peak at various times. While he had a great NBA career, either the teams he played on, their playing styles, or some subtle shortcoming in his game prevented him from becoming a part of the upper echelon of point guards.

Since then there's Stephon Marbury. He is one of the four or five most-gifted point guards to come out of New York. His athletic ability alone was far superior to most of the people we're talking about, but his career has not produced the team results that have to be taken into consideration.

If I am comparing people and one guy has taken his team to a lot of wins, you have to give the nod to the guy who makes his team a winner. All the people who get considered the best have to have done what Magic Johnson, John Stockton, Bob Cousy, Kenny Smith, and Tiny Archibald did—win. Stats aren't enough. Winning isn't enough. You have to have led your team to [a championship].

There are lots of others who came out of New York and are in the NBA right now, but none of them can really be considered of the same quality yet to be a part of this conversation.

Who Was the Biggest Bust?

Rubin says: With nine pro teams and a myriad of major college programs in this town, there would appear to be a lot of candidates from the past thirty-five years, but I think to wear this label requires a great deal.

Many would hang it on a top draft choice who doesn't pan out. Others might put it on a player who fails to meet expectations. A third group could slap it on a coach or a general manager who arrived amid fanfare and failed to right a franchise.

In my mind all of these are merely disappointments. A "bust" has to have a devastating impact, sure, but it can be so much more. Add stupidity in bringing the guy on board. Add a potentially club-crippling high cost. Sweeten it with headline-grabbing big talk. And then have it do exactly the opposite of what was intended. That's a fine stew. That's a major bust.

And as I see it, none compares with the Mets' trade for Mo Vaughn between the 2001 and 2002 seasons. It's a perfect storm: all this and a little bit more.

Vaughn played only one full season and one-sixth of another, even though he was paid for three. His lumbering, slow-footed defense at first base was atrocious, but that's not why the Mets got him. They needed hitting and here's what they got: twenty-nine home runs, 87 RBI, and a .249 batting average. About the only thing he led the league in was trips to Scores.

I'm pretty sure that in the world of sport, $48 million has never bought so little.

New York teams, it seems, frequently shell out big bucks and get a bad return. Heck, Kevin Brown got more than $31 million from the Yankees and, in two seasons, threw barely two hundred innings, disabled himself at a critical time by punching a wall, and imploded on impact against the Red Sox in Game 7 of the fated 2004 ALCS. It's the extra ingredients that set Vaughn apart from serious disappointments like Brown.

Vaughn was supposed to turn the tide for the Mets and send them back to the World Series while simultaneously placating the fans still upset by the failed attempt to bring Alex Rodriguez into the fold.

The Mets were willing to commit enough lettuce to Vaughn to buy two players and created a huge hole in the rotation at the same time. They traded away serviceable Kevin Appier, who'd won eleven games, pitched more than two hundred innings, and posted an ERA under 4.00. The Mets filled the void with one Glendon Rusch.

It's near unfathomable that the Mets didn't have an inkling that this fiasco was coming. The carousing former MVP was shadowed by the issues of his weight and conditioning throughout his career. The Red Sox didn't want to re-sign him after 1998 even though he was extremely popular and hit .412 in the playoffs that year. In two seasons with the Angels, his batting average fell off, but he was still a big run-producer. And then he missed all of 2001 with a torn biceps tendon and still the Mets were hell-bent to get him even without seeing him face big league pitching in over a year.

He was already the equivalent of a hot potato when he joined the Mets. It's just that the Mets got burned.

General manager Steve Phillips and Vaughn set themselves up

with declarations about how a good move it was. Phillips said, "In a typical year, you don't have a chance to get a Mo Vaughn. He had been on a Hall of Fame pace [before the injury], and he has that kind of motivation. We think he's a perfect fit, on the field and in the clubhouse."

Vaughn simply promised to "come back the player I left in 1998." So it looked pretty bad when he turned in his worst season in a decade. Instead of making the Mets a more formidable offensive force, the team actually scored fewer runs per game over the next two seasons. Oh, and Appier? He helped win a World Series championship his first season with the Angels.

When the Mets made the deal for Vaughn, it was celebrated by their fans and front office. The Hit Dog was coming east to save the day. Problem is he never brought the hits. He only brought the dog.

Lennon says: Pound for pound, Rog, there's no question you picked the right guy in Mo Vaughn. It's never good when a player can't hit his weight in the majors, and for an injury-prone slugger who spent much of his free time lounging at Scores, the term "bust" takes on a whole different meaning.

Where I'd take issue with Vaughn is what he was supposed to bring to the Mets in the first place. It was a risky trade to begin with, a salary dump on both sides for grossly overpaid players, and the Mets were hoping Vaughn could resurrect his spiraling career under fellow Connecticut native Bobby Valentine.

So Vaughn basically proved the skeptics right.

But in the case of Johnny "Lam" Jones, the Texas football and track star, there seldom was heard a discouraging word before the 1980 NFL draft. How could anyone dispute his credentials?

Jones, straight out of high school, was a member of the gold-winning 4×100 relay team at the 1976 Montreal Olympics. And after enrolling at the University of Texas, Jones would have had the world record in the one-hundred-meter dash if the electronic timer had not malfunctioned.

Who could blame Longhorns' football coach Darrell Royal for luring Jones to the gridiron, where the speedster was a star running back as a freshman before becoming the school's leading receiver for the next three years—the only one to do so until Roy Williams matched Jones two decades later. In addition, Jones was one of just three players in Texas history to rush for one hundred yards and also have a one-hundred-yard receiving game.

The Jets were infatuated with Jones's world-class speed and, with two picks in the first round of the 1980 draft, possessed the chips to get him. They had visions of Jones becoming the next "Bullet" Bob Hayes, the track star who shined for the Dallas Cowboys, and gladly handed over their two picks—No. 13 and No. 20—to the San Francisco 49ers for the second pick overall.

"His straightaway speed was unreal," former Jets coach Walt Michaels told the *Daily News*. "The theory was to team him up with Wesley Walker, with Mickey Shuler at tight end, and we'd be just about unstoppable in the air."

That was the plan anyway. The Lions selected running back Billy Smith at No. 1 that year, and after Jones went to the Jets, the Bengals chose offensive tackle Anthony Munoz, a future Hall of Famer and arguably the best to ever play that position. The next wide receiver picked in that draft? Art Monk, who the Redskins grabbed at No. 17.

Obviously, Monk would turn out to be better suited for the NFL, and the Jets realized their mistake almost from the moment Jones was unveiled to the New York media. A shy kid from a small town in Texas, Jones had raw talent, but a closer examination may have told the Jets he didn't have the makeup for New York. That unique pressure has caused plenty of players to implode, in every sport, and it eventually broke Jones, too.

"I still recall that day," Michaels said. "The media hit Lam, and it looked like he turned sixteen different colors. He seemed to be saying, 'What did I get myself into?' "

It was a recipe for disaster. Jones struggled badly on the field, along with battling drug and alcohol problems. He lasted five seasons on the Jets, and put together only one decent campaign, catching forty-three passes for 734 yards and four touchdowns in 1983.

The Jets eventually gave up on Jones, trading him to the 49ers, of all teams, and he later signed with the Cowboys before washing out of the NFL in 1987. In his native Texas, Johnny "Lam" Jones is considered a favorite son, an Olympic gold medalist and one of the best sprinters the state has ever produced. But to Jets fans, he will always be branded as the worst draft-day decision in franchise history.

"I know how they remember me in New York: I'm the guy they blew the draft pick on," Jones said after his playing days were over. "That's okay. I didn't live up to their expectations, but I didn't live up to my own expectations either."

Jones eventually moved on with his life. But the Jets fans, they never forget.

THE TEN BIGGEST BUSTS

1. Mo Vaughn (Mets): The only thing as bloated as Vaughn's ridiculous contract was his expanding waistline, and the over-sized "Hit Dog" continued his stunning decline once he arrived from Anaheim. The Mets privately were thrilled when the Hit Dog's knees gave out, letting them recoup half of their $48 million through insurance.

2. Johnny "Lam" Jones (Jets): Regarded as one of the fastest men on the planet after winning a gold medal at the 1976 Montreal Olympics, Jones's NFL career came to a screeching halt in

New York. The Jets traded two first-round draft picks to get him at No. 2 overall, but he was never better than their third-best receiver, and lasted five mediocre seasons.

3. Brien Taylor (Yankees): Unhittable in high school, Taylor had 476 strikeouts in 239 innings, and extorted a record $1.55-million signing bonus from the Yankees after they picked him No.1 overall in the 1991 draft. But after two promising minor-league seasons, Taylor seriously injured his throwing shoulder in a bar fight and never regained his velocity after surgery.

4. Dennis Hopson (Nets): Averaged twenty-nine points during his senior season at Ohio State, which convinced the Nets to pick him No. 3 overall in the 1987 draft. Not only was Hopson a bust—shooting 43 percent in five seasons as a bench player—the Nets passed on Scottie Pippen (5), Kenny Smith (6), Kevin Johnson (7), and Reggie Miller (11) to get him.

5. Blair Thomas (Jets): Yet another mistake at No. 2 for the Jets. Thomas helped Penn State win a national championship as a red-shirt freshman, then rushed for 1,414 yards and eleven touchdowns as a sophomore. In the 1992 draft, with Emmitt Smith on the board—he would later go at No. 17—the Jets grabbed Thomas and he rewarded them with five TDs in five seasons.

6. Bobby Bonilla (Mets): New York native Bonilla threatened to show a reporter "the Bronx" during a clubhouse confrontation. The Mets wished he had played there instead. They made him the sport's highest-paid player with a five-year, $25-million contract, and Bonilla became the face of "The Worst Team Money Could Buy." Also called the press box to complain about an error— during a game.

7. Ron Dayne (Giants): The fact that Dayne, a Heisman Trophy winner, was still on the board at No. 11 should have told the

Giants something. Dayne left Wisconsin as the leading rusher in Division 1A history, averaging 5.8 yards a carry, but couldn't get out of his own way on the Giants. He struggled with weight, annoyed Tom Coughlin, and was gone after the 2004 season.

8. Ed O'Bannon (Nets): Named the Most Outstanding Player of the 1995 Final Four, where he teamed with his brother Charles to deliver a national title for UCLA. But O'Bannon, picked ninth overall, was nearly invisible on the Nets, averaging five points per games on 37 percent shooting in two seasons.

9. Glen Sather (Rangers): A Hall of Famer, Sather is hailed as the architect of the Edmonton Oilers' incredible run of five Stanley Cubs in seven years, alternately serving as both a coach and GM during that span. But after being hired as president/GM of the Rangers in 2004, Sather did not get them to the playoffs in his first four seasons. Filling in as coach after yet another firing, Sather was 33-46-11 in ninety games.

10. Antonio McDyess (Knicks): The Knicks are victims of chronic mismanagement, but the McDyess trade stands out as the most glaring example. Trading Marcus Camby and a draft pick was a dubious move by itself, considering McDyess's medical history, and the Knicks' worst fears were realized when McDyess shattered his knee. He played only eighteen games—for roughly $25 million—scoring 8.4 points per game in his brief MSG career.

Big Blue Wrecking Crew or New York Sack Exchange?

Lennon says: I know it's difficult to imagine now, but there was a time, twenty-five years ago, that four members of the Jets could show up on Wall Street and bring the nonstop frenzy of the trading floor to a screeching halt.

Think about that for a second. New Yorkers ignored the chance to make money just so they could turn away from their computer screens and give a standing ovation to the Jets' defensive line of Mark Gastineau, Joe Klecko, Marty Lyons, and Abdul Salaam.

That's appreciation. And the Jets' front four had become the unofficial mascots of Wall Street from the minute they stumbled upon one of the best nicknames in this city's sports history: "The New York Sack Exchange."

While the origin of that slogan remains open for debate to this day—it appears to have sprung from a bedsheet banner hanging in the stands—there's no disputing that the nickname was a perfect fit. It's rare when a defensive unit has style and substance, and the Sack Exchange had both, from Gastineau's showboating dance to the record rate at which they crumpled quarterbacks.

In 1981, before the NFL made the sack an official statistic, the Jets did it with such frequency that people realized there was a need to chart such defensive dominance. The Jets piled up sixty-six sacks that season, and the NYSE was credited with 53½ of them, a stunning proportion.

"What was created here was this system of defeating opponents by the sack," Salaam recalled. "We would stop the run, put them in a second and long, third and long, and that would change the attitude of the offense. That would cause Joe and Mark to rise, because football is about intimidation."

Joe and Mark, of course, referred to Klecko and Gastineau, who could not be contained by any offensive line. While Gastineau attracted most of the attention due to his antics, it was Klecko who led the charge that 1981 season, with 20½ sacks to Gastineau's twenty. Lyons and Salaam were the two lesser known of that foursome, but in any defensive line, there are always the unsung heroes sacrificing themselves for the glory of others.

That unselfishness was lost on Gastineau, and the gradual alienation from his teammates, along with a few devastating injuries, was a contributing factor to the NYSE soon fading from the spotlight. It didn't help that the NFL outlawed Gastineau's post-sack celebration, penalizing the Jets for his garish behavior, and that was a blow to the cocky self-confidence of the NYSE's ringleader.

But at its peak, the Jets' front four could control a game, which is why they were able to reverse a 0-3 start in 1981 and finish 10-5-1 for their first playoff berth in twelve years. For a franchise desperate for success following the Namath years, the NYSE squeezed respect from opposing quarterbacks, and there's nothing more effective at dismantling an offense than a healthy dose of fear.

I know there have been better defensive units in the history of the NFL, and the Giants, fueled by the fury of Lawrence Taylor, won two Super Bowls on the strength of theirs. But there is something about the sheer exhilaration of a sack, an adrenaline rush that stretches from the chalk-lined field to the farthest seats in the upper deck, and no one did it better than the NYSE.

The most disappointing aspect of the NYSE, aside from

Gastineau's self-destructive behavior, was how quickly it all fell apart. In 1982, Klecko ruptured a tendon in his knee during the second game of the season, and the NFL was put on hold when the players went on strike only two days later. By then, the NYSE's best moments already were behind them. Gastineau achieved a measure of individual glory with a record twenty-two sacks in 1984—Michael Strahan later eclipsed that mark—but the closing bell had pretty much sounded for the NYSE.

Rubin says: I don't know about you, Dave, but I'd prefer a defensive unit that can stop something a little more forceful than a bunch of Wall Street traders.

It's nice that you've glorified The New York Sack Exchange with your eloquent words, but any place where they'd be the choice over "The Big Blue Wrecking Crew" is one where failing to win the Super Bowl has somehow become acceptable. And that's not this town—not by a long shot.

About the only thing The New York Sack Exchange might win is a contest for cleverest nickname. The Big Blue Wrecking Crew won championships for the Giants by dominating playoff opponents from start to finish. Their personnel was better and the unit's performance was, too.

First, here's a little refresher for you on the personnel. The Crew featured linebackers Lawrence Taylor and Harry Carson as its anchors. That would be *two* Hall of Famers where that Jets quartet had exactly none. And they were surrounded by Pro Bowlers and standouts. Carl Banks and Gary Reasons rounded out what might have been the best set of linebackers ever assembled. And the defensive line of Jim Burt, Pepper Martin, and Leonard Marshall completed a front seven that's rivaled only by the group the Steelers fielded in the '70s.

The original version of The Big Blue Wrecking Crew carried

the Giants to a championship in Super Bowl XXI. It KO'd San Francisco's Joe Montana in the first round of the playoffs, pummeled Washington's Jay Schroeder in shutting out the Redskins in the NFC Championship game, and then stifled John Elway in the Super Bowl. In winning those three games against the NFL's best teams, The Crew allowed a total of twenty-three points.

While Marshall once lamented that the BBWC nickname "never really caught on," it did survive to be reborn when the Giants rolled to another championship in Super Bowl XXV with many of the original group still in place.

That year they gave up only 211 regular-season points, the least in the NFL, on their way to the playoffs. There, the Bears, 49ers, and Bills managed a total of only thirty-five points on this big-game unit.

Did The Sack Exchange boast anything similar? Were they nearly as dominant? No, sir. Not even close.

Just the concept of The New York Sack Exchange—the glorifying of an individual accomplishment—would have left Giants coach Bill Parcells and defensive coordinator Bill Belichick nauseated. They were all about putting together a defense that could stop a locomotive in its tracks. And the little dances that the NYSE would do to celebrate a sack? Don't tell me you think Parcells would have tolerated anything like that.

Dave, you are obviously enamored of the nickname and, hey, it's a pretty good one. The guys in the stands with the sheet who gave it to them? Maybe there's a gig on Jay Leno's writing staff for them. But even the most endearing thing about The Sack Exchange, the moniker, belies its inferiority.

When you take a look at the nicknames bestowed on the great defensive units of our time, you'll see exactly what I'm talking about. Minnesota had "The Purple People Eaters." Pittsburgh's was "The Steel Curtain." In Denver, it was "The Orange Crush." And the Raiders claimed "The Legion of Doom." These monikers spoke to their across-the-board success and not just single achievements by single players.

I'm thinking that maybe the four NYSE guys were too busy working on their dance steps to remember that when you play football, it's not about taking a bow. It's about taking a title, which is what The Big Blue Wrecking Crew is remembered for.

So maybe their nickname wasn't as catchy. So maybe they didn't appear in posters that were sold on Forty-second Street. My bet is the guys on The Crew were happier with their Super Bowl rings.

Dave, you point out that the most disappointing thing about The New York Sack Exchange was that it didn't hold together for very long. This brings me to my final reason for going with The Big Blue Wrecking Crew: It never disappointed.

40

Which Was the Worst Trade?

Rubin says: With nine professional sports teams, New York has had more than its share of disastrous trades, but to be the worst, it has to be something special.

A "worst trade" shouldn't just be one you look back at after a year or two, deem it a blunder, and then move on. A "worst trade" also should not be one that doesn't bother you much until you see the player dealt has crafted a Hall of Fame career.

To be a "worst trade" the deal has to punish the team that made it over and over and over again. It has to torment the team as it drags along the bottom as a result of making it. It has to be one that leaves people shaking their heads for decades.

This is why I offer you December 10, 1971, a day that will forever live in infamy for the Mets franchise. That was the day our boys in Queens sent Nolan Ryan to the Angels and, in return, got essentially nothing.

The late Bob Scheffing was the general manager back then, and it is certainly not fair to paint him with this one broad brush stroke. He was an essential part of constructing the 1973 National League pennant winner. But any praise that can be sent his way must be qualified: "Of course, he's also the guy who traded Nolan Ryan."

At the moment the deal was made, there was an incredibly myopic way of looking at it as a good move. The Mets sent Ryan, along with outfielder Leroy Stanton, pitcher Don Rose, and catcher Francisco Estrada to the Angels for infielder Jim Fregosi.

Fregosi was a six-time all-star shortstop, honors that recognized his defensive prowess but ignored his light hitting. And even though he was on the back end of his career, the Mets believed they could move him to third base and shore up their infield defense. Ryan, then twenty-four, had an incredibly live arm but little in the way of control. He hadn't won consistently, going 29-38 in three and a half seasons.

"As for Ryan, I really can't say I quit on him," Scheffing told the newspapers that day. "But we've had him three full years and, although he's a hell of a prospect, he hasn't done it for us. How long can you wait?"

How about one more year?

Ryan had shown more promise in 1971 than in any of his previous seasons, but that didn't seem to matter to the Mets front office. They saw the bottom line of a 10-14 record with a 3.97 ERA and a whopping 116 walks in 152 innings. They chose not to focus on his 8-4 start or the 137 strikeouts he recorded.

So the Mets gave up on him and made the deal. The very next season, they began to see the error of their ways. Fregosi hit an anemic .232, made fifteen errors in eighty-five games at third base, and was well on his way to being traded the next season as the Mets finished third in the NL.

Ryan pitched 284 innings for the Angels in '72, winning nineteen games and striking out 329. Dave, think about how nicely he would have fit into the rotation behind Tom Seaver, Jon Matlack, and Jerry Koosman. Can you imagine?

We all know where this story goes. Ryan becomes one of the greatest right-handed pitchers in the history of the game. He wins 295 games after leaving the Mets, becomes baseball's all-time strikeout king, and throws a record seven no-hitters in a first-ballot Hall of Fame career.

The Mets did win the 1973 pennant—although with little help from Fregosi, who was traded at midseason—and then became a disaster in the late '70s and early '80s, finishing in last place or next-to-last place seven straight seasons. Ryan, by the way, was the strikeout champion every one of those years.

In explaining the thinking that went into the deal, Scheffing said, "I can't rate him in the same category with Tom Seaver, Jerry Koosman, or Gary Gentry."

I think I can voice the thoughts of every Mets fan with two words: Think again.

Lennon says: As you've so eloquently explained, Roger, a title like this is not to be taken lightly. It has to be a deal so cataclysmic that the fallout changes the course of a franchise, alienates the team's fan base, and rains down ridicule on the front office for countless years to come.

Props to you, Rube, for picking the Nolan Ryan trade, a true stinker of a swap that the Mets will hear about until the fall of Western civilization. But I think I've got you beat on this one. I'm going with Bill Belichick, whose name I'm sure is verboten in the hallways of the Jets compound on Long Island.

I know what you're thinking. You're wondering about the legitimacy of my selection. Belichick stunningly resigned from the Jets, and then jumped into the waiting arms of Robert Kraft up in New England, essentially pulling a reverse Parcells, circa 1997.

But I'm staking my claim on a technicality. Belichick, who stepped down as the "HC of the NYJ," was still bound by contract to Gang Green, and thereby had to be traded to the Patriots for a compensatory package of draft picks. Sounds easy enough, but Belichick's attempt to dump the Jets ignited a bitter feud between Hempstead and Foxboro, with Kraft angrily declaring he would not surrender a first-round pick for a coach who wanted out of New York anyway.

That's when Commissioner Paul Tagliabue entered the fray, and ultimately set the parameters for the trade that would free Belichick and still torments the Jets to this day. By Tagliabue's edict, the Jets received the Pats' first-round pick (sixteenth overall) for the 2000 draft and two more picks—a fourth- and seventh-rounder—the following year.

At the time, the Jets figured they pulled a fast one on their AFC East rivals. Getting the Pats' pick gave them a record four selections in the first round, and for what? Belichick was considered a brilliant defensive mind under Bill Parcells, but failed in his only other head coaching job with the Cleveland Browns before coming back to serve again under his mentor in New England.

No one faulted the Jets for extorting what they could from the Patriots, and they made a big splash that April, trading up from No. 16 to draft defensive end Shaun Ellis with the twelfth overall selection. The next year, the Jets used the Pats' picks on defensive back Jamie Henderson and nose tackle James Reed.

Ellis has turned into a standout pass rusher for the Jets, with 43½ sacks in six seasons; Reed is another reliable cog on the defensive line; and Henderson's career got sidetracked by a motorcycle accident that cost him the entire 2004 season. As picks go, you'd have to say that the Jets did okay with those three—though the 2000 draft will forever be known for the Pats stealing Tom Brady in the sixth round.

As for Belichick, well, he's become the Vince Lombardi of the twenty-first century. Belichick already was regarded as a defensive genius, but together with GM Scott Pioli, he has done what the NFL thought impossible—created a dynasty in the salary-cap era. Belichick became the first coach in the eighty-five-year history of the league to win three Super Bowls in four years, and his 11-2 playoff record is actually better than Lombardi's mark.

Had the Jets known that Belichick was destined for such greatness, they surely would have thrown the Tuna overboard and tried harder to persuade his protégé to stay. And as Belichick has flourished in Foxboro, the Jets have been embarrassed by two more coaches, with Al Groh leaving for the University of Virginia and Herman Edwards fleeing to Kansas City. For a team with a serious credibility problem, that's piling it on.

Belichick alone is enough to make this the worst trade ever, but the Patriots not only got the NFL's best coach from the Jets, they also got two draft picks on top of that, a fifth-rounder in 2001 and a seventh-rounder in 2002. Just for the record, those choices became Matt Light—the Pats' best offensive lineman—and Daniel Graham, an athletic tight end who also is a ferocious blocker.

The Jets are hoping they have a Belichick clone in his former defensive coordinator Eric Mangini, now the new Jets head coach. But unless Mangini wins three of the next four Super Bowls, there's no erasing the stain Belichick's departure has left on the franchise.

NEW YORK'S TEN WORST TRADES

1. Nolan Ryan: When they drafted him, the Mets recognized he had great arm, but after three seasons without realizing his full potential, they gave up on him. In return for Ryan and prospects they got Jim Fregosi, who was expected to shore up infield defense and ended up hitting .232 in his one full season in New York. Ryan won 295 games, pitched seven no-hitters, and became the baseball's all-time strikeout king.

2. Bill Belichick: As it turns out, no amount of compensation would have vindicated the Jets for the mishandling of this one in 2000. Belichick won three Super Bowls in four seasons with the

New England Patriots and is now considered one of the greatest NFL coaches of all time. The Jets got three draft picks and had to hand over two others, along with the coach.

3. Julius Erving: This one is almost Babe Ruth-esque. After the Nets completed their final season in Long Island and were moving to the NBA and New Jersey, the club was financially strapped. Believe it or not, they opted to send Dr. J to Philadelphia for cash. Erving went on to become one of the greatest players in NBA history.

4. Tom Seaver: If the Mets hadn't traded Ryan, this would stand as their worst. In the midst of the 1977 season, they dealt the future Hall of Famer and face of the club to Cincinnati for Pat Zachry, Doug Flynn, Steve Henderson, and Dan Norman. Seaver would finish in the top four for the Cy Young Award three more times. Zachary never won more than ten games in a season for New York, Flynn never hit better than .225, Henderson was only a serviceable infielder, and Norman never became more than a part-time player.

5. Ken Phelps: The Yankees sent Jay Buhner to Seattle at the trading deadline in 1988 for the aging slugger and it remains the worst deal made since George Steinbrenner bought the team. Buhner hit more than three hundred home runs with Seattle and was a Gold Glover. Phelps hit seventeen home runs in 122 games over two half seasons and got shipped to Oakland. The deal didn't even accomplish what the Yankees had hoped: They finished fifth in the AL East in 1988.

6. Phil Esposito: The Rangers got the aging legend in the fall of 1975, when he'd already slowed a bit. Esposito played four very good seasons but the Rangers gave up too much in Jean Ratelle, Brad Park, and Joe Zanussi. Ratelle and Park in particular were big reasons why Boston was a perennial contender for most of the next decade, and reached the Stanley Cup finals in 1977 and 1978.

7. Alexi Yashin: The Islanders thought Yashin would finally become a household name when they got him in the summer of 2001. He never did. But the Ottawa Senators made their first big step in becoming one of the NHL's top teams with this move. They turned the draft pick into future star Jason Spezza and got Zdeno Chara, an outstanding complementary player.

8. Pat Verbeek: The Devils haven't made so many trading blunders, but sending Pat Verbeek to Hartford for left-winger Sylvain Turgeon was their biggest. Turgeon scored thirty goals in his one and only season for New Jersey before being dealt for team chemistry reasons. Verbeek became the Whalers' top player and later helped Dallas to a Stanley Cup.

9. Antonio McDyess: It ended up being the last deal in the Knicks' sojourn to the bottom of the NBA a few years ago. McDyess was acquired for Marcus Camby, Mark Jackson, and draft pick Nenê Hilario. A twenty-point scorer with the Nuggets, McDyess reinjured his surgically repaired knee in preseason and he missed the entirety of 2003. In 2004, he played only eighteen games for the 'Bockers. Camby, meanwhile, was finally developing into a big-time player, averaging double figures in points and rebounds the past two seasons in Denver, and Nenê averaged 10.7 points a game during his first three seasons with the Nuggets.

10. Juan Samuel: This 1989 fiasco sent two of the pillars from the 1986 World Series champion Mets—Lenny Dykstra and Roger McDowell—to the Phillies. Dykstra, who had been the Mets spark plug, played seven more seasons in Philadelphia, leading the league in hits twice and making the all-star team three times. McDowell recorded nineteen saves in the back half of 1989 and twenty-two the following year. As for Samuel, he hit .222 over eighty-six games with the Mets that season and was dealt to the Dodgers before the next one.

41

Who Is the Most Damaging "Clubhouse Cancer"?

Lennon says: My first instinct here was to go with the guys who have made our lives miserable, Rog, the media-hating types who find it funny to squirt bleach at reporters (Bret Saberhagen) or swat away TV cameras like King Kong swinging at fighter planes (Randy Johnson).

But as despicable as that behavior may be, I have to keep reminding myself that we're not the story. And on top of that, their teammates couldn't care less, probably enjoying the laugh at our expense—after the reporters are out of sight, of course.

Because of that, I feel the criteria we must use for this debate is the negative effect a player has had on his own employer, to the point where he is shunned by those in the same uniform. And in doing so, like a cancer, it eats away at the team from the inside until it is pretty much dead.

It's not a very flattering label, but bring up this question to New Yorkers and there's one name that always come shooting back: Vince Coleman. To be singled out from that 1993 Mets team, which featured Saberhagen's Clorox antics and Mr. Smiley, Bobby Bonilla, you have to be an especially bad guy, and there was no end to Coleman's malicious streak.

Again, that's the difference with Coleman. He wasn't just annoying for reporters to deal with. He was irritating and sometimes dangerous, to his teammates, the coaching staff, and (incredibly) three different managers during his infamous three-year stay on the Mets. Give Coleman credit for one thing: He crammed a lot of stupidity into a relatively short career in Flushing, and then was shown the door in the January trade for Kevin McReynolds in 1994.

It's amazing that Coleman lasted as long as he did when you check out his ridiculous résumé. In 1991, his first season with the Mets, Coleman apparently was just warming up when he earned fines for verbally sparring with two umpires, and according to umpire Mike Winters, Coleman said he would "get" Winters after the game.

Winters, as it turned out, was just an appetizer. Later that season, Coleman wigged out on batting coach Mike Cubbage before a game, storming off the field and firing his bat and helmet against the dugout wall.

But what Coleman followed up with made those incidents seem like minor traffic infractions. He was among the Mets accused of rape during spring training in 1992, though no charges were filed, and his relationship with new manager Jeff Torborg that season was not exactly warm and fuzzy. In addition to the usual ejections, which Coleman was getting known for, he went from shouting at Torborg to shoving him in September of 1992, which led to a two-day suspension without pay for what the Mets described as "insubordination."

While that already was enough to make Coleman hated within the organization, I've saved the most damning evidence for last. In April of 1993, Coleman nailed Dwight Gooden on his right shoulder swinging a golf club, causing him to miss his start that night. Doc was lucky he didn't get it in the head.

And the showstopper, the shameful event that brought the curtain down on Coleman's Mets career, happened outside of Dodger Stadium, where Coleman allegedly threw a firecracker, maybe even a cherry bomb, toward a group of fans leaving the game. Not surprisingly, Bonilla was with him in the car, and among those injured by the explosion was a thirty-three-year-old woman, a one-year-old girl, and an eleven-year-old boy. Coleman was investigated by the Los Angeles Fire Department and later charged with endangerment, which was appropriate considering he had been nothing but a menace to the Mets. Even his attempt at an apology was ridiculous, and Coleman became more embarrassing to the Mets by the day.

"Most people doesn't know athletes on a personal level, you only know what the media has portrayed us," Coleman said in a statement after the incident. "I personally in the last few days have been portrayed as an insensitive, noncaring athlete."

Wow, Vince. How did anyone get that idea?

Sick of his idiocy, the Mets essentially banished Coleman—they referred to it as a break to allow him to deal with his legal issues—and he never played another inning for them. The Mets wished he never had in the first place.

Rubin says: This question is one of the toughest, Dave, but not for the reason most people think.

When you make a choice on this one, you're going for a truly destructive force. You need someone who drew the enmity of the team's front office or coach or his teammates. He's got to be someone who sucks the life out of a team and drags it on down to the bottom.

My problem is I just keep on coming up with members of the Mets. Rickey Henderson may have been loved by his teammates, but I'm betting no one else in the organization was crazy about him admiring long fly balls that went off the wall, but not over it, or about him starting a card game in the clubhouse during a crucial playoff game. Bobby Bonilla could win in this category. So could bleach-squirting Bret Saberhagen.

With your choice of Vince Coleman, I have to say, you may have gotten the worst of all the Mets' cancers. And I feel like going with another Mets player would just be piling on the franchise. So I'm going to go with "Worst Clubhouse Cancer not on the Mets." And I'm afraid that has to fall to Stephon Marbury. It's not easy to paste the label "cancer" on someone who was once New York's favorite basketball son. But what transpired in the 2005–06 season was pretty opinion-shaping.

Marbury was a delight to cover at Lincoln High School in Brooklyn and a lot of fun for Bobby Cremins and the guys at Georgia Tech. I have no idea how he became the guy who was in the tug-of-war with coach Larry Brown, who's been one of the most successful basketball men of this era.

Now, I'm not going to lay all the Knicks problems down at Marbury's feet. Brown played a big part, too. So did general manager Isiah Thomas. And with these three in play, even owner Charles Dolan himself was left admitting that he looked like an idiot. But the star of the team was front-and-center on this debacle, bringing the team down with his albatross of a contract and even bigger ego.

Marbury has declared himself the best point guard in the NBA, even though he has yet to be part of a team that has won a playoff series. In the middle of the '05–'06 season, he began invoking a self-made alter ego—"Starbury"—in saying that he had been playing too unselfishly, and was too restrained by Brown's style of play.

"I went into this year trying to do something, to put myself in a situation where we can win, okay? To help the team win games," Marbury told the *Daily News'* Frank Isola after the team had sunk to the worst record in the league. "Unfortunately, that didn't happen. So, what do I do now, as far as the way I play? I go back to playing like Stephon Marbury, aka Starbury. I haven't been Starbury this year. I've been some other dude this year."

Brown, lured away from the conference champion Pistons before the season, was less than subtle about where he placed the blame. He held Marbury out of games during critical interludes, telling reporters it was because the team needed to play better defense, and shrugged off the "Starbury" talk by saying it must be the guard's way of challenging himself.

Marbury's been nobody's favorite in the locker room either.

For people who do what we do, Marbury has been great. He's candid with his opinions. He doesn't hold anything back. He has a flare for the pithy word. And his style is still so admired that NBA merchandise bearing his name remains among the league's five best sellers.

The public spat between him and Brown during this past season—in which each has criticized the other's approach to getting the team on a winning track—left Dolan in quite a pinch heading to the off-season. It's clear that the two of them could not coexist to the benefit of the team; and so the owner was left with the difficult choice between his prized coaching coup and his most-talented player.

Marbury prevailed there, but it's hard to see where anyone will end up a winner anytime soon.

Who Is the Best Pitcher?

Lennon says: In most cases, it would be unthinkable to choose a reliever in this situation. There's just a natural bias against guys from the bullpen, mainly because they are generally viewed as rotation dropouts, flawed pitchers simply not good enough to succeed in a starting role. It's probably the only reason Goose Gossage is still waiting for his ticket to Cooperstown.

But there is no debate when it comes to Mariano Rivera, who not only has been the best pitcher in New York during his ten-year stay in the Bronx, but has to be considered one of the most dominating hurlers to ever take the mound for the Yankees.

Was there a more important piece to the Yankees' recent dynasty? No chance. Maybe they win two rings instead of four without Derek Jeter or Bernie Williams. But if the Yankees didn't have Rivera waiting in the bullpen, either as baseball's most effective setup man in 1996 or as closer in the years immediately after, there would have been no renaissance in the Bronx. We'd be saluting the Mariners or Indians instead.

And when it comes to awards, Rivera is in the running for the Cy Young every year and frequently gets votes for the MVP, the latter being an extremely rare honor for pitchers, especially those of the relief variety. Though he's never won the Cy Young, Rivera finished second in 2005, and third in 1996, 1999, and 2004. He's also only the second pitcher since 1997 to place in the top ten for the American League MVP voting, finishing ninth in 2004 and 2005.

"To me, he's the greatest modern-day weapon I have seen or played against," said Alex Rodriguez, a two-time MVP himself. "He has been the heart and soul of the New York Yankees dynasty."

This is not meant to be a knock against Joe Torre, but how do you think he got to be such a great manager? Is he really that different than he was with the Mets, Braves, and Cardinals? Or is Torre just incredibly lucky that his career path veered into Rivera's at the right time in history?

With Rivera as setup man to John Wetteland in 1996, the Yankees were 70-3 when leading after the sixth inning. After taking over for Wetteland the following season, Rivera had the second-best conversion rate (87.9 percent) among closers with at least 150 saves.

I think Torre would be the first to admit that he owes his rings, in large part, to Rivera—as does everyone else in the Yankees organization.

"Without question we're talking about the best reliever, in my opinion, in the history of baseball," general manager Brian Cashman said. "This guy has become branded with the Yankee logo. People are going to remember this man for so long for what he's done."

What has he done? Rivera, armed with his lethal cut-fastball, has put up unprecedented numbers during his pin-striped reign of terror, becoming one of baseball's most feared pitchers, especially in October. He has the all-time lowest postseason ERA (0.81) and his thirty-four saves are the most in playoff history. Rivera also owns the postseason record with 34½ scoreless innings. If official scorers kept track of broken bats, he'd be the record-holder in that category, too.

Rivera's dominance has illustrated how a lights-out closer can be the key to a championship, even when he's surrounded by an all-star cast like the $200-million Yankees. He's the only reliever to win the ALCS MVP (2003) and World Series MVP awards, and there is no minimizing the feeling of hopelessness for the opposition when Metallica's "Enter Sandman" blares from the Yankee Stadium loud-speakers.

It's amazing to think how close Rivera came to never becoming a Yankee legend. The club considered trading him twice—once for David Wells during his rookie season in 1995 and again in the winter of 1997, after Rivera, in his first year as John Wetteland's replacement, allowed the home run to Sandy Alomar Jr. that knocked the Yankees out of the playoffs.

But they wisely chose to stick with Rivera, and that turned out to be one of the best decisions the Yankees have ever made.

Rubin says: Well, you've made it pretty hard on me, Dave, but I think I am up to the task.

Mariano Rivera is practically a lock to give you a great inning or two every time he is summoned into a game and has perfected the specialty of closing games during an awesome ten-year run in New York. How does anyone make an argument against someone like that?

The answer is simpler than it seems. You go with a guy who gives you nine great innings every time he is in the game and is probably the only pitcher who had a better decade in the Big Apple. You go with Tom Seaver.

I'm sorry, but what Rivera does for the Yankees today is something that only has become valuable in the last twenty years. Though he is a sure bet for Cooperstown, it is worth noting that when he gets there, he'll be among only about a half dozen pitchers that do his thing. Seaver was a starting pitcher—one of the best ever—and starting pitching has always been the more fashionable commodity. One of the top right-handers ever to take a mound, when Seaver was elected to the Hall of Fame on his first ballot, he was selected by 98.8 percent of the voters, which was a landslide like almost no other.

Rivera is nearly unhittable for about seventy-five innings a season. Seaver was nearly unhittable for almost 275 innings a season during his first ten with the Mets before his unfortunate trade to the Reds (one of the worst deals a New York team ever made). And all that hardware that Rivera keeps missing out on? Seaver won three Cy Young Awards—1969, 1973, and 1975—and finished ninth or higher for the MVP four times. In 1969 he was edged out for it by Willie McCovey, even though they had the same number of first-place votes.

Moreover, Seaver is the guy responsible for giving the Mets a winning tradition. In '69 he went 25-7 with a 2.21 ERA, and the Miracle Mets, who'd never won more than seventy-three games, triumphed in one hundred and then took the World Series. He had nineteen wins in 1973 when the team captured its second pennant.

Here's a look at a decade of dominance by the guy: From 1967 to 1976 he averaged nineteen wins, was an all-star nine times, a victories champ twice, an ERA champ three times, and a strikeout champ all ten seasons.

"What was special about him as a pitcher? You'd have to write a novel," said Jerry Grote, who caught him with the Mets. "Nolan Ryan left guys shaking their heads, believing they were overmatched. With Seaver, they'd get struck out and credit him with having made a good pitch. They'd come up again, strike out again, and credit him with having made another good pitch. Then, the game would be over and Seaver would be in double figures in strikeouts. The guy didn't make bad pitches."

Seaver had the overpowering fastball and the precision slider, but he also used his changeup and curve very effectively. Even though he was a power pitcher in the truest sense of the words, it was his guile and smarts that set him apart from the other greats who wore that label.

"He had such presence of mind," Grote said. "He never had to be reminded of anything. He was always ahead of hitters. I don't mean in the count. I mean in his thinking."

And if all that weren't enough—and it is—Tom Terrific also was great ambassador for the game. His style, placid demeanor, and class were not only an example to be followed, they seemed to hark back to the humbler roots of the game when players didn't browbeat cameramen or talk about themselves in the third person.

The former commissioner of baseball, A. Bartlett Giamatti, once wrote this for *Harper's* magazine: "With consummate effortlessness, his was the talent that summed up baseball tradition; his was the respect for the rules that embodied baseball's craving for law; his was the personality, intensely competitive, basically decent, with the artisan's dignity, that amidst the brave but feckless Mets, in a boom time of leisure soured by divisions and drugs, seemed to recall a cluster of virtues seemingly no longer valued."

That was Tom Seaver: Carve 'em up on the field and kill 'em with class off of it.

Greater Accomplishment: Three Straight World Series Crowns or Four Straight Stanley Cup Titles?

Rubin says: There haven't been that many dynasties during the past thirty-five years. That makes us lucky in New York: We've had two—the 1980–83 Islanders and the 1998–2000 Yankees. Each did something stupendous and should be hailed for it. But this question calls for a comparison and, Dave, I am afraid that when you stack them up, it's no contest at all.

Picking the Yankees' achievement over the Islanders is easier to do than naming the teams that lost any of the seven titles in question.

To measure the grandiosity of any accomplishment, my friend, context is needed. Allow me to provide it.

When the Bombers finished off the Mets in 2000, they became the first team to win three straight titles since the Oakland A's did it twenty-six years earlier. When the Islanders swept the Oilers for Lord Stanley's Cup in 1983, they became the first team to win four straight titles since . . . the four years before their string started.

That's right, Dave, the Montreal Canadiens won four straight ending in 1979. In fact, winning three or more in a row practically happens all the time in the NHL. It's happened five times in the last fifty-five years. Kinda takes away from the luster of it all, doesn't it?

While this could very well be the "I rest my case, your honor" moment, allow me to underscore exactly how tough what the Yankees did was.

There are a handful of things that usually prevent baseball teams from repeating twice or three times. One is injuries, something luck obviously plays a role in. Another is egos, of which there is no shortage in baseball, particularly around the Yankees' clubhouse. A third is keeping a winning unit together, and with free agency running amok beginning in the late '90s, it's no easy task.

Ask the current editions of the Yankees how easy it is to keep pitchers—particularly older ones—off the disabled list. The Bombers were a fortunate group with respect to injuries during 1998, 1999, and 2000, if you take a good hard look. David Cone was thirty-five, thirty-six, and thirty-seven years old yet made ninety-two starts during those seasons. Orlando (El Duque) Hernandez made eighty-three starts even though he was in his mid-thirties (we think). Roger Clemens was thirty-six and thirty-seven during the last two of those seasons and made sixty-two. It's not too often you get three guys of that age in one rotation and no one suffers a breakdown.

The other part of keeping the team together is re-signing those players who become free agents. At just a cursory glance, you can see that Cone was inked to new deals twice and Scott Brosius, Bernie Williams, and Mike Stanton once each. Of course, an argument could be made that the Yankees had the unnatural advantage of having free-spending George Steinbrenner as an owner, but good players always have more than one suitor.

That egos never derailed the Yankees juggernaut is a credit to manager Joe Torre. These teams were laden with stars, but Torre found a way to get everyone to put winning ahead of himself, something that doesn't happen very often. Dave, I'd love to tell you that the Islanders dealt with a similar issue, but I just don't see it. It's hard to get a big head on skates, especially when you're playing the No. 4 sport.

There are lots of other reasons that what the Yankees did was the greater accomplishment. They had to contend with being one of the most scrutinized teams in sports while the Islanders, from their safe haven in Nassau County, never got the analysis that the Yankees did. They had to play a grueling 162-game season while the Islanders had an eighty-two-gamer. They had had to play in a tougher division—with the archrival Red Sox—than the Islanders and they also had to deal with the emotional weight of Torre's prostate cancer diagnosis during the 1999 season.

Dave, my intention here is not to belittle what the Islanders did over four magnificent seasons. The Yankees won only three titles to their four, but they still did them one better.

Lennon says: Time out for a second, Roger. I want to make sure I've read this correctly. You're trying to dis the Islanders by saying their four-peat is the type of thing that happens all the time in hockey? Just because the Montreal Canadiens did it right before them? And such a streak has been done five times in fifty-five years?

Correct me if I'm wrong, but the Yankees have won twenty-six world championships, including nine in a fourteen-year span that ended in '62, and five straight, from 1949 to 1953. Obviously, that was a different era, with fewer teams and a different playoff format. But every sport evolves over the years, and creates its own unique challenges for defending champions.

Here's how the Yankees adapted to that Darwinian concept: George Steinbrenner ultimately decided to outspend everyone else. When you have the most money, it's a logical strategy, especially when any four of the Yankees' players make as much as the entire rosters of some teams.

I'll give the Yankees props for their 1998 title, when their $72-million payroll was not the highest in the sport—that dubious honor belonged to the Orioles—and they won 114 games during the regular season. That's downright economical, a miserly $630,000 per victory. Not bad.

But once The Boss got a taste of the champagne again, he was addicted, and the Yankees' payroll jumped to $97 million in 1999 and $114 million in 2000. By then, the genie was out of the bottle, and the Yankees left their more fiscally responsible rivals in the dust.

Don't tell me that balancing egos was the difference during that three-peat, Rog. Steinbrenner can't even balance his checkbook.

So that brings me to the Islanders, a dynasty that basically was built from scratch. They started out as an expansion team in 1972, had the worst season in history when they finished 12-60-6, but a decade later, the Islanders were the class of the NHL.

The Islanders didn't even win their first division title until 1978, and a year later, they became as close to invincible as anyone in hockey—including the prestigious Canadiens, otherwise known as the Yankees of the NHL.

Like Torre with the Yankees, the Isles had Al Arbour, the coach responsible for keeping the machine running at optimum levels. The Islanders had plenty of talent, too, with three eventual Hall of Famers—Mike Bossy, Dennis Potvin, and Billy Smith—as the guardians of the dynasty.

But hoisting a cup is no skate in the park. Just to get to the finals, the Islanders had to win four playoff rounds, including the first two against divisional rivals. Remember what those wars were like against the Rangers?

Sure the Yankees and Red Sox are supposed to hate each other, but they can keep a safe distance from each other on the field. That's not the case on the ice, where you can freely express your hatred by jamming the butt end of a stick into someone's mouth or splattering them into the boards. Just surviving those early rounds doesn't sound so easy to me.

The Islanders also continued their dominance during the NHL's realignment for the 1981–82 season, when they ran off a record fifteen consecutive wins. Somehow, despite the grueling nature of the sport, the Islanders also appeared to get stronger as the playoffs wore on, winning their last two Stanley Cups with sweeps of the Canucks and the mighty Oilers—an explosive offensive team that featured Wayne Gretzky and Mark Messier.

How special were these Islanders? They made it to the brink of tying the Canadiens' record of five straight Stanley Cup titles—winning nineteen consecutive playoff series—before the Oilers got their revenge by beating them in five games in the 1984 finals.

You're right about one thing, Rog. The Islanders, way out there in Uniondale, only get a tiny fraction of the attention focused on the Yankees. But what they did during that Stanley Cup four-peat is a greater accomplishment in my book. And by last count, four world titles is one more than three.

"We're not the Yankees," Islanders center Butch Goring said after winning that fourth Cup. "We don't go running around telling everyone how great we are. We just go out on the ice every night and show how good we are."

You tell 'em, Butch.

Who Is the Most Overrated Athlete?

Lennon says: Give me a minute here, Rog, to set the scene for you. Lights dimmed at the Garden, another sellout crowd, music thumping, and here comes your answer.

"At center . . . No. 33 . . . Paaaaatrick Ewwwing."

By the end, was there a bigger buzz-kill for the World's Most Famous Arena than seeing a gimpy Ewing slowly rise up off the bench and trot out to high-five his teammates? It's never pretty for any professional athlete running on fumes, but for Ewing, his final days in orange and blue just felt a little emptier.

For all Ewing accomplished in those fifteen seasons with the Knicks, the one thing he did not do will always loom larger than his seven-foot shadow, and that is win an NBA championship. Ewing is the face of the Knicks' failure during his tenure, and despite a well-decorated career, there's no sugarcoating the fact that he was never quite as good as he was supposed to be. And no bargain, either. Ewing raked in about $120 million.

Conspiracy theorists still insist the NBA rigged the 1985 draft lottery so the nation's top media market—I mean, the Knicks—could select Ewing as the No. 1 overall pick. Commissioner David Stern got his wish when Ewing provided instant credibility for the previously woeful Knicks, and the former Hoya's arrival sparked a roundball renaissance at the Garden.

Here's the problem: While the Knicks were good with Ewing, they were never good enough, and that falls on the wide shoulders of the Big Fella. If Ewing truly is one of the NBA's fifty greatest players, as he was voted, shouldn't that include a critical basket or two along the way?

But Ewing's specialty wasn't winning titles. It was predicting them. Incorrectly, I might add. Every time the Knicks were headed for a Game 7 or a Game 6 or a Game 5, someone would inevitably ask Ewing about his thoughts, and then came the "guarantee." Being a reporter myself, I have to admit that's cool with me. That's the kind of talk that sells newspapers. But after a while, you need to deliver, otherwise things get ugly.

And ugly is what always happened to the Knicks. The enduring image of Ewing, unfair or not, is the one of him missing that potential tying layup at the buzzer in Game 7 against the Pacers during the 1994–95 playoffs. There was Ewing, tiptoeing into the lane, flipping up a finger-roll, and then—*doink*—bouncing it off the back rim. Knicks lose, series over.

At least Ewing took a shot that night. The previous year, in the NBA Finals against Houston, Ewing virtually disappeared in the fourth quarter of Game 7, scoring four points and missing the only two shots—both jumpers, of course—he took inside three minutes. Many blame John Starks for the series-clinching loss because of his 2-for-18 performance from the field, but Ewing should have asserted himself with a title on the line. I don't have the list in front of me, but I'm guessing that's what everyone else on that Top 50 list would do.

That 1993–94 season was supposed to be Ewing's year, too. Michael Jordan did the Knicks a favor by retiring to pursue an ill-advised baseball career, and Ewing still couldn't get a ring in his absence. To me, there's just something missing there. The truly great players find another gear when it matters most, not spin their wheels. And toward the end of Ewing's reign at the Garden, when the injuries set in, it seemed like the Knicks, spurred by Allan Houston and Latrell Sprewell, were better without him.

And how good was Ewing compared to his contemporaries? He was never the most dominant player in the league, or even close. Ewing did win Rookie of the Year in 1985, but from then until he retired in 2002, he was twenty-second overall in points per game (20.98) and fifteenth in rebounds per game (9.81)—which, ironically, was the same rebound total Charles Oakley averaged during that time frame.

I don't see Oakley's number hanging from the Garden rafters, and he helped the Knicks win as many NBA championships as Ewing did.

Rubin says: You and I are quite a pair, Dave. Nothing like taking a few moments out of the day to tear down some icons. For our most overrated athletes we've chosen to go after two of the most famous. At least we're aiming high.

You had to go with Patrick Ewing because he never delivered a championship, and you make a hell of an argument. My pick is both more daring and more accurate. The choice here is Brooklyn's own Mike Tyson, and that's in *spite* of his becoming a champion.

Ewing, at least, was playing against the very best competition the sport had to offer, especially when the Knicks were in the playoffs. Tyson? When he wasn't taking out fading greats he was pounding on no-names. And anytime "Iron Mike" got matched with a serious contender, he got beat like a drum.

It would seem every great boxer has something in his arsenal that makes him superior: a jab or a hook, foot speed, or the ability to take punches and wear opponents down. Tyson's best weapon was his ability to intimidate, and his handlers always made sure he was matched up against someone who was vulnerable to it.

When he first won the WBC championship, he took out an aging and frightened Trevor Berbick, who lost every shot he got at a world title afterward. He then had title defenses against contenders like Pinklon Thomas, Tyrell Biggs, Tony Tucker, Tony Tubbs, Frank Bruno, and Carl Williams.

Let's face it: This wasn't exactly Ali taking on Frazier and Foreman and Liston. None of these guys was truly champion material.

I almost forgot about some of his other marquee fights as champion. There was a four-round knockout of ancient Larry Holmes and a first-round knockout of 'fraidy cat Michael Spinks, a former light-heavyweight champion.

It wasn't until he fought James "Buster" Douglas in Tokyo on February 11, 1990, that Tyson was completely exposed. Douglas was a 42–1 underdog, which explains why the fight took place at 1 A.M. Eastern time; no one was interested. But Douglas did things other fighters had failed to do: really tag Tyson with some punches. Iron Mike folded like an aluminum lawn chair.

"Mike Tyson was a terrific fighter," boxing writer Jose Torres told the *Baltimore Sun*. "He knew when to punch, where to connect, and he knew the application of power and speed. But when he began to get hit, he lost all determination [and] confidence in himself."

The Buster Douglas fight produced the enduring image of this so-called "great fighter": Douglas dancing around and Tyson on all fours trying to put his mouthpiece back in. As soon as he'd been dethroned, the meteoric decline began. His marriage to Robin Givens fell apart. He filed for bankruptcy after earning more than $300 million. And, of course, there was the rape conviction that landed him in the clink.

Take a good hard look at the fights Tyson won after he was released from prison. There was his comeback bout over Peter McNeeley (this guy actually lost to Butterbean) and the first-round downing of Bruce Seldon, who appeared to go to the canvas without getting hit.

But when Tyson finally came up against another true contender, Evander Holyfield, he was back in trouble. Holyfield was not only unintimidated by Mr. "I'm gonna make you my girlfriend," but also hit back. Hard.

Holyfield battered Tyson in an eleven-round TKO that clearly shook the last of his confidence in the ring. When the two were matched again, Tyson freakishly bit one of Holyfield's ears, getting himself disqualified rather than taking another whupping from a superior fighter.

By the end of his career Tyson was a real loser. He dropped three of his final four fights—all by knockouts—to Lennox Lewis, Danny Williams, and Kevin McBride. Not exactly Ali going out by dropping a twelve-round decision to Leon Spinks.

In fact, there was nothing about Tyson that really compared with the other truly great fighters of the modern era, including Ali, Frazier, Foreman, and Holyfield.

45

Is There a More Dominant Defensive Force Than Lawrence Taylor?

Rubin says: Every sport has had superior athletes and superlative performers, Dave. It's the reason guys like you and me are always being asked for our Top 10 athletes from this sport or that, who played this position or the other. But when you look down such lists, chances are you're only going to see the names of those who piled up great numbers.

How many of them did so while changing their sport or revolutionizing their position?

These athletes are rarities; they come along once in a generation. Lawrence Taylor was one of them and we are all lucky to have been able to see him play. He combined abilities we'd never seen before with incredible instincts and unmatched ferociousness to become the most feared player in the NFL for a decade.

There hasn't been a defensive player—before or after—who could have an impact on a game the way he did for the Giants.

Taylor changed the way people think about outside linebacker, and turned a complementary position into one of the most important on the field. It was the ridiculous athleticism of Taylor—a 6'4" freight train of a man—that reshaped all that.

Taylor made it seem like the norm to pursue a running back across the entire length of the field to make a tackle. He made it appear commonplace for a member of the front seven to cover a wideout on a deep route. On a pass rush, he could throw an offensive lineman aside like a rag doll with his strength or leave him falling over in his tracks with his speed and fancy footwork.

"Lawrence Taylor was one of the first guys that an offense actually had to try to take him out of a game," Indianapolis Colts coach Tony Dungy told *Newsday* shortly after Taylor's retirement. "Usually it's the other way around, where you're looking to take a running back or a wide receiver out of the game. Just look at all the things he can do. He has that tomahawk from the back side where he'll force a fumble. He has the spin moves, the speed rush around the corner to the quarterback. You didn't see all that in one player before Lawrence Taylor came along."

It was noticeable, too, and not just to the coaches and coordinators who were asked to devise a way to stop him or mimic him. Taylor became only the second defensive player to be named the NFL's MVP when he recorded 20½ sacks in the Giants' 1986 championship season. In a thirteen-year career, he amassed 142 sacks and almost 1,100 tackles and was selected to the Pro Bowl ten times.

John Madden once said of him, "Lawrence Taylor, defensively, has had as big an impact as any player I've ever seen. He changed the way defense is played, the way pass-rushing is played, the way linebackers play, and the way offenses block linebackers."

There are two things about Taylor that never showed up in the stat sheets that were almost as valuable as the contributions he made after a ball was snapped: his leadership and his ability to intimidate.

Taylor is well known for running his mouth, but when he spoke in the Giants' locker room everyone listened. How many times did we see him whip The Big Blue Wrecking Crew into a frenzy during the Giants' run to the Super Bowl in 1986?

And no one could describe the way he could terrorize an opposing team like he did. As Taylor has told it on a number of occasions, during one game, Philadelphia quarterback Ron Jaworski was lining up behind center and having trouble picking up Taylor's location. Jaworski began barking out "Where's fifty-six?" and Taylor stood up from his stance to respond, "Don't worry, big boy, I'll be right there."

Taylor just got into an offensive player's head that way, making an already devastating player even more lethal.

Bottom line is this, Dave: If we were going to hold a mock draft of all the players from pro football history, who would be the first defensive player chosen? I'm betting each of us would take LT before any other.

Lennon says: There's no denying LT's greatness, and I can't help but agree with you, Roger, when you say he revolutionized the position of outside linebacker. His Hall of Fame résumé speaks for itself, and watching Taylor sack an opposing quarterback was like seeing a great white shark devour a baby seal. In football, no one was higher than LT on the food chain, and anyone who stood between him and the QB was considered an appetizer before the entrée.

Where this debate gets sticky is calling Taylor the most dominant defensive player during our contemporary time frame of the last thirty-five years. And there are a few reasons why he has to share the title with a handful of players who possess the same blend of intimidation and talent.

First off, like many of the elite, Taylor benefited from playing in a superior defensive scheme with the Giants—engineered by head coach Bill Parcells and coordinator Bill Belichick—that included plenty of Pro Bowl–caliber players.

Harry Carson, the outstanding middle linebacker between Taylor and Carl Banks, was the team's captain for ten of his thirteen years and made it to Honolulu nine times. In the Giants' 4-3 defense, it was up to the front four to tie up the offensive linemen, leaving

Carson as the primary run-stopper and giving an edge rusher like LT a free shot at the quarterback.

Obviously, Taylor still thwarted every effort to stop him, or even slow him down, but it's not like LT was the only one opposing teams had to worry about. Brutish defensive tackle Jim Burt, another Pro Bowler, anchored the D-line for the two championship teams in 1986 and 1990.

With so much specialization, along with more and more complicated defenses, it's difficult for one player to be singled out in football, like Michael Jordan or Barry Bonds. Taylor did just that when he was voted MVP in 1986—only the second defensive player to win the award—but that is a nearly impossible feat in this era, which always chooses to recognize the glitzier offensive stars such as Peyton Manning.

Take the Ravens' Ray Lewis, for example. Many consider him a modern-day LT, and without him, Baltimore is nothing, as they showed during the 2005 season when he was sidelined because of a torn hamstring. Lewis was named the MVP of Super Bowl XXXV, in which the Ravens embarrassed the Giants, 38–7, and that was after he won Defensive Player of the Year honors that same season. Then there's Reggie White, Bruce Smith, Jack Youngblood, and Deacon Jones.

How about the menacing characters of Pittsburgh's "Steel Curtain" defense during the '70s? Could anyone dictate the course of a game better than Mean Joe Greene? Like Taylor, the Steelers' defensive tackle is a Hall of Famer, and he had help, too, playing on the same line with L.C. Greenwood, Dwight "Mad Dog" White, and Ernie Holmes.

As far as linebackers, Jack Lambert's gap-toothed sneer was the last thing many opposing QBs saw before getting flattened. Unlike Taylor, Lambert played the middle, but he doled out punishment like few before or after him. And it's impossible to make a statistical comparison, because the NFL didn't chart many of those defensive numbers before 1981, which is when counting sacks became official. In Lambert's case, his domination had to be seen to be believed, and those who witnessed it at the time would stack him up against anybody.

"He had no teeth and he was slobbering all over himself," Broncos QB John Elway once said of his first meeting with Lambert. "I'm thinking, you can have your money back. Just get me out of here. Let me go be an accountant."

Domination can be interpreted many ways on a football field, and that's why Taylor doesn't get to wear the belt all by himself. Guys like Lambert and Lewis are every bit as important to their teams as Taylor, perhaps even more so during their particular eras, and can hit equally as hard.

Which Was the Greatest Championship?

Rubin says: I've got six words that make it clear that no championship in our time frame here stands above the New York Rangers' 1994 Stanley Cup: "Now I can die in peace."

These six words—which appeared on a sign that was held up as the Rangers put the wraps on the Game 7 triumph over the Vancouver Canucks—summed up the anxiety and frustration of a people who had gone fifty-four years without a championship celebration and finally had one.

Rangers fans are among New York's most passionate and loyal. They consistently sell out the Garden, they flock to player appearances, and they relish every opportunity to disparage a rival.

Over those fifty-three seasons that they went without a Stanley Cup, Blueshirt faithful got more than their share of torment. While they saw their team come close and fall short on so many occasions, they had to endure seeing just about every other team reach a pinnacle. During the drought, the Yankees won fourteen titles, the hated Islanders four, the Giants three, and the Mets and Knicks two apiece. Heck, even the Brooklyn Dodgers and New York Giants won a World Series and the Jets captured a Super Bowl.

And you want to talk about frustration? The Rangers lost in the Stanley Cup finals three years—1950, 1972, and 1979—and in the Conference championship four others: 1971, 1973, 1974, and 1986.

Some of these defeats came under the most aggravating of circumstances. None probably stands out more than the seven-game defeat in 1950 at the hands of the Detroit Red Wings. That year, Madison Square Garden wasn't available for playoff games because its owners had an agreement to host the circus. The Blueshirts had to play "home games" at Toronto's Maple Leaf Gardens and, even though they were robbed of that advantage, still took it to the limit.

The 1994 Stanley Cup championship was New York's greatest not only because it finally brought an end to the torment, but it did so in such a satisfying way. You know how Boston Red Sox fans say that winning the 2004 World Series became even more satisfying because they eliminated the Yankees? The Rangers had their own version of that a decade earlier.

En route to that spectacular moment when team captain Mark Messier hoisted the Cup over his head, the Rangers got to vanquish both teams in the neighborhood rivalry. They opened with a sweet first-round sweep of the Islanders and ousted the New Jersey Devils in a seven-game conference championship that culminated with a postseason contest some call the greatest in the sport's history.

Messier actually set the table for that incredible game when, with the Rangers down three game to two against the Devils, he guaranteed a Game 6 victory. Then he delivered the win with a hat trick.

In the series clincher, the Rangers took their fans on the ultimate roller-coaster ride. Who can forget that they took a 1–0 lead into the final period? Or how they gave up a goal to Devil Valeri Zelepukin just 7.7 seconds before clinching a berth in the finals? At that moment, all the long-suffering Rangers fans were just staring into the abyss with "this is not happening again" on the tips of their tongues.

And then their heroes brought them back. Stephane Matteau's goal in the second overtime was the clincher.

There were so many bold things that happened on the way to

the Promised Land. Some will look at the 1990 acquisition of Messier as the key. Others will point to the trading deadline deals for Matteau, Brian Noonan, Glenn Anderson, and Craig MacTavish. And others still will suggest it was just clutch guys like Matteau and Brian Leetch who got it done.

What they'll all agree about is that it was the triumph that let an entire segment of our population finally breathe.

Lennon says: Well, Roger, I can trump your argument in six words or less. Two, in fact: Who cares?

The Rangers winning the Stanley Cup is not exactly the Red Sox conquering the Curse of the Bambino, an eighty-six-year-old hex that sent a generation of New Englanders to their graves without a title.

And why do I bring that up in this discussion? I'd be willing to bet that New Yorkers cared a whole lot more about the Red Sox finally earning a ring than any hockey season, whether it ended with a championship or not.

In NHL circles, and for the eighteen thousand or so puckheads that fill Madison Square Garden for their beloved Blueshirts, the Rangers' magical run to the Cup certainly was the thrill of a lifetime.

As for everyone else in New York—yes, even Mets fans have to admit—the Yankees are the gold standard for greatness, and no team was greater than the stellar group that rolled to the 1998 World Series crown.

Don't believe me? Says so right on the ring, "Best Team Ever." I've seen it with my own eyes. And in this case, it's not George Steinbrenner merely flaunting a self-important streak as wide as Broadway. The 1998 Yankees not only won the Fall Classic, after a one-year hiatus, but they went a jaw-dropping 125-50 en route to their twenty-fourth world championship.

For those scoring at home, that's a .714 winning percentage, and a level of excellence unheard of in baseball, where even good teams lose once every three games. Those Yankees, however, rarely lost. They set an American League record with 114 wins during the regular season, topping the 1954 Indians (111), and their 125 victories overall blew away the previous mark of the 1906 Cubs (118).

Once the Yankees moved into first place in the AL East on April 21, 1998, they stayed there for 159 consecutive days, and finished twenty-two games ahead of Boston. Only the 1902 Pirates had a bigger margin over the runner-up, burying Brooklyn by 27½ games.

To be honest, the constant winning robbed the regular season of any real drama, aside from that May 17 afternoon in the Bronx, when David Wells fired a perfect game, the first for the Yankees since Don Larsen's gem in the 1956 World Series.

But that special Sunday was merely the teaser of what was to follow, and I don't mean Wells's loathsome autobiography, *Perfect I'm Not.* The Yankees clinched the AL East on September 9, beating the Red Sox for win number 102, kicked around the Devil Rays for the record-clinching 112th victory on September 25, and then had to cope with the sobering news that Darryl Strawberry had been diagnosed with colon cancer.

Though unnerved by their teammate's illness, these Yankees showed their affection for Strawberry by steamrolling whoever stood in their way from that point. They swept the Rangers in the Division Series, dismissed the Indians in the ALCS, and the Padres never had a chance in the World Series.

Well, let me take that back. San Diego had a sliver of hope in Game 1. The Padres' Kevin Brown—yes, that Kevin Brown—was clinging to a 5–2 lead through six innings in the Bronx before Chuck Knoblauch's three-run homer tied the score in the seventh.

Later that same inning, with the bases loaded, reliever Mark Langston appeared to have struck out Tino Martinez on a 2-and-2 pitch that definitely looked over the plate. Instead, Martinez swatted the next pitch for a grand slam—the first in a World Series game for the Yankees since Joe Pepitone's blast in 1964—and the Padres never recovered.

In Game 2, El Duque became the first Yankees rookie to win a World Series start since Jim Beattie in 1978; and Scott Brosius belted a pair of homers in Game 3, the second a three-run shot off closer Trevor Hoffman.

Brosius, playing in his first postseason series, was named MVP, mostly for his Game 3 heroics, but he also batted .471. And then there was a budding star named Mariano Rivera.

Nearly traded the previous off-season after serving up that crushing home run to Sandy Alomar Jr. in the ALDS loss to Cleveland, Rivera pitched 13 1/10 scoreless innings during the 1998 playoffs. He was 6-for-6 in save opportunities, with a 0.51 ERA.

Greatness? C'mon. Who's kidding whom here.

47

Who Is the Darling of the U.S. Open?

Rubin says: The real darling of the U.S. Open is the only tennis player who could raise the volume at Arthur Ashe Stadium to near-painful decibel levels. He is the only one who could turn a throng's hatred to love with his effort and guts. He is the only one, Len-o, who could make hometown hero John McEnroe—who grew up in Queens—into a villain for a championship match.

Jimmy Connors may not have started as the Open's most beloved player, but he certainly ended up that way, replete with an incredible send-off. He won five U.S. Open titles, but Connors remembers the 1991 tournament most fondly because that was the year his minions propelled his thirty-nine-year-old body through to the semifinals with their adulation.

The Grand Slam events and their fans are each entirely different. Wimbledon is stuffy and its crowd seems to enjoy a polished champion who is as good with his strokes as he is with etiquette. The Open is more like hardscrabble New York. We like character. We like heart. We want a showman who can make us gasp at his effort one minute and then make us laugh with his antics the next.

Connors was like that. He could finish a ninety-second volley by diving for a ball and then—perhaps in an effort to get some rest—pop into the stands to take a swig of a spectator's drink. He was adored for the way he left everything on those courts. He repaid our love by channeling our energy right into his game.

Connors's act did not play well here when he debuted at the Open in the early '70s. He was one of tennis's bad boys, a brazen and overconfident talent who occasionally swore at match officials and made obscene gestures to heckling spectators. He won the 1974 and 1976 titles, but when he lost in the finals in 1975 and 1977 at the West Side Tennis Club, spectators booed him off the court.

Then something odd happened to change the relationship between the New York fans and the man. Connors lost his national No. 1 ranking and somehow fell behind rival Björn Borg. With his charisma and the label of an underdog, Connors had an opening to win over the Open fans. On the court and off, Connors played the part of the underdog with aplomb. He whipped the fans to a frenzied pitch and then used the electricity to vanquish an opponent.

He needed the fans to win and they wanted him to.

The thing that really doesn't make sense is why it took so long to win them over. Connors always had been the kind of overachieving performer New York went for. He wasn't the most talented. He was never overpowering. He used a tiny steel racket and a two-fisted backhand and returned just about every smash hit his way. His sense of humor was appealing and he was good-looking enough to make women swoon.

He also had an attitude that was simply irresistible. He never quit, no matter how dire the circumstances. During his legendary 1991 sendoff, Connors was down two sets and trailing 4–1 in the third and took a single game off Patrick McEnroe. It was the spark in winning a five-setter that lasted more than four and a half hours.

"I hate losing more than I love winning," he said then.

Before Connors at the U.S. Open, much of tennis had the stuffy country club feel. He could turn any of the Tennis Center's courts into Giants Stadium, make his fans a weapon to use against an opponent.

In the years since he stopped coming, Open fans have come to appreciate him more. The last fifteen Opens have been by-and-large a parade of colorless greats (Andre Agassi excepted). They are spectacular talents, but there's nothing to connect with and nothing to attract us to them.

That was never a problem with Connors. We couldn't keep our eyes off of him. And once we fell for him, he became all good things in our eyes. Boorish behavior at Wimbledon or the French Open? Just Jimmy being mischievous, we'd say. Our favorites never do anything wrong.

"Once New York accepts you for what you are and what you can give them and the enjoyment that they can get from you, that can turn a lot of ways," he said in an interview during the 1991 Open. "These people here today made me what I am, and I appreciate that."

They all got as much out of him as he got out of them.

Lennon says: Hmmm. Not so sure about your enthusiasm in calling Jimmy Connors the "darling" of the U.S. Open, Rog. Personally, when I think "darling" of anything, a woman usually comes to mind. Maybe that's an outdated, 1950s way of looking at this question, but I doubt that I'm alone in picking Chris Evert as the overwhelming favorite—dare I say "darling?"—of the U.S. Open.

Call me a caveman, but much of Evert's early appeal stemmed from the fact that she was a pint-sized assassin in a blonde ponytail when she burst on the scene as a sixteen-year-old amateur in 1971 at Forest Hills. I circle September 4 of that year as a red-letter date for the Open because Evert won over the crowd with a tenacity and never-say-die spirit that New Yorkers adore.

That's when Evert knocked off Mary Ann Eisel, the world's fourth-ranked player, by fighting back from six match points. After losing the first set, 6–4, Evert trailed 6–5 in the second and was down 40–love before mounting an improbable rally. She won that game, took the tiebreaker 5–1, and then cruised to a 6–1 win in the deciding third set. That earned Evert the label "Cinderella in Sneakers," and she thrived on the role of teenage underdog.

Evert finally succumbed in a semifinal loss to eventual champion Billie Jean King in her Forest Hills debut, but that was the start of an untouched run of greatness. She reached the semis in seventeen of her nineteen Open appearances, and won 101 matches, which still is a record, for both sexes. Evert also took four straight Open titles from 1975 to 1978 and, in her time away from New York, throttled the competition in every corner of the globe.

She was especially brilliant at the French Open, where her baseline game thrived on the red clay of Roland Garros, and Evert left her mark there with a record seven titles—one more than her six in Queens. She was nearly unbeatable on clay, winning 125 consecutive matches on that surface, but that success wound up backfiring on the once beloved player who soon became known as the "Ice Maiden."

"I was the ice queen and they wanted to see me melt," Evert said. "They wanted to see me cry, probably show some emotion. But I carried it inside myself."

In her sport, there was no one more visible than Evert, and she created a media firestorm by hooking up with your guy, Rog—Connors. They were known as the "golden couple" of tennis, and even played mixed doubles together at the U.S. Open in 1974. At that point in their careers, Connors received second billing to Evert, and that may have had something to do with their wedding plans dissolving the following year.

Think Evert was big back then? She shrugged off Connors to date Burt Reynolds—at the height of *Smokey and the Bandit* fame—and the son of a president, even if he was Gerald Ford's offspring.

As Evert solidified her No. 1 ranking, she became less of a

crowd favorite, which is what happens to dynasties. By coldly dispatching opponents, Evert was more machine than the ponytailed teenager the tennis world fell in love with, and it took the arrival of Martina Navratilova for her to become a favorite again.

Matched up against the bigger, stronger Martina, Evert's underdog status was restored to some extent, and deservedly so. Navratilova would end Evert's unchallenged reign over women's tennis, but she also allowed her to exit the stage as a beloved figure. It was fitting that Evert played the last match of her career in the very same tournament that launched her to stardom, and she gracefully bowed out after losing to Zina Garrison in the quarterfinals of the 1989 U.S. Open.

Evert walked away with eighteen Grand Slam titles, and earned at least one every year from 1974 to 1986. Her .900 winning percentage is the best of any player to pick up a racket professionally, and when you realize that Evert was born on the grass courts of Forest Hills, her legacy endures at the Open like no other.

As testament to her celebrity, Evert became the first female professional athlete to host *Saturday Night Live* after she retired. She was an obvious choice. After shining on one New York stage for so long, it was only natural to have her perform on another.

Where Is the Most Hallowed Place for Hoops?

Rubin says: About the only thing more New York than a Nathan's hot dog is a pick-up basketball game. They call it "The City Game" and there's no place where more of it is being played than right here in the five boroughs. These places can't be beat for catching creativity and competition, and when they host a big tournament—as so many of them do—you can add the pulsing rhythms of music and the classic in-game shtick of a dude on the microphone calling the game.

In every corner of the city, you find great basketball in the playgrounds, from the Lost Battalion Rec Center in Queens to Dyckman Park in Upper Manhattan to Foster Park in the Flatbush section of Brooklyn, made world famous in Rick Telander's book *Heaven Is a Playground.*

Even the nicknames of the places can be great. The court at the Surfside Gardens project in Coney Island is "The Garden," home to Stephon Marbury and Sebastian Telfair. The one beneath the Martin Luther King Jr. Towers at Lenox Avenue and 114th Street is "The Kingdome," named for the elite tournament it hosts. The court at the Israel Putnam playground in Bed-Stuy is "Soul in the Hole."

Now, The Rucker may draw the big names from the NBA, and Goat Park at West 99th and Amsterdam may have been home to

Earl "The Goat" Manigault—the city's most famous playground legend—but for my money there is no greater way to experience New York streetball than at "The Cage."

It's the perfect nickname for the court at the intersection of West 4th Street and Sixth Avenue, right above the subway station for the A, B, C, D, E, F, and V trains. The court is short and cramped and it is lined with a high chain-link fence. There's hardly any room between the sidelines and the fence, so a hard foul might end up hurting you twice: once on contact and again when you hit The Cage walls.

The level of play is excellent. Lakers point guard "Smush" Parker grew up playing in The Cage and was dubbed "The Grim Reaper" there. Lloyd "Swee' Pea" Daniels was a regular. So was Rod Strickland—"The Future"—and Anthony Heyward (aka "Half Man Half Amazing").

But the reason I love this place is the scene. When the games are good, people are hanging all over the fence that surrounds the court. And I'm not just talking about other ballers, I mean guys with briefcases who were walking by and tourists who have never witnessed a scene like it and kids from nearby NYU.

There, inside the hooting and hollering, the game is a circus. Big guys with big game are operating in a small space. Players looking to "get next" pack the sidelines. You can hear the urban rhythms blend: the squeak of sneakers against concrete, the honking of horns of Sixth Avenue traffic, the hawking of sidewalk vendors selling their goods.

That's vintage New York and the reason The Cage is probably the most photographed playground in the country, and a backdrop for so many movies that are shot in New York. You can't find anything like it anywhere.

The other thing I like about The Cage is that it's democratic. Yes, a lot of the time you'll see games that feature reams of former college and high school stars—usually the most entertaining stuff to see. But lots of other times it's a place where every man can go to play. There are plenty of chances for guys like me and you, Dave, to get a posse together and get into a game.

All you've got to do on those occasions is show up, lace 'em up and holler "I got next." But you'd also better bring some game with you. This is New York, the city of players, and that's a hot spot for basketball. Winners hold the court, and if you lose, it could be a long time until "next" comes around to you again.

Lennon says: Charles Dolan should be thankful the NBA season runs from November to April, and New York is too far north of the equator to support an outdoor basketball league in the dead of winter. Otherwise, Madison Square Garden would be as empty as Penn Station at 3 A.M. and Harlem's Rucker Park would be charging stockbrokers $100 a pop to sit on stone bleachers.

Until someone builds a roof over that hoops cathedral at 155th and Frederick Douglass Boulevard, the Knicks' expensive brand of mediocrity will remain safe for mass consumption. But for those who want to see street ball in its natural habitat, there's no better locale in the five boroughs than the playground named after Holcombe Rucker, the Harlem community legend who started it all back in 1947 as an altruistic way to help kids through basketball.

More than half a century later, Rucker probably wouldn't recognize the tournament he helped create. Since 1980, the run has been dominated by the Entertainers Basketball Classic, an event that is part hip-hop, part show biz, and every bit street ball at its best. It's stocked with playground legends, college stars that never cleared the next hurdle, and NBA phenoms looking for a little off-season burn.

Where else but on the green-and-red asphalt of Rucker could you find the likes of Stephon Marbury and Rafer "Skip to My Lou" Alston running the court with Corey "Homicide" Williams and

Larry "Bone Collector" Williams. With more than 1,500 gawkers pressed into the tiny fenced-in space—some watching from trees and rooftops—the action is broadcast live with a microphone plugged into a streetlight. The play-by-play is more Jay-Z than Marv, but the beat (nicknames only) is the perfect sound track to the freestyle action on the court.

The games may be anything goes, and the rules loosely enforced, but the talent shines through. And you won't find the dozens of college coaches and pro scouts complaining. The city's elite ballers make a pilgrimage to The Rucker every summer because everyone knows that's where the best showcase their skills. It's strictly A-list for players and entertainers while the other playgrounds are D-league by comparison.

Maybe The Rucker is a bit flashier these days, reflecting the continuing mutation of James Naismith's peach-basket game, but its history is unmatched by any other court in the nation. In the late '60s and '70s, NBA stars like Wilt Chamberlain, Walt "Clyde" Frazier, Tiny Archibald, and Bernard King would regularly match their talents against playground legends like Pee Wee Kirkland, Joe Hammond, Earl Manigault, and Herman "the Helicopter" Knowings. That latter group never made it to the NBA, but at The Rucker, they were all-stars of their backyard game.

"Guys were just dunking the ball all over the place, it was wild," Frazier recalled to the *Village Voice*. "You also have to realize that playing against NBA competition was their NBA season. We were just up there playing in the off-season and not as serious as they were. They certainly had more incentive than we had."

That pride is what elevates The Rucker, where the heart and soul of the game is on display every night, transforming a small square of concrete into a slice of hoops heaven. Call it a *Field of Dreams* for the roundball set, and it just seems right that the court sits across the street from the site of the old Polo Grounds. Both are special places that captured the imagination of its loyalists.

In New York City, reputation is king, and The Rucker, through the years, has only enhanced its five-star rating. The playground continues to invite only the hottest names in the game, and the show is basketball's version of Broadway. Don't believe me? Take the B train up there and see for yourself.

Was Reggie Jackson Truly a Great Yankee?

Lennon says: Some people are just born for the New York stage, and Reggie Jackson knew it before he ever signed with the Yankees. As Jackson once said, "If I played in New York, they'd name a candy bar after me." Call it a self-fulfilling prophecy, but Jackson was right, and fans got their first bite of the Reggie Bar on opening day of the 1978 season.

With an ego as big as the Bronx, Jackson was an acquired taste, as Billy Martin and George Steinbrenner were quick to discover. But for all of the in-fighting, name-calling, and general nastiness, Jackson is one of only twenty-five players in franchise history to have a plaque and his number in Monument Park.

If sharing immortality alongside Babe Ruth, Joe DiMaggio, and Mickey Mantle isn't a mark of Yankee greatness, I don't know what is. There's also irrefutable evidence in Cooperstown, too, where Jackson is sporting the interlocking NY on his Hall of Fame plaque.

While it's true that Jackson played a relatively small fraction of his career with the Yankees—five seasons out of twenty-one—his pin-striped résumé launched him into larger-than-life status. Jackson himself said, "I didn't come to New York to be a star, I brought my star with me." But even the bombastic slugger couldn't have imag- ined how big he would get in the Bronx. Jackson went from twinkling star to fiery supernova in those five years, and his influence on those Yankees—both good and bad—extended beyond the white lines.

The New York tabloids couldn't draw up a better character than Jackson, who nearly had a fistfight with Martin on the dugout steps at Fenway Park, swapped insults on a regular basis with Steinbrenner, and, by the way, possessed a flair for dramatic home runs. To be a great Yankee means to be entertaining on and off the field—even the quiet DiMaggio had Marilyn Monroe—and Jackson was money on both counts.

Never mind the five-year cameo in the Bronx. All Jackson really needed to cement his Yankee legacy was the 1977 World Series, when he hit five home runs during the Fall Classic, including three on consecutive pitches in that memorable Game 6. It was before that World Series, in fact, that Thurman Munson, no fan of Jackson's, referred to him as "Mr. October" to a TV camera crew.

Never was a nickname more dead-on. Jackson later won the World Series MVP in that six-game conquest of the Dodgers, and not only did Mr. October drill three home runs in the clincher, the last was a 475-foot blast off knuckleballer Charlie Hough that landed in the blacked-out hitter's-eye in center field.

Jackson hit 563 home runs in his career, but it seems like every one of his 144 for the Yankees carried some extra significance. Every time Jackson stepped to the plate in the Bronx, it was an event, whether he whiffed for one of his record 2,597 strikeouts or launched a deep drive into the right-field upper deck.

And when it came time for October, no one looked better in pinstripes. Jackson played thirty-four of his seventy-seven postseason games for the Yankees—less than half—but hit twelve of his eighteen playoff homers and supplied 29 of his 48 RBI during his days in the Bronx. Jackson won as many World Series rings with the A's as he did with the Yankees—two—but few remember him in the gold and green of Charlie Finley's dynasty.

To New Yorkers, Jackson will always be a Yankee, and that was clear when he returned to the Bronx as a member of the Angels in 1982. In his first game back, with the crowd chanting, "Reg-gie, Reg-gie," Jackson homered off former teammate Ron Guidry. That quickly changed the chants to "Steinbrenner sucks" and even The Boss would come to regret letting him go.

When Jackson was inducted into the Hall of Fame in 1993, Steinbrenner said that not re-signing him was his biggest mistake as owner of the Yankees. You don't hear Steinbrenner say that very often. Only for the great ones.

Rubin says: Just listen to yourself, Dave. Getting into fistfights with teammates? Nearly getting into one with a manager? Going on and on about "the magnitude of me"? This guy doesn't sound fit to be listed with truly great Yankees like Gehrig, DiMaggio, Mantle, and Jeter. He sounds more fit for a straightjacket!

Being a great Yankee isn't just about hitting home runs, Dave. If it were, then Dave Winfield would have his number retired because he hit sixty-one more in pinstripes than Jackson did. And it's not just about being a key part of championship teams, because then this discourse might be all about Moose Skowron.

The great Yankees did—and do—more than just that. They are leaders like Phil Rizzuto and Yogi Berra and Derek Jeter. They helped build the franchise's reputation for being the best in all of sport, like Ruth and Gehrig and Mantle did. They were dignified and glorious like DiMaggio.

Does any of that sound like Reggie Jackson to you, Len-o?

When Reggie showed up in New York, he gave an interview to *Sport* magazine in which he discussed Munson and unforgettably described his own role with the Yankees as "the straw that stirs the drink," something the Yankees captain took correctly as disrespectful. Munson even confronted Jackson, who tried to say he'd been misquoted. Munson's memorable response: "For four pages?"

Just think what it would be like if any of the huge stars recently brought into the Yankees fold had dissed the current captain like that. They'd immediately become Public Enemy No. 1 with the fans at the stadium and with teammates in the clubhouse. Everyone knows these Yankees are Jeter's team the same as everyone knew that those Yankees were Munson's.

Now, don't get confused here and go thinking that I don't believe Jackson was a great player. There's no argument here that he is one of the greatest talents ever to play the game and that his place in Cooperstown is more than well earned. He has the best nickname in baseball—Mr. October—and lived up to it during all his stops in the majors. I agree with you, Dave, that his three home runs on three swings in a World Series game also ranks with the greatest single-game performances.

Still you've got to do a lot more to be a great Yankee if you're going to spend less than a quarter of your career here. One incredible night like that doesn't get you there. One incredible season like his forty-one-homer tear in 1980 doesn't do it either.

The opinion here is that Paul O'Neill was more of a great Yankee than Jackson. He was not only a terrific player who delivered in the clutch and helped the team to four World Series championships, he added to the clubhouse environment with his competitive nature and his teammates loved him for it. That's what being great is.

It's not getting into a fistfight with third baseman Graig Nettles at the team celebration dinner after winning the 1981 AL pennant in Oakland or being nice enough to start the fisticuffs with his wife and four kids in attendance.

You can't hold Jackson's many confrontations with George Steinbrenner against him because The Boss was an impossible person to deal with back then. And while I don't condone the time he ignored manager Billy Martin's signs and ended up with a five-game suspension, I am sure playing for Martin was no picnic, either.

There is some concern here that Steinbrenner's decision to re-tire Jackson's number 44 is being used as some kind of standard or proof of something. Everyone knew from the timing of the an-nouncement that it was more an inducement to have Jackson put the interlocking NY on his Hall of Fame plaque.

Big Stein might have publicly lamented his decision not to re-sign Jackson when he saw his former slugger help the Angels win the AL West the following year, but he was publicly disparaging him right before he made that call. The Boss had been grousing about how Reggie's fight with Nettles was just another thing he'd be considering at contract time. And Jackson emptied his locker like there was no chance he'd be back.

They both knew the marriage was over. This wasn't some sad parting of a team and one of its greats: It was good riddance.

50

What Were the Best and Worst Endings We've Seen?

Rubin says: Here we are, Dave, with the last seconds running out in the third period and two outs in the ninth inning. With forty-nine topics dispatched, we've brought our readers to the final pages. Can you think of a better way to finish this Great New York Sports Debate than a bit of dialogue about endings?

There are so many candidates here that the task seems daunting. In truth, they can be whittled down to a select few in each category. To me, New York's most fantastic finish should be one that the fans love to watch over and over again. The most horrific should be exactly the opposite, something that brings on physical illness when the video gets cued up.

That's why I am going with Aaron Boone's Game 7 blast to end the AL Championship Series against the hated Red Sox, and one of the Giants' all-time lowlights, a play New Yorkers know simply as "The Fumble." I always try to finish on a positive note, so it's the bad news first.

There are two sides to every story, so it should be noted that not everyone calls Joe Pisarcik's 1978 bungle against the Eagles "The Fumble." In Philadelphia, and probably most of the country, the play is dubbed "The Miracle at the Meadowlands" because the Eagles snatched victory from certain defeat.

The Giants held a 17–12 lead, had the ball on their own twenty-nine with only thirty-one seconds left to play, and Philadelphia had no time-outs to stop the clock. Taking a knee would have run out the clock to end the game. Instead Pisarcik attempted a handoff to running back Larry Csonka. A blown exhange resulted in a fumble and the Eagles' Herman Edwards plucked it off the turf. Edwards returned the ball for a touchdown as Philadelphia prevailed 19–17. This play right here is the reason quarterbacks take a knee to end a game.

While Pisarcik has shouldered the blame for this fantastically stupid event, that's not really fair. Offensive coordinator Bob Gibson actually called the play and it cost him his job the very next day. Of course I suppose if Pisarcik had realized the idiocy of it, he could have changed the call in the huddle.

Giants fans can take one comfort in recalling this ghastly gaffe: It affected some of the most important changes in the organization. This is the play that sent the season rolling downhill. The Giants could have been alive in the playoff picture at 6-6 with a win that day; instead they spiraled to a 6-10 finish and coach John McVay and GM Andy Robustelli were fired. George Young—your pick for the top executive—came in and rebuilt the franchise.

On to the good news: The Yankees have a pantheon of great moments in their long and illustrious history and Boone cemented himself a place with that blast on the first pitch of the eleventh inning from Boston's Tim Wakefield. The context makes the moment all the richer.

Not only were the Yankees going head-to-head for a spot in the fall Classic with their archrivals, they already had snatched their dignity and the game's momentum three innings earlier.

New York trailed 5–2 going into the eighth when Sox manager Grady Little carved himself a little place in every Yankee fan's heart by sending Pedro Martinez back out to the mound after, some reports say, he'd told his ace his night was over. Alan Embree was ready in the bullpen, but Little went back to Martinez and then, even after he'd allowed a run on two hits, made a visit and stuck with him. New York knotted the score with two more hits and that was the beginning of the end.

Joe Torre had Mariano Rivera and, in 2003, that meant Boston had no chance. Boone, who didn't even start the game and had played poorly in the postseason, crushed Wakefield's first pitch.

That night would have to rank near the top of any list of Boston's most heart-wrenching finishes, and if that doesn't add to its greatness in New York, well, nothing really can.

Lennon says: Thanks for the fine set-up job, Roger. Now, as I try to summon my inner Mariano Rivera to close this one out, I fear I'll wind up pulling an Armando Benitez instead. Fortunately, I'm alone at a kitchen table with my laptop, not standing on a mound with fifty-five thousand maniacs whose happiness depends on the location of my fastball.

Or the accuracy of my kick, jump shot, or deep throw.

Nope. For me, the pressure's off. By the end of this chapter, the buzzer sounds, and the back cover closes. But before this debate is through, I'll finish it with my own classic New York finishes—one good, one bad—both memorable in their own distinctive fashion. Since there's no sense ending on a down note, let's start with Charles Smith's four missed layups at the end of Game 5 of the 1993 Eastern Conference finals against the Jordan-era Bulls.

So how does a nondeciding game take on such a greater significance? I'll tell you why. These were the Michael Jordan-Scottie Pippen Bulls, and the Knicks were on the verge of slaying the dragon after taking a 2-0 series lead with them to Chicago. Even though they dropped the next two to the Bulls, when the series returned to the Garden, Smith had the basketball—and his own fate—in his hands in the waning moments.

This truly defied explanation. The Knicks, trailing 95–94, inbounded the ball with 28.8 seconds remaining and Patrick Ewing, falling down, managed to shovel a pass to Smith in the low post with about thirteen seconds left. That's when the Garden became completely unglued. Listen to how Marv described it:

"Smith stripped. Smith stopped. Smith stopped by Pippen *again*! It's *over!*"

What Marv failed to point out was Smith's first aborted attempt, when he was stripped clean by Horace Grant. All the 6' 10" Smith had to do was lean forward and drop the ball in, which for him was like paying the toll at the Triborough Bridge before E-ZPass. Even if he tripped, Smith probably had a 50-50 chance of making the go-ahead basket.

But Grant's swipe was only the beginning. After Smith grabbed his own loose ball, Jordan got him next, and then it was Pippen's turn. This was torture. Both Jordan and Pippen teaming up to torment the Knicks, tag-team style. When Pippen knocked it away for the final time, the Bulls flipped a full-court pass to B.J. Armstrong, who scored on a layup at the buzzer to complete the shocking 97–94 victory.

For the record, the Bulls took Game 6, then rolled over the Phoenix Suns for their third straight NBA championship. But you already knew that.

As for the greatest ending, I'll give you one guess.

Of course it's Game 6 of the 1986 World Series. Was there ever any doubt? Aaron Boone clubbing a Tim Wakefield knuckleball deep into the Bronx night is great entertainment for Yankee lovers, but even New Yorkers who hate the Mets had to appreciate the events of October 25, 1986, at Shea Stadium.

The big bad Mets were goners, already bracing for a cold winter of second-guessing and backstabbing when the Red Sox headed into the bottom of the tenth inning with a 5–3 lead. Oil Can Boyd was popping champagne in the clubhouse, and with the Mets one strike away from oblivion, DiamondVision flashed CONGRATULA-TIONS 1986 WORLD CHAMPION RED SOX.

Well, I don't even need to tell you what happened in that tenth inning, but in deference to the late Bob Murphy, I'll give you the happy recap. Three straight singles by Gary Carter, Kevin Mitchell, and Ray Knight cut the lead to 5–4 and a wild pitch by Sox reliever Bob Stanley tied the score at 5, putting Knight at third base.

Then, with two strikes, Mookie Wilson chopped a ground ball that made the hobbling Bill Buckner, on two bad ankles, look one hundred years old as the roller skidded between his legs. In came Knight, and the rest is history.

The Mets went on to win the World Series and somebody actually paid $93,000 for the baseball at auction.

Now that's a great ending.